Charles Francis Adams, Jr.

1835–1915

THE PATRICIAN AT BAY

D1516413

THIS FIRST BIOGRAPHY of Charles Francis Adams, Jr., is an absorbing portrayal of a remarkable man and a vivid account of his time. Descended from two presidents of the United States and a son of America's Civil War minister to England, Adams led a far more active and varied life than his renowned brother Henry. A financier who despised Wall Street and yet emulated its methods, an overseer of Harvard, and an historian, Adams yet devoted the major portion of his life and his greatest energies to one of the paramount public issues of his day, the growth and regulation of the railroads.

When he returned to Massachusetts after years of distinguished military service in the Civil War, Adams began to write on railroad problems. Mr. Kirkland traces in detail Adams' investigation of railroad operation and regulation, his term of service on the Massachusetts Railroad Commission which became a model of its kind, and his presidency of the Union Pacific Railroad. Adams ultimately lost his control of the Union Pacific in a direct confrontation with Jay Gould in which the reader becomes aware of the curious streak of admiration that colored Adams' attitude toward this "pirate" he so detested.

In other sections Mr. Kirkland tells of Adams as reformer, particularly in edu-

Edward C ... , Bowdoin
College, wa: ... A.B. from
Dartmouth (... d an M.A.
from Cambri lowing Adams to tell his own story and l books on
the history to convey his own inimitable mixture of *History of*
American Ec melodrama and relentless self-evaluation. *ommunity,*
1860–1900; a ... *w England*
History, 1820–1900 (Harvard University Press, 1948). He has also edited
Andrew Carnegie's *The Gospel of Wealth* for the John Harvard Library
(The Belknap Press of Harvard University Press, 1962).

Charles Francis Adams, Jr.

1835-1915

THE PATRICIAN AT BAY

❖❖❖❖❖❖❖❖❖❖❖❖❖❖❖❖❖❖❖❖❖❖❖❖❖

Edward Chase Kirkland

Harvard University Press

Cambridge, Massachusetts

1965

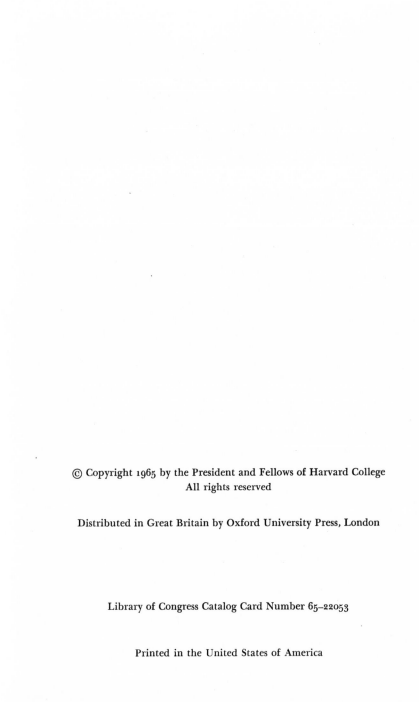

TO

Thomas Boylston Adams

Preface

MY frame of reference is simple. I admire Charles Francis Adams, Jr.; I even have a certain affection for him, a feeling I have an uneasy suspicion he would not reciprocate. Whether or not he would approve the result of my researches, I am sure he would commend my method, for he wrote to his brother Henry in 1864: "The English are getting to understand the art of biography for they let a man tell his own story and reflect his own character in his own words." In the case of as gifted and as prolific a writer as Adams, this method is as inescapable as it is interesting.

Though correspondence of Charles Francis Adams, Jr., is in widely scattered depositories, the diaries and a large accumulation of letters are in the Massachusetts Historical Society. Quotations from this body of material are of three kinds: (1) from the microfilm edition (which is copyrighted and extends through the year 1889), by special permission of the Massachusetts Historical Society; (2) from the post-1889 files ("Adams Papers — Fourth Generation"); and (3) from the Diaries and Memorabilia of C. F. Adams, Jr., which, like the post-1889 files, are not included in the microfilm edition. Permission to quote from the second and third of these groups has been kindly given by Mr. Thomas B. Adams, trustee of the former Adams Manuscript Trust, and by the Massachusetts Historical Society, to which the Trust gave the entire Adams family archives in 1956. I also wish to acknowledge gratefully permission to quote from the Brander Matthews and Frederic Bancroft papers in the Columbia University Library; from the General G. M. Dodge papers in the Iowa State Department of History and Archives; from the Charles Elliott Perkins papers in the possession of Richard C. Overton; and from the Charles W. Eliot papers and the Records of the Harvard Overseers, both in the Harvard Archives. To the hospitality and generosity of owners or custodians of Adams material, there has been one exception. Deplorably, the Union Pacific archives at Omaha are kept closed to scholars.

Oscar Handlin has read the manuscript of this volume and his editorial suggestions have contributed greatly to its improvement. My wife, Ruth Babson Kirkland, has done occasional research assignments, typed the whole manuscript, and helped prepare it for publication. I am under deep obligation for assistance to the staffs of the Dartmouth College Library and of the Massachusetts Historical Society, and to the editorial staff of the Adams papers. While the last has answered my many questions, it has never given directives or imposed restraints. Nor have members of the Adams family read any portion of my manuscript, expressed any wishes about what I should write or not write, nor authorized this biography in any way.

Thetford, Vermont   E.C.K.

CONTENTS

ILLUSTRATIONS

Charles Francis Adams, Jr.

1835–1915

THE PATRICIAN AT BAY

CATCHING THE STEP

1835-1869

ACCORDING to his diary, Charles Francis Adams, then living in Boston on Hancock Avenue, was awaiting on May 27, 1835, the birth of his third child. The young father kept at bay whatever anxieties he may have had not by pacing the floor but by reading Duclos and Madame du Deffand and by rewriting an essay of political speculation. He ended his entry for the day by pouring out "my soul in gratitude" for the safe delivery of a "fine boy." [1] Eventually the baby, named after his father, was one of four brothers, constituting the nineteenth century generation of the most notable family dynasty in the United States.

The first genuinely eminent member of the family had been John Adams. A Boston lawyer, turned revolutionary, he served in the Continental Congress where he advocated Independence. Later he drew up the Massachusetts Constitution of 1780, was one negotiator of the peace treaty ending the Revolution, and served as first envoy of the new nation to the Court of St. James. Elected as the first Vice President under the Federal Constitution, he presided over the Senate in its formative period. When Washington refused to serve longer, Adams was chosen the second President of the United States. He had a single term. John's son, John Quincy Adams, after a career as diplomat and

Secretary of State almost unprecedented in variety, length, and distinction, became the sixth President of the United States in 1825. Within a short time after his defeat by Andrew Jackson in 1828, Adams' constituents elected him to the House of Representatives. During successive terms until his death in the Capitol building in 1848, he became the most forceful spokesman for the antislavery cause.

His youngest son, Charles Francis Adams, would spend a term and a little more in the House on the eve of the Civil War. Then Lincoln would appoint him minister to the Court of St. James; in the early 1870's he would be an American member of the commission that arbitrated the Alabama claims arising from the Civil War. At the time of the birth of his third child he was only a young man of twenty-seven, a Boston lawyer who felt an obligation to enter politics, in which "If it were not that I was under the perpetual stimulus of family pride, I would never mix." [2] By 1835 he had not gone much farther than formulating opinions and expressing them in contributions to newspapers and periodicals. He had also made a fortunate marriage to Abigail Brown Brooks, the youngest daughter of Peter Chardon Brooks of Medford and Boston.

Brooks, at his death reputedly "the richest man in New England," left behind a fortune of $2,500,000 acquired in insurance, in fortunate maritime adventures during the Napoleonic wars, and in money lending. Though John Adams was well enough off to bequeath land and funds to institutions in his native town and John Quincy Adams had left to his son "a tolerably ample fortune," the Brooks marriage brought a new affluence to the Adams line. Consequently Charles Francis Adams, Jr., visiting his parents in Washington during the eventful pre–Civil War session of Congress, was able to write to his brother Henry, "The governor is doing well. Character, ability, wealth and family all rank high in Washington and all of them he has." [3]

The long years of political eminence and the large American families of this era meant that the Adamses had an extensive connection of relatives and friends. They knew everybody and could assume that everybody wanted to know them. On the whole this was an advantage. The doors of editors, publishers, diplomats, Justices of the Supreme Court, and bankers opened to the Adams name without need of further introduction. On the other hand the position of being an insider naturally stirred the envious and censorious. On this count, at least, Charles sympathized with his father. "Constant reference" to the first and second Adamses "in connection with himself annoyed and at times irritated him. He could not habituate himself to it, nor learn to take it lightly and as matter of course, — at one time the commonplace utterance of some not unkindly man, devoid of good taste, and at another the obvious retort of a coarse and commonplace opponent, quick to avail himself of a telling personal allusion. For all such it was so very easy to refer to a noticeable family deterioration, — 'sharp decline' was the approved form of speech, — and the reference was sure to elicit a sneering laugh, and round of blockhead applause from the benches of the groundlings . . . To have one's ancestors unceasingly flung in one's face is unpleasant, and listening to the changes incessantly rung upon them becomes indubitably monotonous." [4]

Perhaps this constant yammering eventually impressed even C. F. Adams, Jr., for in his mid-fifties he was musing: "Why is [it] that the tendency in the family is toward the development of the elements of weakness and deterioration; while in the mass a distinct improvement is perceptible?" This generalization was based upon a false premise. No member of Charles' generation attained the presidency or congressional office, but its massed talents represented the flowering of the family's genius. The eldest of Charles' brothers, John Quincy Adams, 2nd, two years the former's senior, has left the dimmest record.

Like most first sons in the Adams family, he was a lawyer, but in politics he moved only on the local and state levels. For years he shared with Charles an office in Boston and participated in the same business affairs. On John's death in 1894 Charles wrote: "Early in life he dominated me; later, I dominated him, but as a whole, our relations were not only close but brotherly in their friendliness." This affection did not prevent Charles from adding that his brother "lacked persistence and will" and was "curiously wanting in the spirit of adventure and desire of novelty . . . thus, he systematically narrowed himself down and rusted." [5]

Charles' junior by three years was Henry Brooks Adams of the famous *Education*. Henry became a professor, historian, and dilettante, and the idol of a coterie among his contemporaries and later writers. The relationship between the two boys in youth was extraordinarily close. They grew up together in Quincy, and as young men shared living quarters off-Yard at Harvard. During the long affectionate correspondence that flowed between them during Henry's wanderyears in Europe it was Charles Francis who recommended to "My dear little boy" the autobiography of Gibbon "as a *vade mecum*." Months later Henry wrote from Rome that he had at last read Gibbon and had been stirred. "I feel much as if perhaps some day I too might come to anchor like that. Our house needs a historian in this generation and I feel strongly tempted by the quiet and sunny prospect." Later the intimacy cooled. One reason was Henry's marriage to Marion — "Clover" — Hooper. On her death Charles wrote, "Me she never liked; nor can I blame her much for that; — I trod all over her, offending her in every way." In later years the old relationship was reknit. When Henry had a stroke he recuperated in a cottage on Charles' Lincoln estate; Charles moved to Washington when Henry bought a house there; and Henry wrote the just epitaph for Charles' gravestone in Quincy. Less formal was Henry's outburst on his brother's death. "In truth, Charles was worth three of me, and leaves me utterly helpless." [6]

Charles' relationship with Brooks, the youngest of the four brothers, was marked by tension. Thirteen years younger than Charles, Brooks started out as the conventional small-boy nuisance, "such a disagreeable little sculpin," in Charles' words. When he grew up his conversation, slicing abstractions thin, bored or irritated Charles, and a prolonged exposure, such as a day's sail, was apt to end in "a thorough blow out" and Brooks's abrupt departure from the boat. Nor apparently did his marriage improve him in Charles' eyes any more than had theirs improved John and Henry. When Brooks called on Charles subsequent to this event, he "astonished me by his ungartered Hamletlike demeanor and greeting." In the troubled times of the early nineties Charles was so driven "frantic" by Brooks's "egoism," "pessimism," and worn-out wisdom that he concluded Brooks "is either out of balance or something serious is the matter." [7]

In writings which were almost coextensive with his lifetime and which formally valued nearly everyone he knew, Charles makes singularly little reference to his mother. An attempt by Henry, when the boys were just out of Harvard, to arouse in his brothers a sense of affection and respect for her Charles rebuffed with a blast of icy rationality: "As for mamma the real difficulty must out — all her children who have grown up are stronger than she & accordingly often in taking stronger views & more independent positions are very apt to overcrowd her more than is consistent with the respect due to her . . . I am now too old and too independent to be ruled." [8]

In the 1890's Charles brought himself to a long-considered, formal appraisal of his father. "In plain language, I do not like my own father." His was "a strong not generous, kindly or sympathetic nature, self-contained, introspective, Puritanic in the English, and virtuous in the Roman sense . . . In his family circle he was intense. It never occurred to him that he might have been wrong or pursued an unfriendly course to his children, though he at times even late in life, inflicted on me frightful mortifications." When Charles looked over this estimate filling eight or nine pages, he found "it fails to touch the root of the matter." Consequently he tried again but only succeeded in repeating the indictment. Though there is evidence that "the governor" was less aloof and unkindly than his son asserted, he certainly gave the impression of unpleasantness. "I thought that in all my life I had never seen but one other face as cross as his," wrote a younger man.[9]

During most of his youthful years in Boston, Charles lived at 57 Mount Vernon Street in a house given by Peter Brooks to Charles' mother. Wearing one of the most charming exteriors of Beacon Hill residences, it still stands within a short distance of the State House. In 1889 when he cleaned out the house after his mother's death, Charles noted in his diary: "It was 46 years ago that we moved into that house, and I have not one pleasant association connected with it. I went out of it today with a sense of relief." Part of his aversion sprang from his dislike for Boston weather and the childhood diversions and tedium of the city in general. He concluded, "My boyhood wasn't very attractive, anyhow." [10]

Formal schooling began with dame school and continued at various small private schools in Boston and elsewhere. Charles later described the numerous mistakes his father made in this sequence. When Charles was thirteen he entered the Boston Public Latin School and, at the direction of his parents, began to keep a diary. Later he burned the diary for those years; he would have gladly inflicted the same fate upon the school. Many graduates agreed with him. Certainly Henry did. To celebrate the virtues of the masters of the school in his own and Adams' generation put so great a strain upon the integrity of Phillips Brooks, a Boston Latin School graduate, that he rather slid by them in a commemorative address. On the other hand George Santayana found excellences in the school, and Charles W. Eliot, a Boston Latin School graduate and a man with as ingrained a tendency toward innovation as had Charles, detected virtues in the "conservative tradition" of Latin, Greek, mathematics, and English declamation. It gave and would give "a welcome means of systematic discipline for boys and young men whose parents are competent to give their children a prolonged education" and provided "a good foundation for a larger number of subsequent professional pursuits than any other." [11]

Adams did not agree then or later. His grudge lingered on. In 1889, walking about Groton where his two sons were students, Charles "saw all that is here done for these boys, and thought of my own boyhood and what I lost, and was wroth." Though his indictment of the Boston Public Latin School was specific — "a dull, traditional lifeless day-academy in which a conventional, commonplace, platoon-front, educational drill was carried on" — a subjective factor crept in. In 1851, a year before his graduation, his father withdrew him from the school, for he was not doing well, and sent him to a private tutor. Here was a failure Charles could not forget. Instead of blaming himself, he blamed the school and blamed his father for sending him there in the first place. His *Autobiography* gives the impression that the paternal decision was largely personal willfulness. Really it was Bostonian karma. Historically the city had established this classical school to prepare students for college and the "old custom of our school at the close of ceremonial occasions" of singing "Fair Harvard" demonstrated which college was intended.[12] It probably never entered the head of an Adams that Charles should go anywhere else than to the Latin School.

Harvard was an Adams inheritance. John Adams, the first of the clan to go there, graduated in 1755; John Quincy Adams graduated in 1787, was the first Boylston Professor of Rhetoric and Oratory, and for eighteen years served on the Board of Overseers; Charles Francis Adams, class of 1825, was president of that board from 1869 to 1881. Of his sons, John Quincy Adams, 2nd, graduated in 1853, Charles in 1856, and Henry in 1858. John became in 1877 a member of the Board of Fellows, the real governing body of the college; Charles was an overseer with only a year's interruption from 1882 to 1907; Henry and Brooks both held appointments on the faculty.

The truly Olympian Harvard man can decide whether a degree beyond those in course is appropriate in his case. The institution had conferred honorary degrees upon the most eminent in earlier Adams generations, but Henry and Charles preferred to consult their own convenience in the matter. In 1892 Charles, having "for some time felt a wish to have the present generation recognized and the succession maintained," managed to have Henry invited to receive an LL.D. Henry, after replying that he would be unable to attend commencement because of a sprained ankle, arrived in Cambridge on the afternoon of the day, eliciting thereby from Charles the opinion: "A more brutal, unnecessary, and more ingeniously offensive and aggressive discourtesy never was perpetrated on the College, — all out of pure Miss Nancy affectation." The next year the Corporation announced its intention to nominate Charles — "Honestly I am pleased — greatly pleased." Then misgivings set in. Adams' financial situation was so precarious he feared the bestowal of the degree might prove mortifying. "Decided with John not to take the LL.D. — am not in the mood"; he refused. Unlike Henry, however, Charles had a second chance. His LL.D. in 1895 continued the family tradition. Charles found that commencement "on the whole an agreeable day." As a degree recipient he had to "sing for his supper," and his address at the commencement dinner observed, "Memory reverts to other days, — other scenes." [13]

8

When Charles was an undergraduate the worn-out phrase "a stage of transition" certainly applied to Harvard. The Augustan age of Presidents Kirkland and Quincy had passed and the age of Charles W. Eliot was still "waiting before." In the 1850's the student body fluctuated between 326 and 365; and the college consisted of a few plain buildings set in a quadrangle, gracelessly fenced. It looked like a New England academy. Still the faculty of thirteen or fourteen members contained many eminent men. In modern languages a changing of the guard in Adams' day substituted James Russell Lowell for Henry Wadsworth Longfellow. The professor of mathematics was Benjamin Peirce; of rhetoric and oratory, F. J. Child, the emerging pioneer scholar of ballads and Chaucer; of Greek, C. C. Felton, a humanist and Hellenist; of natural religion, moral philosophy, and civil polity, Francis Bowen, a puckish figure who taught history and economics as well as philosophy with a mind and sharpness of his own; of chemistry, J. P. Cooke. The question was whether the Harvard arrangements permitted the genius of these and other men to function. Cooke, for instance, had two rooms for a laboratory in the basement of University Hall which in his estimation were "entirely unsuitable" and "there is also a manifest incongruity and impropriety in placing a Chemical Laboratory in immediate proximity with the Chapel and recitation-rooms of the College." [14]

Charles Francis Adams, Jr., entered Harvard as a sophomore the year James Walker became president — a position which Walker occupied until 1860. Walker's was the third of six short caretaker reigns. During this time the college on the whole ran on inherited momentum and along traditional grooves. Walker believed in the middle way. On the one hand he made a "rule not to preach about anything until they have done talking about it in the omnibus"; on the other hand, later in life as an overseer, he was one of the most aggressive advocates of the election of Charles W. Eliot to the presidency of

Harvard. As a reformer President Walker was content to introduce a hymn into the morning services and abandon evening chapel. He met the requirement of keeping students in attendance or at work by scheduling classes as late as possible in the afternoon even when it meant the use of gaslight in the recitation rooms. He also reduced French from the status of a required subject with the commendation that "this is not an innovation but a return to the original plan." Adams later observed that caution and compromise in a college president stir suspicions. "Walker was regularly set down as a lying old Jesuit." [15]

The curriculum, which had come down from President Quincy's day largely unaltered, was a core curriculum extending over the four years. The core tapered. At the base in freshman and sophomore years all subjects — Latin, Greek, mathematics, rhetoric and oratory, ethics, and a taste of ancient history — were prescribed; at the top in the senior year required courses were history, philosophy, rhetoric, and physics. Along the path, generally in the last two years came various electives in modern languages and science; but the rules and requirements often penalized those who chose these novelties in preference to further work in the prescribed studies. Finally the official descriptions of courses were quite as apt to conceal as to reveal what undergraduates studied. Senior-year philosophy, for example, included study of the Federalist papers and lectures on the English and American constitutions; and on one occasion those who chose Longfellow's Italian listened in the first term to lectures on Goethe's *Faust*. On the surface the studies young Adams took at Harvard were fairly well balanced. French, German, Italian, and chemistry accompanied the more traditional requirements in Greek, Latin, mathematics, rhetoric, and physics. His later accusation that Harvard cut him off from modern life was exaggerated.[16]

No doubt Adams failed to distinguish between course requirements and the methods of instruction. The latter were admittedly dreary. Under the "Scale of Merit" system each student was required to recite at every class meeting and was given a determined number of points for his performance. The president totaled these weekly, after making stated deductions for absences or other offenses. As classes grew larger faculty members, hard put to conform to the system, resorted to routine and memorization. Graduates in these years agreed that the college hit bottom. Charles joined the critics, often rather unjustly. According to his recollections he had a minor aptitude for Greek, but Professors Felton and Sophocles ruined it. Felton had the reputation of being one of the most friendly, charming, and interesting scholars on the faculty. The Scale of Merit, however, compelled him to hear and grade recitations for twelve hours a week; for transmitting his enthusiasm for Greek civilization and institutions, he had weekly an hour's lecture part of the year.[17]

Though Adams was not sufficiently charitable to Felton, he was acute enough to realize that professors and students were victims of a system. "The educational trouble with Harvard in my time was the total absence of touch and direct personal influence as between student and instructor. The academic, schoolmaster system prevailed; and, outside of the recitation room, it was not good form — it was contrary to usage — for the instructors and the instructed to hold personal relations. Our professors in the Harvard of 'the fifties' were a set of rather eminent scholars and highly respectable men. They attended to their duties with commendable assiduity, and drudged along in a dreary humdrum sort of way in a stereotyped method of class room instruction." [18]

On the whole, however, young Adams' opinion of his Harvard career was more amiable than for the earlier phase of his education. The ease of the curriculum afforded the undergraduates a great deal of free time, part of which was spent socially. The great grandson of the John Adams, whose social rank had placed him fourteenth among the twenty-five members in the class of 1755, now "belonged easily and of right, to all the clubs and all the societies, literary and social." He was a member of the Institute of 1770, president of Alpha Delta Phi, and secretary, poet, and odist of the Hasty Pudding Club. There was one drawback to these pleasant associations; Charles' classmates were rather run-of-the-mine; later their "chief distinction was contributing two inmates to the State's prison." Still it was "a goodly company" from which Adams learned a great deal.[19]

Since he had much time to himself, he turned to "infinite reading and much writing." The "prophet voices . . . Tennyson, Thackeray, Emerson, and, perhaps most of all Carlyle" were his intellectual enthusiasms. He contributed to the *Magazine* pieces on Whittier, Hawthorne, and Charles Reade. In his second year he won a Bowdoin Prize with a dissertation on "Juvenal's Satires as Illustrative of Public and Social Changes after the Establishment of the Empire." Charles was so proud of this achievement that he spent part of the forty-dollar prize for a signet ring which he wore for over forty years. On graduation he was in the lower half of his class — at least according to the calculations of the Scale of Merit.[20]

Adams missed at Harvard the interest and directing hand of his teachers. He resented the permissive system which left him to discover his own aptitudes and shape them as best he could. At least that is what he wrote. He had made the same complaint of the earlier phases of his own education, and in later life worked at Quincy for the introduction of more personalized and individualized instruction in the public schools. But the lack of better instruction, as Adams understood it, hardly seems the whole explanation for his disillusion. Perhaps there is a further key in the savagery with which he destroyed the literary evidences of school and college days. Less than ten years after his commencement he was burning a manuscript of an old Hasty Pudding poem — "a monument of folly." In 1889 he systematically read over his youthful diaries and manuscripts, "far from a pleasing or creditable record," and threw them in the fire. These *diei irae* he later looked back upon as "the pleasantest days I then had." The record he read was "silly. That it was crude, goes without saying. *That* I didn't mind! But I did blush and groan and swear over its unmistakable unconscious immaturity and ineptitude, its conceit, its weakness and its cant." [21] Charles did not resent having been born; he simply resented having been born young. If one could only have started life at middle age, all those youthful years of nonsense and frustration would have been avoided.

If he lacked a wholly commendable education, Adams in facing a career and society had the support of a prominent family, some property of his own and the assurance of more, and, with his shock of black hair and impish eyes, an appealing personal appearance. He probably had too many brains to put most people at ease with him; whether he had the talents and resolution to make a living was another thing. The transition from college to occupation is a severe test for any young man; it was doubly difficult for a youth with a distinguished name. Not every activity or employment was open or satisfying to him. Charles knew he should have a plan in life and that all his force and his efforts should be directed toward "the attainment of that ultimate end." The great handicap was that he had no special "aptitude." So, like his brother John, he fell into the Adams pattern and started to become a lawyer. [22]

In October 1856 he entered the office of Dana and Parker to read law. Both men were Harvard graduates. Dana also had a traditional relationship with the Adams family for his grandfather, Francis Dana, had served John Adams as secretary at one time during the Revolution and in turn later employed John Quincy Adams in the same capacity. Indeed Charles' middle name, as that of "the governor," was a reminder of the Dana association. Richard Henry Dana, who had recovered his health and gained a literary reputation with *Two Years before the Mast*, was a court lawyer who prepared and presented his cases with immense thoroughness and tirelessness. Not all his cases were trivial, for he was among counsel for the fugitive slave Anthony Burns in 1854. His partner, Francis E. Parker, on the other hand, rarely appeared in court. Worldly-wise and with a store of New England common sense and a gift for epigram — "The mission of America is to vulgarize the world" was his best — his career surprised one of his Harvard classmates. "Frank Parker, our first scholar, might naturally, we should all have said, reach the Supreme Bench in rapid strides . . . but that he should, instead of this, become the greatest business lawyer in Boston, that he should have charge of vast estates, that he should die rich, that his pallbearers should be bank presidents and millionaires, this was something that no one could have credited in advance." [23]

For twenty months Charles slaved at the law, reading; listening with pained impatience while the senior partner "pumped into me for two stricken hours, talking law which he himself didn't understand and which, I'm sure, I didn't"; wolfing down heavy midday dinners in the cheap restaurants spread about the Court House on Pemberton Hill; and wondering whether Dana and Parker saw through him and discerned his inadequacies. In spite of misgivings Adams decided to take the bar examinations, a series of questions on one sheet of letter paper, nonchalantly administered and graded by Judge Bigelow, a Quincy neighbor and friend of the Adamses. Charles passed and was sworn in. "I was no more fit to be admitted than a child . . . Bigelow's personal knowledge of me had something to do with it." Charles at first shared an office with John; then took one of his own, "a gloomy, dirty den in my father's building, 23 Court Street," and there he waited for clients none too

hopefully: "God never meant me for a lawyer & nothing short
of a miracle will ever make me one." [24]

"I turn from thoughts of love to deeds of law with a calm-
ness which proves that my heart must be pure and my hands
clean," Charles wrote his brother Henry, absent in Europe.
For Charles was, along with John and other eligible young men,
busy not only in offices but in society. In this arena Charles
fancied himself "a sort of Major Pendennis." Of the season of
1859 Charles wrote: "Never since I have been in society have
I seen a winter go off with such a sort of shriek & howl, so drunk
with wine & excitement, so ram full of canvas-back duck &
oysters, so slop up in jollity, so jam down in fatigue." This
bacchanal reached a peak at the Tiger Ball, "the event of
this century . . . I assure you we all stepped round there like
ram's tails in fly time. It was the grand overwhelming Waterloo
victory of dancing. The Tiger Ball you know is vulgar; young
ladies couldn't think of dancing, of course, they must go & sit
in the galleries and wear bonnets and look on . . . The theatre
really looked magnificently & was crowded to the full extent
— the floor was alive with dancers & the music clashed away
like fun. Did you ever dance with a woman as knew how to
dance to the music of drums and cymbals? . . . The young
women at first were pretty quiet, by & by they began to think
how nice it would be if they could dance to that music on that
floor, then they grew wild to dance, finally they looked down
and saw Martha Chadwick placidly waltzing away & then they
went crazy. Regardless of paternal injunctions and maternal
entreaties, regardless of criticism & regardless of dress, they
one by one flung away their bonnets & cloaks anywhere & anyhow, & rushing onto the Tiger floor danced away like mad."
When the "small hours began to grow large" Charles "retired
into the manager's [John's] room to drink brandy & waters,
finally at half after four John & Arthur & I . . . went to Par-
kers, where we finished the night on turkey & champagne until

15

Lieut. Dexter grew very drunk and Manager Adams was disguised in liquor and Private Adams alone preserved his echelon. Finally the clock was striking six before I rested my pillow upon my head. This lasted for four days, during which the morning was devoted to cocktails and oysters, the afternoon to conversation and humor & the evenings to supper, music, and dancing." [25]

Sometimes these gay doings were strictly male. To celebrate the weekend of the Fourth of July in 1859 Charles sailed with four other young men to the Isle of Shoals. Their high jinks proved so vexatious to the landlord of a hotel there that the young men returned to Boston. "I have rarely seen a prettier sight than Boston harbor & the country round as we beat up to the city on the evening of the 4th, the whole being alive with fireworks & the night being one of the finest you can imagine. We got in at 10 o'clock and I went up to the Tremont, where, of course, I found a drunken crew who seemed . . . to be trying to blow up the hotel with torpedos and firecrackers. I ended the night of the 4th by supping with Hollis Hunnewell who also seemed to me from his sprightly conversation and admirable frankness to be perceptibly under the effects of wines. I left him finally at one o'clock. I amused myself for the next hour by washing my face, long since become about the color of a lobster, with raw whiskey." [26]

Never does a person grow older faster than in his twenties. After two or three years out of Cambridge, Charles felt like an old man when he revisited Harvard where he knew no one except the professors — and he felt older still as social season succeeded social season and the debutantes seemed so young he wondered how they "found their way out of their nurseries." For these were the years when he wondered whether he was in love, and if not, what were the reasons; the years when he and his friends placed bets who would marry whom and when, and what new wives were going to "litter" or "foal." At one time he reflected, after an appraisal of current marriages: "Copulation may vigorously proceed, but assuredly conception is at a standstill." [27]

But all this gaiety and cynicism did not advance Charles in the law or ease the fundamental discomfort of his position. He was living at home in the fourth story of 57 Mount Vernon Street; his father continued his allowance. Though there were savings in these arrangements and he had the companionship of John, he was still under family surveillance and was still dependent. The Boston rule then was that a young man's first latchkey should be that to his own household. So when Charles returned late from one of his gay parties, he had to "ring" his father out of bed in order to get in and possibly face a censorious comment. Lacking a successful life plan of his own, he dreaded succumbing to his father's expectations of him. Possibly if "the governor" could have looked into Charles' mind, he would have been quite incredulous at what his son conceived as the paternal wishes. Charles was certain that his father "wanted us to be thoroughly commonplace, — to remain at home, apply ourselves studiously and discreetly to our chosen vocations, to marry early, to lead always correct and domestic lives, and to develop into comfortable middle aged men as soon as possible after graduation." The whole tradition of the Adams family contradicts the notion that fathers intended such a limited ambition for their sons; and "the governor," to take a case, fell far short of attaining it for any of his boys except John Quincy. Meanwhile Charles' life remained undirected. When pressed to marry, he snapped back that he could not "go into the market place & buy a wife as easy as I could buy a horse. 'Go & get in love' — isn't it what I've been trying to do for two years." There were moments of despair lest he be an idler and surrender to that "fatal magnetic risk for us, the knowledge that our family is wealthy and that for us there is no real object in labor. God knows I would as soon die as live overcome by this deadly influence and indeed if I fail to struggle against it; & if no happy misfortune occurs to wake up my energies, I shall not much care how soon I do die — an objectless life is more bitter than death." [28]

On a small scale Charles cracked the circle of his limitations, alike dismal and frivolous, by applying his lawyer's talent and leisure time to business adventure. He had inherited a "little property," and the family had invested on a considerable scale in Boston lands and buildings, particularly in the Court Street neighborhood. Charles now "put up" his father to the purchase of the Melodeon estate on Washington Street and proposed to put "my own small property" into this joint enterprise. "I expect to make a very good thing out of it." Soon he was enlarging his capital investment. "I really can't say that I have any worldly objection to borrowing money at 6 per cent & receiving therefor, at a later period, 10." The plan was to erect a granite front building with stores, offices, and a hall to rent; by the spring of 1859 Charles wrote Henry he was "rapidly becoming a Croesus." Within a few months the note of certainty and braggadocio died down as he found himself a "real estate agent" quarreling with workmen and chaffering with tenants. "For this work it is possible God may have made me, but if he did, I would almost rather that in my infancy he had taken me to himself." In the end Charles found himself in the same old dependence upon "the governor" who, since he did not want his children harassed in money matters, loaned them money as a sort of advance on their inheritance. "And if your heroism would tempt you at any future time to relieve yourself of a fancied obligation to your natural friend and guardian, you remain at liberty to pay back the debt in such sums and at such times as you may find convenient." [29]

In the midst of this vexatious busy work, current politics suddenly preoccupied the young man. He was too young to hope for political office for himself, but the success of his father

Charles Francis Adams, Jr., in 1855
— Harvard College senior picture.
"It was at Harvard that my aptitude, such as it was, began to develop." (*Autobiography*)

Adams in 1861. "My visit to N.Y.
made me esteem myself as pump-
kins, but coming back to Boston
takes the conceit out of one."
(*Diary*)

Adams (third from left) and the officers of his regiment. "They talk of the horrors of war; we have made them a jest." (Letter to F. W. Palfrey, February 7, 1862)

The Old House. "The stone cutters . . . look upon [me] as an aristocrat, and the old homestead about which all my pleasantest memories cluster, as a mere hindrance to growth." (*Memorabilia*)

stirred him. Through the turbulent forties and fifties Charles Francis Adams had continued the antislavery traditions of his father. He threaded his way with shrewdness and conviction along an obscure path through old and new parties, through factions and schisms, until the Republican party emerged in Massachusetts to hold out promise of antislavery success. In 1858 the Republicans nominated Charles Francis Adams for the House of Representatives and his election was a triumph. About a year later the family moved to Washington.[30] When Lincoln won the presidency in 1860 Adams was re-elected to Congress.

Early in 1860 Charles, who had been left at home to wait for clients, manage the Adams real estate, and keep a welcome "bachelor hall" on Mount Vernon Street, went to Washington to visit his parents. The national capital in its slapdash appearance, its rough politics, and its society left him gasping. "Washington is a bear garden it is true and the tone of morals and manners is disgustingly low." Charles met the "leading minds" of North and South, wrote letters to the press in his father's behalf, and attended endless balls, receptions, and dinners. "This is the charming, the fascinating — the life of lives for me." As he wrote to Henry, "Now probably you don't know what a flirtation is. — I didn't — in fact I never saw one except in Washington . . . I went there green — the first time a young woman trod on my toes, as I talked to her, I drew my foot away and looked at her reproachfully. When she insisted on my holding her hand, I insisted on letting it go. When she pressed my hand in the dance, I didn't return it and only offered the end of my fingers. I came there cold & impossible and then I found it paid. They didn't understand and it bothered them and they laid themselves out to subdue me . . . I haven't seen a Boston girl for six weeks but shall tonight, & really don't know how they'll seem — they are so very virtuous." Whatever their differences of opinion on other matters, the brothers were of one mind on Boston girls. Charles apparently had come around to Henry's complaint: "There is not one of them with salt enough in her corporation to keep her over Sunday." [31]

Later in the summer William H. Seward, a former governor of New York who had failed to win the Republican nomination for the presidency, came to Quincy, announced his admiration and allegiance to the ideas of John Quincy Adams, and invited the elder Charles and his son to accompany him on an electioneering swing through the West. In these years Seward was the political lodestar of the Adamses. The elder Adams could not take the whole trip, but Charles could and did. By steamboat or team, the party got as far west as Lawrence, Kansas, and covered the midwestern states pretty thoroughly. This discovery of the country Charles declared "invigorating." He was the companion of Seward and less reputable statesmen and met a whole host of candidates and politicians including Trumbull, Douglas, and Lincoln. Charles concluded that the "eye" of Lincoln "never belonged to a man great in action; it is neither the quick sharp eye of a man of sudden and penetrating nature, nor the slow firm eye of one of decided will; but it is a mild, dreamy, meditative eye which one would scarcely expect to see in a successful chief magistrate in these days of the republic. *Mais nous verrons.*" All in all, the young Bostonian encountered men, communities, and happenings "strange, unreal, almost weird." [32]

In February 1861 Charles was again in Washington on a visit to his parents. Henry, back from Europe, was already at the capital, serving as his father's secretary. As spasms of secession seized state after state in the South, Washington was filled with rumors, alarms, and panic. The Republicans developed two factions: extremists who would stand firm and teach the South a lesson, and conciliators who would make some concessions to keep the border states in the Union and thus so discourage the southern fire-eaters that even the seceded states would crawl back into the Union. Seward was the leader of the conciliators and in his cause Adams joined; Sumner from Massachusetts led the radicals. Young Adams felt in retrospect that both opinions ignored southern feeling and sentiment and overestimated the extent of southern unionism; but at the time he showed the same waves of optimism and fear as did his elders whom he was glibly judging according to whether their ideas jibed with his father's. Sumner was, of course, "an agitator, a rhetorician, and a theorist." Seward was "an able, a specious, and adroit and a very versatile man; but he escaped being really great." Of Lincoln, though he could not hear a word of the inaugural address, Charles formed a somewhat more generous opinion than previously. In any case the family soon moved back to Boston and Quincy, "all of us nourishing this delusive hope of peace and a restored Union." On March 19 the family was dumbfounded to learn that Lincoln had appointed Charles Francis Adams as minister to Great Britain. When Adams returned from a Washington briefing he was still hopeful of peace, but his son was not so sure — "Without a furious snow-storm raging, within, for me at least, doubt, hesitation and gloom. War, I felt, confronted us." With Fort Sumter "the Confederate whip came down across the Northern face." On the first of May, after waiting to attend the marriage of John to Fanny Crowninshield, Charles Francis Adams, minister to the Court of St. James, sailed for Great Britain.[33]

Meanwhile Charles was taking steps in "getting my bearings." In the *Atlantic* of April 1861 his "first well-considered, carefully prepared and laboriously copied-out" magazine paper appeared. In "The Reign of King Cotton" the young author relied upon the observations of Olmsted and Helper about the South and seasoned the mixture with a dash of Adam Smith. Cotton production was a monopoly. Like all monopolies it was bad, bad for the South's development and for those white farmers of the South outside the privileged circle. The solution was competition, competition from other producing areas, notably India, and from the diversity of occupations in the South. Olmsted complimented Charles on the article.[34]

So did other friends. An unidentifiable dissenter in Cambridge, however, warned Charles against the cosmic tone. "There is really no new light in it. This is the fault of all young men who think and write. They want to get to the bottom of things and make an exhaustive statement. In my themes I always arrived after the first page at the creation of the world and original sin." Charles received forty dollars for the article; more important, "it caused me to be recognized as a young man of somewhat nebulous promise." [35]

Though "The Reign of King Cotton" concluded with an apocalyptic quotation from the book of Revelation, Charles' personal response to the secession crisis was at first prudential. Immediately after Sumter he was writing, "War is no plaything, and, God knows, I have no wish to trifle with it. I, therefore, shall not now volunteer, or expose myself to unnecessary service . . . To-day, I shrink from the idea of a skirmish." These reservations sprang from a habit of reasoning and also from a sense of obligation, for "the governor" had left the family affairs in his hands. This may have been a shrewd stratagem on his father's part. The minister to England was not the first father nor the last, no matter how ardent his principles, to cherish "an earnest wish" that his sons "keep out of it. No man who dips his hands in this blood will remember it with satisfaction. And I confess my aversion to see any of my blood either a victor or a victim in this fratricidal strife." He thought himself scrupulous in not confiding this attitude to his sons; [36] curiously they seemed aware of it.

John served on the military staff of the governor of Massachusetts, Henry accompanied his father to England, and Charles debated his course. Enlistment would undoubtedly break the dreary routine of his office and spare him the mortification of his "failure" at the law. A brief militia service on garrison duty at Fort Independence in Boston Harbor showed him that he enjoyed military service and an outdoor life. Still he could not break loose. Then on October 30 "I went out to ride. It was a clear, windy afternoon, and the autumn leaves gleamed through the crisp October air in the afternoon sunshine. As I was walking my horse through the Braintree woods and meditating on my enforced staying at home, it suddenly flashed across me, Why do I stay at home? . . . The first sensation was not pleasant; and I found myself instinctively clinging to my old, old reasons, now only excuses; but in another moment I was all aglow." [37] He applied for and received a commission, and a day or so after Christmas, 1861, as a first lieutenant he was mustered into the First Regiment of Massachusetts Cavalry Volunteers. The outfit proceeded almost at once to Hilton Head and Beaufort, South Carolina, pieces of the Confederacy early occupied as a result of the superiority of the Federal navy.

Throughout his life Charles always admired the boldness and drama of his decision. "God! What an escape! I was swept off my feet, out of my office and into the army. Educationally and every other way, it was the most fortunate event in my life . . . Think of my life without that experience!" Here the hint of posing is inescapable. At a time when thousands of young men were enlisting, to stay out was more distinctive than to go in. What really lifted Charles' enlistment above the commonplace was the family setting. The young man ignored or defied his father's wishes as neither John nor Henry had. As an activist Charles felt superior to them both. On one occasion he condescended to John over the latter's civilian comforts of wine, fire, and gaslight, while we "poor devils" are in the mud and cold of active service.[38] Under ordinary circumstances Charles would certainly have stigmatized this most childish of all military poses by his favorite word, "vulgar."

While his brothers were holding back, Charles felt he was

fulfilling a family tradition. Could the Adamses, the most "American" of families, with their record of antislavery sentiments be "wholly unrepresented in the field"? Of this rhetoric his father had observed dryly, "But none of his predecessors has been soldiers. Why should he?" With shrewdness he attributed his son's choice to a personal trait: "With abilities and character much above the average he lacks continuity of purpose, which is shown in his beginning an object vigorously and becoming discouraged if not soon successful. He has now taken to an occupation for which he has little fitness." [39]

In his jubilation over his "escape," his "blessed break," Charles did not stop to inquire whether this was what actually happened. In reality he took Boston and Harvard along with him. Little demonstrated this better than the manner in which he obtained his commission. To get it he probably had to pass the scrutiny of Henry Lee, Harvard, class of 1836. Since the Commonwealth was raising these early troops, its governor, John A. Andrew, had the right of appointment. A representative of the "plain people," he nevertheless believed that positions of leadership should be held by the educated and well-born. Since he had neither the acquaintance nor experience to choose such, he relied upon Henry Lee. So much a Massachusetts man that he would have died "if he could not very regularly see the dome of the State House," Lee became eventually a senior member of Lee, Higginson, and Company. He knew the Commonwealth and its families, their history, their strengths and weaknesses. Candor and wit saved him from making weak but impressive choices.[40]

The original suggestion to Adams that he seek a commission in the First Massachusetts Cavalry came from Horace Burney Sargent, another Harvard graduate, who was to become its lieutenant colonel. Later his brother, L. M. Sargent, Jr., a fellow alumnus, became lieutenant colonel and at intervals commanded the regiment. Three out of ten majors in the First and seven out of twenty-eight captains were Harvard graduates. No wonder Charles could write to a companion of "old Bohemian days" that the "Parker-house [is] all over creation." Among the officers his best friends were Lieutenant Colonel Greely Curtis, not a Harvard man; Major Henry L. Higginson, whom weak eyesight prevented from graduating from Harvard, and Captain Caspar Crowninshield, recent Harvard graduate and brother of the wife of John Quincy Adams, 2nd. As for the men, they were not like "those god-forsaken Michiganers and Pennsylvanians" billeted next door; they were natives of Massachusetts, largely Americans, "young, athletic, ingenious, surprisingly alert and very adaptive." Charles sought from military service an education and, as in Boston and Cambridge, was dissatisfied with what he found. "What I most needed I never had — a competent and kindly instructor, a military preceptor and model." Nor did he outgrow his slowness to see opportunities and his timidity in grasping them.[41]

Adams had not chosen the hard way in military service. He was not a foot soldier but a cavalryman. The cavalry was an elite service. Its members rode horses rather than tramped the miles away. The common query "Did you ever see a dead cavalryman?" expressed a popular and unjust attitude. Nor did Charles, a self-conscious young man, always deny himself the excitement of giving the episodes of his career the conventional aspect of a set piece. In any case this treatment relieved the humdrum of army life. At first Federal commanders used cavalry as the eyes and ears of the army. Thus the assignment of the First Massachusetts to the islands off South Carolina was essentially picket or guard duty. "The governor" in London, however, sighed when he learned Charles' tour of duty was at Port Royal: "I much fear I shall never see him again." A year later his son was writing, "They talk of the horrors of war; we have made them a jest — so far. Talk of luxury — you should see our tents. Here on my table is a bundle of flowers which one of my men brought which at home would be worth yellow gold. I write on a mahogany table and behind me is a looking glass & a sofa. I sit on horsehair chairs and my feet rest upon carpets, — & all the spoil of the Philistines loaned by a paternal government to its gallant defenders." Regrettably missing were ice, champagne, the cocktail, oysters — features of the quondam "festive scene" in Boston.[42]

A little later when the First Massachusetts transferred to Washington after the failure of McClellan's peninsular campaign, the "picnic" was over. Antietam followed. During that "veritable charnel house," according to his admission, Charles "dropped quietly asleep — asleep in the height of the battle, and between the contending armies." In October he got his captaincy. A photograph of the successful young officer sent Boston friends into "merry shouts" because of "its grave expression, its steady earnest power, its grim severity, clad so in the panoply of war. No one seeing it can but feel that the man inside is an ardent soul wielding the 'sword of the Lord and of Gideon!' " [43]

The next year, 1863, Adams looked back upon as "my best period in the service." As Lee moved northward through the Shenandoah on his invasion of Maryland and Pennsylvania, he sent his cavalry to the east to protect passes and keep in touch with the Federal army. For much the same purpose the northern cavalry formed a screen to the west as the Federal command moved to keep between Lee and Washington. In June the First Massachusetts and other units encountered Virginian cavalry regiments at Aldie near a pass in the Bull Run mountains. In the course of the deadly helter-skelter of charges and countercharges one hundred and fifty-four of the First's officers and men were killed, wounded, and taken prisoner. This was the most sanguinary conflict it ever fought. In the subsequent convergence of the two armies at Gettysburg the remnant of the First Massachusetts participated; it did not, however, take a momentous part in the battle. Adams' contemporaneous narrative pictured his outfit moving inconclusively about the battlefield and hearing and seeing conflict at a distance; his *Autobiography* introduces the nap taken during crises; and other recollections by inference juxtapose Pickett's charge with Adams' private recitation of lines from Milton's *Samson Agonistes*. The year ended with picket and scout duty about Warrenton, Virginia.[44]

The bulk of military service is monotony and boredom. Perhaps an undue share of details came Adams' way, for he was often the commanding officer's adjutant. Consequently life seemed a string of orders, reports, appeals; the "sabre yields to the pen." Furthermore the care of horses was exacting. Men had to feed, groom, and clean their mounts and when the animals fell into misfortune cure or kill them. Worn out with this routine, Adams felt like a horse doctor.[45] As trying as beasts were human beings. Currents of intrigue ran everywhere; insubordination was developed into a fine art, and the constant pillaging made him ashamed of his uniform.

The only consolations were letters from home — "It's like fresh water in an August noon" — and reading. Adams laughed when his father sent him a copy of *The Golden Treasury*. But he soon found that he and his friends read it. "It is very pleasant to lie down in all this dust and heat and to read some charming little thing of Suckling's and Herrick's." Better than letters was home itself. Adams steadily rejected furloughs until early in 1864. Then when his company re-enlisted, Adams returned to Boston with them. Charles must have found satisfaction in the tribute Governor Andrew, in his welcome to the unit at Faneuil Hall, paid him as an eminent representative of a distinguished family. The "last of the Adamses" was no longer a term of opprobrium. Everywhere Charles found his friends and relatives were the embodiment of warmth and kindness, but, of course, the Quincy homestead was the magnet. "Walked over the house and sat and smoked a cigaret and drank a glass of my old whiskey in the old familiar rooms." [46]

Charles' leave was long enough to permit him to visit the family in England. Henry met him at Liverpool, and as the new arrival gazed out of the train window on the journey to London, he could not help being impressed by "the wonderful development of this country. This country is actually finished!" His other reactions to England varied. A dinner "with about a dozen young liberals of the Oxford stripe" left him with the impression "they were all highly informed and very generally informed but they lack vivacity, humor, and companionship to a most lamentable degree." As for London it was "only a big and formal Boston." But when he crossed the channel with Henry to Paris, the young New England soldier abandoned all reservations. Though he later came to dislike Paris, on his first visit he savored a "city for pleasure, the whole air is full of it." Everyone was gay and lively and the women were beautiful. On the fourth day he concluded his visit with "one more dinner with Burgundy, and started for London smiling and happy with wine." [47] Within five weeks he was back in the army.

To return to the old role and the old subordination was not to Adams' taste. Charles and his coterie had fallen out with the Sargents, their commanding officers. The somewhat obscure causes of friction had been capped by a dash of Adams nonchalance. Summoned by his commander to explain his actions, Charles answered "in that airy manner which makes me a universal favorite" and endeared himself further by "winking pleasantly at [Sargent's] orderlies." Adams apparently begged Theodore Lyman to rescue him from the repetition of such encounters. Lyman, who had been at Harvard in the class ahead of Charles and like him had been a member of the Hasty Pudding Club, was now attached as a "headquarters guest and personal aide" to the staff of General Meade. As a result of Lyman's intercession Charles and his Company D were detached from the First Massachusetts to serve at General Meade's headquarters.[48] During the great drive through the Wilderness and the siege at Petersburg this was also Grant's headquarters.

Though not a staff officer, Charles was now in a position to observe how grand strategy was executed. In the Wilderness "Grant smoked and whittled all the time and he is the coolest man I ever saw." "All Grant's staff sit in a circle under Grant's fly and look at Grant." By the end of the summer Adams was an outright admirer; Grant "certainly has all the simplicity of a very great man, of one whose head has in no way been turned by a rapid rise. A very approachable man, with even, unaffected manners, neither stern nor vulgar." [49]

Meanwhile Adams' military career entered a third phase. In 1864 the Commonwealth of Massachusetts, to fill its quota of soldiers, had recruited the Fifth regiment of cavalry from Negroes smuggled from Canada or brought north from occupied territory in Virginia. The white colonel was Henry S. Russell, a cousin of Robert Gould Shaw, a more famous commander of Negro troops. In July 1864 Charles received a lieutenant-colonel's commission in the Fifth Massachusetts. In September he joined the regiment, "nigger all over," which, dismounted, was guarding prisoners at Point Lookout in Maryland, a post "established on a low, sandy, malarious, fever-smitten, wind-blown, God-forsaken tongue of land dividing Chesapeake Bay from the Potomac River." By this step Charles escaped his boredom and disillusionment with the First Massachusetts, secured a promotion, and was able to satisfy his curiosity about "The Everlasting Nigger Question," as he had called it in his "The Reign of King Cotton." There was a touch of idealism, too, in his conviction that the enlistment of Negroes would ensure "the freedom and regeneration of the African race." This idealism was muted, however, for his previous contacts with Negroes incited misgivings. He was convinced the "nigs" were docile, cheerful, lacking in initiative, skillful as workmen, and possessing "an immeasurable capacity for improvement . . . I have little hope for them in their eternal contact with a race like ours." [50]

To the end of his life Adams always marveled how his health had withstood the army's ignorance of the laws of health and sanitation. Little by little in 1864 dysentery, jaundice, and malaria whittled away his robustness, and doses of opium and quinine did little to ease his miseries. After a sick leave at Boston and Quincy he returned to his Maryland post, not entirely cured, for a "mild, dull Christmas." Mistakenly, as he afterward thought, his initial dynamism had driven him to secure mounts for his troops and to have his men assigned to active service. In mid-February on the resignation of Russell, Adams became a colonel of the regiment, and thus had the distinction of leading his blacks into "burning Richmond at the moment of its capture . . . the one event which I should most have desired as the culmination of my life in the army." There was a touch of feebleness in this elation, for Adams' physical complaints had returned. A few months later he left his command. In August 1865 he resigned and was discharged — a physical wreck weighing 130 pounds. Already he had been brevetted brigadier general.[51]

His service years had followed the course his father had anticipated. They began with elation. After his first experience under fire in 1862 he wrote his father, "I would not have missed it for anything . . . the sensation was glorious . . . Without affectation it was one of the most enjoyable days I ever passed." This mood ebbed away until the close of the experience "was for me a Dead Sea apple." Thirty years after Appomattox, Adams recorded with approval Caspar Crowninshield's "natural description" of how he felt then. "The news of the surrender reached him about 11; he said he went away, and cried, and then said his prayers — the tension was so intense. I can well understand it — we were so sick of the whole thing! The feeling that it was really over was too much. The life had become hateful." [52]

But as part of his education, for as such he judged his military service, the army years had taught Charles something. He was fond of saying, time after time, that the war made a man of him. This generalization was as banal as it was formless. Undoubtedly the service had strengthened his love of the out-of-doors, and by bringing him in contact with a variety of men had taught him a certain humility. As he informed Governor Andrew at the formal welcome to his outfit at Faneuil Hall in 1864, he had learned that the men were better than the officers, and his army training had given him a renewed faith in democracy and mankind. This lesson, however genuine at the time, he did not always remember. But the habit of command and decision and of meeting emergencies gave a shy and untried young man a measure of confidence and poise. Curiously this war service, undertaken in part as a break with the family, also gave Adams an appreciation of his heritage. In a rather belated but nonetheless generous acknowledgment, he wrote his father in 1864, "To be egotistical, I think I see the old family traits cropping out in myself. These men [who were re-enlisting] don't care for me personally. They think me cold, reserved and formal. They feel no affection for me, but they believe in me, they have faith in my power of accomplishing results and in my integrity." [53] Adams had begun, however partially, to fulfill one of his own prescriptions, "Know thyself."

The war had seen other beginnings. On his first leave Charles, just before sailing for Europe, had gone to Newport to see his married sister. There at an evening dinner he met Mary Hone Ogden. The young cavalry captain fell at once under her spell. "With her I was charmed, — as pretty as a French picture." The dispatch with which the preliminary protocol to these family affairs was run through suggests also that the matchmakers were at work. Charles needed no urging.

"Miss Ogden . . . runs through my head infernally. She persuades me that my sensibilities are not dead but sleeping! Hora! I'm not played out." At the end of the year when on sick leave he went to Newport again. Although elders were always present and in the way, he found himself still "aglow." "A pleasant night of waking dreams suggestive of perennial youth" followed his decision to continue the romance.[54] Back again in New England in February 1865, he slipped away from John's Boston house, went to Newport, and became engaged. On November 8, 1865, Miss Ogden, the Minnie of the diaries, and Charles were married.

Though he felt warmly when he mentioned his sweetheart and wife, Charles did not forswear the Adams' habit of appraisal — affectionate in this instance — when it came to Minnie's family. Her father, Edward Ogden, a New Yorker, descended from colonial ancestors and possessed of inherited wealth and position, "was very handsome and a gentleman and a man of the world in society." Her mother, nee Caroline Callender, came of an old family which traced back to Princeton and the Knox-Witherspoon-Smith connection. She was "as pretty as they make them . . . She was a thoroughly good woman but Lord! — how Scotch and matter of fact." [55]

The role of an Adams wife was no easy one. She must be prepared to accept long absences from her husband and to accompany him to distant places and in restless changes of abode. She must face with composure sudden changes of temperament and purpose, and at the same time endure an absorption in work and activity which might well cheat her of attention. She must manage her family and household with flair and sophistication. It is perhaps not discreet to probe too relentlessly the reasons why one woman speaks well of another, but in this instance, in view of the evidence, there is no need to question the enthusiasm of a lady in their Washington coterie: "He found the one woman of his generation fit to marry him, so

beautiful, so self-possessed, so nearly his equal in every way." [56]
With Charles the Adams good fortune in marrying still held.
The governor realized it. Commenting upon a letter from
his son at the time of his engagement and upon other letters
about Miss Ogden, the father wrote: "Of all the incidents that
go to make up the happiness of life, one of the greatest is that
of being blessed with good children. When I saw these letters
I am afraid I was a little foolish." Then in a kindly matter-of-
factness he wrote on: "You are right in judging that the circumstances attending the worldly resources of the lady you propose
to marry have no weight with me whatever." "For reasons well
known to you in the state of my fortune and your mother's, I
can scarcely give you capital. That is locked up either in trusts
or in large interests in land. But I can give you income, on
the same footing which I gave to your brother, when he took
the same step. It is my intention to give $3000 per annum to
each of my sons in succession on their marriage. I wish I could
do more." With this assurance and Minnie's money, the bride
and groom went abroad where from Rome to Paris they saw
foreigners and fellow Bostonians. In 1866 they were back. In
after years Charles remembered it as the "worst of all" of his
many crossings. "Where to go? What to do? pah!" The young
couple stayed for a spell at the Mount Vernon Street house and
then moved to "the little house on the Neponset road" in
Quincy. "I had not yet caught the step." [57]

RAILROAD REFORMER

1869-1890

PROBABLY the most pleasant single aspect of Charles' "great unacknowledged debt to the Civil War" was the cessation of any further serious effort to make a go of the law. As to what to put in its place, Charles had undertaken by letter a dialogue with Henry as early as 1859. Like most correspondents Charles was talking to himself. He began by urging Henry to become a "sophist." "What this country needs, what it has not yet got, & what it will willingly pay for is a body of trained thinkers, — men capable of directing public sentiment. To be this you must be a philosopher, a lawyer, a writer & a speaker. It is not a thing to be attained at once; it is a profession." From London in 1862 Henry caught up and enlarged this suggestion. "But what we want is a *school*. We want a national set of young men like ourselves or better, to start new influences not only in politics, but in literature, in law, in society, and throughout the whole social organism of the country — a national school of our own generation." [1]

The advantage or the obligation of playing the sophist was a persistent theme with Charles. As late as his presidential address before the American Historical Association in 1901 he invited his fellow historians to hold at least one of their meetings in the July "preceding each presidential election. The issues of that election will then have been presented and the opposing candidates named. It should be understood that the meeting is held for the purpose of discussing those issues from the historical point of view, and in their historical connection" — an elevation of political discussion and the rejection of partisan arguments would result.[2]

Meanwhile in the sixties Charles was busy with the practical problems of how he, as an individual, could participate in realizing this noble dream. "My future," he once wrote, "must be business and literature." On another occasion he added: "All my natural inclinations tend to a combination of literature and politics and always have. I would be a philosophical statesman if I could and a literary politician if I must." Perhaps staying in the army would have afforded him the means, position, and leisure to write and exert an influence, but ill-health and his marriage turned his efforts in another direction. As he wrote in the eighties, "As long ago as when I left the army . . . I made up my mind to devote fifteen years to making my way into a position." "I endeavored to strike out a new path, and fastened myself, not, as Mr. Emerson recommends, to a star but to the locomotive-engine. I made for myself what might be called a specialty in connection with the development of the railroad system." [3]

To play the sophist for the railroads was a shrewd stroke. American inventors and investors had begun in the late 1820's and early 1830's to experiment with the railroad as a means of carrying freight and passengers. By the 1850's transportation by rail had reached a certain level of maturity. At the end of the decade the rail network contained 30,626 miles and had pressed from the seaboard to Chicago, to the Mississippi, and beyond. In Massachusetts alone there were 1264 miles of railroad and the Commonwealth led all the states in the proportion her mileage bore to her area. Indeed the density of railroads in Massachusetts surpassed that of the industrialized countries of Western Europe.[4]

In the 1860's when Adams cast his lot with them, the railroads nationally were about to enter upon a new phase. Immediately after the Civil War construction, which had slowed during the conflict, leaped ahead. Between 1865 and 1873, when panic chilled further expansion, the railroads had doubled their miles in operation. The most conspicuous event in this remarkable period of growth was the completion in 1869 by the Central Pacific and Union Pacific of the first transcontinental line. The immensity of this achievement, accomplished in good measure through subsidies from the Federal government, captured the popular imagination. Growth at such a rate was hardly to be expected in Massachusetts, which had been working at railroads for decades, but mileage did increase in this period. More importantly the state pursued a wide program of state aid to railroad enterprises, of which the incompleted Hoosac tunnel route was the most noteworthy. In part the state's policy was a reaction to Boston's dissatisfaction with her traditional route to the West, along which the Boston and Worcester and the Western railroads had been consolidated in 1867 into the Boston and Albany.[5]

Adams did not attempt to hitch his wagon to the locomotive engine in the most obvious way by seeking employment on a railroad. The daring and ingenuity of his strategy lay in his belief that he could make a living by wedding railroads and reform. There was a need for reform. Railroads were a business experiment; correct principles of construction and, more important, administration had neither been formulated nor understood. Furthermore railroads had not always fulfilled their promises nor had they always brought benefits. Security holders had not received dividends and, in some cases, interest; the rate structure, by its general level and by departure from it in discriminations, perplexed and outraged shippers and travelers. In short, communities, which had largely looked upon railroad corporations as agencies to achieve public purposes, failed to perceive the gains from their existence or operation.[6] How to make a living from these disappointments and agitations was a problem. The obvious path was politics. In this area Adams was "convinced that I have no aptitude, I lack magnetism frightfully, & have no facility of doing the right thing at the right time. I am frightfully deficient in tact; I never can remember faces or names, and so I am by nature disqualified. I never could be a popular man." Nor was there available, then or for decades later, the possibility of academic employment as a teacher or scholar in the field of railroads. Railroad journalism promised more. The number of journals devoted to the business had increased in the 1850's, and Henry Varnum Poor was demonstrating through the *American Railroad Journal* that an editor could advocate railroad reform and still make a living. Though such prospects might have appealed to one as facile with the pen as Charles, he apparently regarded publication as a part-time thing or a last recourse.[7]

Though prospects of a livelihood from railroad reform were narrow, Charles had the advantage of knowing how to be a reformer in general. Any impressionable young man growing up in his family was bound to learn from antislavery agitation and the formation of the Republican party the importance of stirring the deeper emotions as a prelude to decisive action and the way to stir emotions through speech and essay. He knew how to make sure these appeals would reach the public, or at least its leaders. Otherwise Adams was unprepared for his role. Some engineers, legislators, judges, journalists, businessmen, and investors knew about railroads. Adams was not one of these. With the exception of what his despised legal background had taught him, he was as innocent about railroads as a new-born babe. The series of essays he wrote over the five years after his return from a European honeymoon served the purpose of educating himself as much as informing the public. He learned by groping.

In April 1867 the *North American Review* published the first fruits of his effort — a review article, "The Railroad System." This periodical had been a favorite mouthpiece for his father, and Charles turned to it naturally. In a manner reminiscent of his prewar essay on "King Cotton," the "Railroad System" at once sounded a magisterial note. With two exceptions, not stated, the "application of steam to locomotion" is "the most tremendous and far-reaching engine of social revolution which has ever either blessed or cursed the earth." The reason its benefits were not more fully realized was a conflict of interest. "The owners of roads naturally prefer that tariff of prices which will insure to them the largest net profit, whatever may be the amount of travel or transportation over their lines . . . The community equally naturally desires cheap as well as abundant transportation; but, on the other hand, are far too much disposed to forget their own rights, and to look upon corporations, not as their servants and trustees, but only as self-interested traders." [8]

Having begun with the cosmos, Charles ended with Boston. He gave guarded approval to a suggestion of Josiah Quincy, Jr., ex-mayor of Boston, Harvard graduate, and a neighbor of the Adamses. Quincy proposed that the state recapture the Boston and Worcester and the Western railroads under their charter provisions and run them as a railroad for the prosperity of Boston. Upon this "startling" proposal, Adams commented: "There is no difficulty of law or precedent to be encountered, and all goes smoothly on until we come to the question of management." This objection proved insurmountable. "Corporations can never compete on equal terms with individuals, and governments always exemplify the most expensive way of not doing things." [9]

On the whole this first salvo of the young Adams was more cogent on railroads "as an abstract question" than on concrete details. Along with the other articles in this period of incubation, it showed the author was becoming expert by reading railroad reports, agitational and promotional literature, government reports from various states and European countries, and newspapers. Great gaps still remained in his and the public's knowledge; the railroad question "is not yet ripe for any satisfactory solution through the absence of any reliable statistical tables. The first measure, therefore, looking to any future legislation, should be the creation, in the various States, of bureaus of railroad statistics, under the superintendence of competent commissioners." This prescription appeared in a footnote.[10]

If "The Railroad System" never got off dead center, the succeeding articles on Boston were sharper and more interesting. In two installments in the *North American Review* of 1868, Adams had a gay time teasing Boston about her decline into a second-class "large town" like Lowell and Manchester. While admitting that Boston had made efforts to arrest her descent into "decadence," Adams thought these had been misdirected. The chief remedy was a channel which could do business cheaply with the West. The way to discover that channel was for the community to "organize its intelligence." This should be "the labor of a new commission, composed of such men in material life as Story was in law, Mann in education, and Bache in science. These men must study causes, point out effects, and indicate remedies . . . Whatever is attempted, let it be attempted knowingly and systematically; in obedience to some natural law." [11] Then and only then could Boston rival Chicago.

Adams lifted the commission idea out of a footnote into a central position in his text because he was trying to persuade the Massachusetts General Court to establish a railroad commission. If he could get one authorized and secure an appointment on it, he could solve his personal dilemma. He would be a sophist within the government and he would have won his position not through popular election, which he was unfitted to face, but by gubernatorial appointment. While waiting for the political gods to move, instructing and inciting them as best he could, Adams tossed off three essays on subordinate features of the railroad system.[12]

After he moved to Quincy, Adams set his pen to what has proved his best-known and most enduring work in the field of railroads: "A Chapter of Erie." This was well titled, for it described an episode in the history of the Herculean efforts by Commodore Vanderbilt, president of the New York Central, to secure control of his great cross-state rival, the Erie Railroad. The managers of the Erie, Daniel Drew, Jay Gould, and James — more conventionally Jim — Fisk, not only resisted the attack but sought to make money out of it. The struggle began on Wall Street where Vanderbilt tried to buy a majority of Erie stock, and where the Erie managers contrived to manufacture so much new stock that even the courage and resources of the Commodore could not cope with the flood. Then the contestants moved into the courts, where each had not only counsel but captive judges. Finally both sides rushed to Albany to secure the legislation they wanted. "A Chapter of Erie" was an exposé of the stock exchange and of corrupt government as much as it was of railroads.[13]

It was impossible to ruin the drama of these proceedings. Even though Adams thought his narrative "too long," the story lost nothing in his telling. He cut down the cosmic in favor of details. The elegance of his epithets — the rascals were usually designated "gentlemen" — and the ironic air of disbelief in the ludicrous incidents along the way created the impression that the shenanigans here set forth were worse than corrupt and dangerous, they were vulgar. Part of Adams' delight in the exposure must have arisen from the fact that these were New York doings. While he was writing the article, he had visited the New York Stock Exchange and seen "men as nature made them with every affectation cast aside."[14]

Where did he get his material? Apparently he scoured the

newspaper files, particularly the *Tribune*, in the Boston Athenaeum. But journals could not furnish the "inside" story as Adams told it. The gaps in his information which he so much lamented were filled in by a communication from a New York broker and perhaps by conversations with some of the principals involved. There is a piquant note in his diary for 1872: "Heard of the murder of James Fisk, Jr., — the damned rascal was a good friend to me but the state's prison has been cheated of an inmate!" At the time and in retrospect Adams thought the essay was "the hardest piece of work I ever did." Though he had his customary misgivings in the course of composition, when it was done he knew "it is good, very good! Much better than I thought." And when he sent it off to the *North American Review*, Minnie and he dined with his parents on Mount Vernon Street; "The goose hangs high — in a day or two it will drop a little." His elation slackened when the publishers paid him only $150. This struck Adams "as a little too mean" and he sent the check back. Actually he soon realized the *Review* was on its uppers and consequently to make the stir to which he felt entitled, he busied himself with getting a revised "chapter" published as a brochure. Within six months it seemed "to have sold only 2000 copies." [15]

From the short-range point of view it made little difference. Early in 1869 the General Court passed "my railroad commissioners bill." Adams mobilized every influence, Richard Dana, Edward Atkinson, and others, to get an appointment, and on June 28 Judge Bigelow, who had passed Adams in his law examination, called to report that Governor Claflin had nominated him. In the little cluster of days when June gave way to July, successes came crowding in. Years later Adams still felt the thrill. "Careful preparation told . . . That Fourth of July, 1869, was, distinctly, one of my life's red-letter days . . . The preliminary struggle at last was over; the way was open before me. At last I had worked myself into my proper position and an environment natural to me." In the afternoon he celebrated his day of happiness by taking a walk with Henry and dining at the old house in Quincy.[16]

In after years as he examined the act of 1869 Adams was apt to mingle censure with incredulity. It was "clumsily drawn"; "in theory an experiment, in reality it was a makeshift." Certainly the statute was vague. The General Court established a railroad commission of three members appointed by the governor and assigned it no specific power, except that of investigating accidents. The bill declared the "Commissioners shall have the general supervision of all railroads in the Commonwealth," and were to make an annual report in January to the legislature, "containing such facts, statements, and explanations as will disclose the actual working of the system of railroad transportation in its bearings upon the business and prosperity of the Commonwealth, or as to any part thereof . . . as may seem to them appropriate." [17] In brief the statute seemed to authorize a fishing expedition into the railroad business. If such abstractions were not likely to arouse antagonism from the railroads, they were equally unlikely to stir enthusiasm among reformers bent upon a different order of things.

This permissive tone stemmed partly from Adams' ignorance of railroad matters. He wanted time to learn; the exercise of a state's power to collect testimony, evidence, and reports certainly furthered that end. Thus equipped with knowledge and wisdom, sophist Adams could hope to shape public affairs. "The board of commissioners was set up as a sort of lens by means of which the otherwise scattered rays of public opinion could be concentrated to a focus and brought to bear upon a given point . . . In fact . . . the law could not have been improved. Had it not been a flagrant legislative guess, it would have been an inspiration." [18] Whether the presence of a rapidly growing railroad system and the pressure for action upon its rights and wrongs would wait upon a long period of self and public education was another question.

Looking back upon the beginnings of his bureaucratic phase, Adams felt the commissioners "could hardly save themselves from falling into contempt." His anxieties arose from the limitations of the statute of 1869, from his estimate of his fellow commissioners, and from uncertainty as to whether he could take over the commission and make it an Adams enterprise. Of his original associates, James C. Converse, chairman of the commission, was a dry goods commission merchant who obviously represented the interest of the Boston Board of Trade in improved communication with the West. Adams at once concluded he was "the damndest fool I have met lately — such an ignorant bag of wind — he makes me blue." His second associate, Edward Appleton, a Harvard man, Adams at first suspected as a "clear-headed business man of doubtful associations." His clairvoyance was justified, for in 1872 it was revealed that while Appleton was commissioner, he accepted funds from railroads for engineering advice. No wonder Adams thought he was "the poorest of them all." [19] Neither Converse nor Appleton was reappointed when their terms expired.

Whoever his associates were, Adams relied upon one of the fundamental laws of bureaucracy to manage them. He did not think his colleagues would stand in the way "of my doing as much work as I please." Almost at once he discovered they were perfectly willing to assign the writing of the annual report to him; and still later he found they were not only willing to accept it but they did so with alacrity. "And so my views may be considered as successfully launched." Of course many of his difficulties were eased when Adams became the chairman of the commission in 1872, and secured associates who would accept his leadership without exhibiting that "restive jealousy" and those "ruffled feathers" Adams once had to smooth down. Adams was particularly at ease with Albert D. Briggs of Springfield, Massachusetts. He thought him "a very simple, true man," though his innocence was so complete it failed to perceive a conflict of interest obvious to the General Court. From the mid-

1870's to the end of the decade the personnel of the commission remained practically unchanged. This permanence was "singularly fortunate" for the group "had a chance to outlive its inexperience and profit by its own blunders, which naturally were at first neither trifling nor infrequent." [20]

Since the commission was intended primarily to plan and appraise, the General Court regarded it as a substitute or supplement for legislative committees on railroads and frequently solicited its opinion on proposed legislation. Governors anxious to know whether to veto or approve railroad bills also sought advice. Furthermore the commission often proposed legislation supplementary to the original act or to put into effect its own recommendations.

In the early years two enterprises recurrently tested the Massachusetts concept of a railroad commission as thus organized. One was the Boston, Hartford and Erie Railroad, projected to run southwest from Boston and then directly westward to the Hudson River. Its promoters thus sought to bisect the territory lying south of the Boston and Albany Railroad and north of New England's southern coast. Adams, before the commission came into being, had once seized upon the enterprise as a whip to chastise Boston's promotional inertia and lack of imagination. According to his analysis, Boston capitalists were neglecting a road "starting from their own doors, running through the most populous region of the continent, leading to double termini, to New York and the great West, furnishing Boston the shortest road to each through an open country, swarming with a busy population, — an unmade road which is at once a through road and a road between great cities." Actually the route traversed a difficult terrain nor did its direct or "air-line" character enable it to challenge already adequate avenues of transportation. The promotion and management of the road had fallen into the hands of a bunch of adventurers as unsavory and as irresponsible as the Erie ring of Fisk, Drew, and Gould; indeed the Bostonians occasionally gave these New York colleagues aces and spades and still won the game. In 1867 the Boston, Hartford and Erie induced the General Court to grant them a state loan of $3,000,000, and thereafter they came back, importunate and shameless, for additional appropriations. The day the money stopped came in 1870.[21]

The other enterprise — the Hoosac Tunnel route, had a longer history. Projected to run through the northern tier of Massachusetts counties, the line reached the Connecticut River at Greenfield over a succession of end-to-end roads, and it was intended to continue westward by the Troy and Greenfield Railroad and to pierce the Berkshire barrier by the Hoosac Tunnel, whose length of somewhat over four miles made it the longest bore in the United States. At Troy and Albany the road was to connect for the West, as did its rival the Boston and Albany, over the New York Central. As early as 1854 the state had granted financial assistance to the Hoosac route; one way or another construction kept going during the Civil War; in the postwar years the new inclination of the state toward railroad subsidies poured millions into the Hoosac enterprise and in effect transferred to the Commonwealth the ownership of the tunnel and of the railroad beyond the Connecticut River. In 1873 the tunnel was holed through; two years later the first trains passed through the "great bore." So long had been the history of this Massachusetts institution that one wit remarked many believed the Hoosac Tunnel had come over in the Mayflower. Between 1873 and 1875 the debate between tunnelites and anti-tunnelites as to how to utilize the route came to a head in the press and on Beacon Hill. The immediate result was that the state in 1875 established a toll system under which it retained the ownership and operation of the Troy and Greenfield Railroad and tunnel and charged a toll upon their use by connecting railroads.[22]

Amidst these turbulent seas, Adams swam as best he could.

He did not get much help from the governors. Claflin, who had appointed Adams to the commission, "is so slow and tired that I can't do business with him." He did feel somewhat kindlier when the governor finally brought himself to veto a bill for further aid to the Boston, Hartford and Erie. Adams rejoiced: "The B.H.& E. got a dreadful black eye and seems to be gone up which is a great gain for me." [23]

Of Governor William B. Washburn, Claflin's successor, Adams had a better opinion. "The Governor's judgment is sound and he thinks slowly and talks around." If Adams' private advice on the Hoosac was of the same tenor as his public utterances, it is little wonder the governor hemmed and hawed. This opinionated young man on the railroad commission was proposing to consolidate the various lines running from Boston to Troy by the recapture provisions of their charters or by other means and then have the state operate the lines. Granting this proposal was an "innovation," Adams justified it not as a universal policy but as a measuring rod for existing private enterprises. "We rely on competition to preserve us from red tape on one side and corruption on the other, and so we do not want to destroy competition by State ownership, but we want to get back to it through mixed ownership." The toll system, the alternative adopted as politically feasible, filled Adams with rage. At first he hoped Washburn's successor would veto it. But Gaston "is weak, he wants to veto it, has and confesses that he has excellent grounds for doing so, and yet does not." [24] With the remaining governors during his commissionership Adams was more content. At least they had the merit of keeping General Benjamin Butler out of the governor's chair. Butler's military and political career had been so equivocal that reformers of the Adams persuasion viewed his defeat as the triumph of political righteousness.

Often Adams thought the General Court and its agencies were a greater cross to bear than the Executive. Yet there were moments when Adams had fun in his contacts with the people's representatives. The 1870 hearings on state aid to the Boston, Hartford and Erie were crowded with playful ironies. One lawyer who appeared for the road was R. H. Dana, in whose office Adams had read law. Dana continually referred to his former pupil as "my young friend." When he brought out the fact that Adams had once endorsed the enterprise, Adams dismissed this approval "as one of the crudities of my youth . . . I don't profess now to be infallible. I only say that my opinion is worth a great deal more now than when I wrote that nonsense." Characteristically Adams was satisfied with this performance. "I woke up the blockheads of the Board of Trade by my evidence & they are all about my ears of course, my colleagues have gone back on me, this vexed me a little." Eventually he wrote the report for the committee minority opposed to a continuance of state aid. Analytically and rhetorically this was a devastating document.[25]

As the basis of his general theorizing about railroads, Adams always relied upon "the eventual supremacy of an enlightened public opinion." From day to day, however, it proved hard to enlighten the public; nor did the light of pure reason always guide its decisions. However gratified by sportive intervals and personal triumphs, Adams never ceased being amazed by the State House "where business is flapping round in its usual loose way & it remains to be seen how far we can influence it." A year later he was groaning, "This being six months each year under a legislative harrow is simply execrable; it destroys all ones nerves." Apparently by the mid-seventies the General Court was less of "an incubus"; it had stopped hazing the commission and admired it.[26]

Meanwhile the commission proceeded to its assigned tasks. If it were to report upon the railroad system of the state, more particularly upon whether it was conforming with the charters and laws of the state, the commission and everyone else had to

47

know what these charters and laws were. The complexity of this task was well illustrated by the legislation of 1869. In that year the General Court had established the railroad commission; it had also passed seven other laws of general application to railroads and 145 special laws incorporating new roads, amending the charters of old ones, and directing or permitting certain acts, operational and financial. A chaos of uncertainty, contradiction, and privilege resulted. Consequently Adams at once pressed the General Court to authorize a codification of general railroad legislation and a compendium and index of the acts applying to particular organizations. Though the authorization was forthcoming, the General Court refused to pass until 1874 the consolidated statute the commission had drawn up. It filled nearly sixty pages of the *Acts and Resolves*.[27]

Another step in the inauguration of order and system was an act to terminate the grant of special charters and substitute a general act for incorporation under whose provisions any group of incorporators after filing plans and demonstrating their seriousness of intent and financial abilities by stock subscriptions and after obtaining approval from the railroad commission could secure a charter and build. Such an act would not only do away with the helter-skelter of the past, it might systematize through uniformity the launching of future railroad enterprises. The General Court passed a general incorporation act for railroads in 1872.[28]

To discuss the railroad system the commission had, however, to know something more than legalities. Technical, financial, and operational details were also necessary. Theoretically the annual returns which the railroads under their charters made to the secretary of the Commonwealth provided this information. While he was educating himself and others, Adams had sensed the misleading and ambiguous character of the information thus provided: in his official capacity as commissioner he soon expressed a breathless incredulity over the irrationality and opaqueness of railroad affairs. He could not, for instance, learn from the returns so common a matter as the mileage of railroads in the Commonwealth, "an item of information perhaps, as important as any, and one in respect to which accuracy would seem not very difficult of attainment." In fact the returns were full of contradictions and divergencies and the railroad officials neither took them seriously nor filled them out carefully. At Adams' bidding the General Court proceeded to introduce a reformed order of things. In 1870 a statute stated the returns were to be made to the commission rather than the secretary of the Commonwealth, set penalties for tardiness and inaccuracies, and authorized the commissioners "to order such changes as they shall deem expedient," and also require from the railroads "alterations in the method or form of keeping their accounts." [29]

Though the commissioners were for the moment satisfied that their innovations produced at least accurate engineering statistics, they were certain that the new form of reports did not reveal operational data. This was a vital matter. "Every proposal for a reduction of rates will always be met with an answer (whether sound or not on other grounds is here immaterial) that the corporations, under their present tariff, earn only enough to pay operating expenses and moderate dividends." [30] As far back as the early charters, a frequently included clause limited earnings to 10 percent per annum on the cost of the road; if the percentage exceeded that figure, rates were to be reduced. Adams was convinced that the more favorably located and better run roads were in effect avoiding a rate decrease by financing their expansion and improvement through the reinvestment of earnings. In other words they had closed their construction account and put permanent improvements into their operating account. Hard pressed roads did the opposite. As long as the methods of keeping railroad accounts differed because of each road's financial exigencies, a valid comparative study of costs and rates was out of the question.

Consequently Adams began to press the General Court to

authorize the commission to draw up a standard system of keeping railroad accounts and impose it upon the railroads. If the legislature did not respond, doom was around the corner. "The Commissioners feel it incumbent upon them to warn those interested in railroad investments in Massachusetts that the books of the corporations are, in many cases, far from properly kept. It may be that the officers concerned are exceptionally honest, but this is certainly the only safeguard against fraud which the stockholders possess. If the banking business were conducted with the same looseness in accounts, defalcations would be even more frequent than they now are." [31] Whether such vague caveats would have toppled a system of keeping accounts that conservative opinion and the inertia of railroad accountants preferred is doubtful.

The financial collapse of the Eastern Railroad in 1875 gave force to general arguments. Adams pointed out that the railroad had charged to its construction account the damages resulting from the Revere wreck, described below, as well as the discount on the sales of its bonds. "It would seem to be mere waste of time to dwell upon the preposterous character of such entries . . . It is as if a man who was so unfortunate as to have his barn burned to the ground were to get rid of his loss by charging it off into the cost of his house." Perhaps such outcomes were due to fraud by management; perhaps the explanations were variables in the accounting system. "Indeed discretion and good judgment enter so largely into railroad accounting, that it has been in no way unusual for corporations to find themselves hopelessly bankrupt before those who managed their affairs were aware that they were in a position of danger." In 1876 the General Court capitulated. It authorized the commission "to prescribe a system upon which the books and accounts" of railroad and street railway corporations "shall be kept in a uniform manner." Furthermore the commission, to determine whether a corporation was keeping its books

Portrait of Mary Ogden Adams (Mrs. Charles Francis, Jr.) by
Francis Millet (1876). "Millet painting Minnie and getting along
well." (*Diary*)

Portrait of Adams by Francis Millet (1876). "Began to sit for my portrait in earnest . . . tremendous likeness." (*Diary*)

properly, could employ a full-time auditor. In cooperation with the railroads' accountants a form of return taking twenty pages of the annual report was drawn up. The commission's five years of agitation for "correct knowledge" had apparently been realized.[32] Into few aspects of his railroad program did Adams throw himself with as much zest and persistence as into this quest for a "correct system"; nationally his example had exceptional influence.

In at least one other feature of railroad operation, railroad accidents, Adams found a comparable but belated success. When the commission came into being, trains were run on schedules of fixed meeting places and the telegraph was not generally employed to regulate conformity to these schedules; automatic signals had not been invented; hand braking a train to a stop was laborious and slow; the wooden rolling stock telescoped in collisions and promptly flamed into a "holocaust," ignited by stove heaters or open-flame lighting; wooden bridges gave way and let trains fall into rivers and ravines; crude hand couplings between cars maimed employees and exasperated them into taking chances; a self-reliant and undisciplined public insisted upon alighting from moving trains and upon competing with the locomotives at grade crossings. Not accumulated incidents but great calamities, measured either by the number or importance of persons killed, horrified the public and compelled state action. For instance, Connecticut's commission, which preceded Massachusetts' by a decade, was established when a train plunged through an open draw at Norwalk.[33]

The provisions of the Massachusetts act specifically gave the Massachusetts commission a chance to derive from the seeming chaos of particular accidents some generalizations and to make usable recommendations for safe practices. While the commission was still feeling its way, the Revere disaster of 1871 pitchforked it into action. On an August Saturday passenger trains on the Eastern Railroad had become so congested that the system of operation, whatever it was, practically collapsed. In the evening of that day a Portland-bound express ploughed into the rear of a local passenger train at Revere station. The trains caught fire. Twenty-nine people were killed and fifty-seven were injured. Horror and indignation swept the state. At a mass meeting Wendell Phillips, another Massachusetts reformer, declared, "This terrible disaster, which has made the last thirty-six hours so sad to us all, is a deliberate murder." Naturally someone was guilty. For such "bathos of extravagance" Adams had little use, but the public excitement of the time compelled the early publication of an *ad hoc* report and the consideration of general safety measures. The first was one of Adams' finer performances. It analyzed luminously the complicated series of events which culminated in the disaster, yet caught and communicated the drama and horror of the event itself.

Over the long run Adams was skeptical of what legislation could do. Relying instead upon the advisory and voluntary devices of the act of 1869, he assembled a committee of railroad officials. They recommended, among other things, "the general adoption . . . of brakes operated from the locomotive," "the construction of all new passenger cars in such a manner as to prevent telescoping in case of accident" and the change of existing cars to conform to that standard, "the adoption of some approved standard heating apparatus," the disuse on passenger trains of any illuminating substance other than candles or a fluid incapable of ignition at less than 300 degrees Fahrenheit, "and finally the general use of the telegraph in aid of the present time-table system." Such brakes were Westinghouse air brakes and such cars were equipped with the Miller platform, whose buffers were backed by the heavy lengthwise sills under the car and whose couplings held the cars tight to each other, but the commissioners deliberately avoided designating the devices by name. Adams dreaded lest specifications freeze technical experimentation and also give a business advantage to the holders of patents. As for the human weaknesses Revere had revealed, damage suits would make managers prudent; in the case of operatives, Adams had already expressed doubts as to whether "caution can be legislated into engineers, and presence of mind into signal men." [34]

Since Adams felt it extremely desirable to put railroad accidents into perspective, he fell back upon his favorite method, comparative statistics applied to an area larger than Massachusetts. After a survey of other American states and European nations, he discovered that fatalities in proportion to passengers carried and to passenger miles traveled in Massachusetts were generally less than in the United States or overseas. Indeed one of the safest places on earth was a Massachusetts train. Sunstroke, murder, and accident in the city of Boston accounted for more fatalities. Facts such as these filled Adams with awe. "A practically irresistible force crashing through the busy hive of modern civilization at a wild rate of speed, going hither and thither across highways and by-ways and along a path which is in itself a thoroughfare, — such an agency cannot be expected to work incessantly and yet never to come into contact with the human frame." These observations Adams published in 1879 as a little volume on railroad accidents. It was a sort of swan song to his years on the commission. He claimed correctly that this book made accessible for the first time "material buried in newspapers and contemporaneous sources." He also restated his enthusiasm for the Miller platform and buffer, the Westinghouse air brake, and the interlocking and electric signal systems. It was up to the public to "hasten their more general adoption." Neither the public nor railroad officials nor railroad legislation, however, really got around to dealing effectively with accidents until the 1890's.[35]

One result of the Massachusetts commission's way of doing

things was that occurrences rather than abstractions compelled the formulation and application of principles. The fundamental acts of 1869, for instance, had said nothing about railroad labor. The Revere disaster raised this issue in at least a tangential manner. One of its causes had been a lack of discipline and responsibility in the labor force.[36] Suddenly in 1877 a strike of engineers and firemen presented the labor issue in a direct and general fashion.

This dramatic episode was the New England manifestation of a national discontent with the methods railroad managers had taken to meet the aftermath of the depression of 1873. Throughout the nation there had been pay cuts — often successive ones. Strikes in Pittsburgh had taken on the aspect of an armed rebellion against the Pennsylvania Railroad; in Massachusetts a few Boston and Maine strikers had abruptly stopped trains in transit and dumped the fires in locomotives. Since the railroad was prepared to run trains with strikebreakers, there was little inconvenience. But the abruptness of the strikers' procedures as well as their attempt to dissuade those who had taken their places aroused considerable excitement. Adams, "much troubled," consulted railroad officials, held a hearing at which the strikers presented their case, and then after a "fine brisk walk up through Braintree revolving the strike question in my mind," wrote his report the following day. His colleagues approved it and it was printed at once. He thought at the time it was "a good, square, blow well got in," and in later years he still thought it was "as creditable a piece of work as I ever did."[37]

As was customary, the report began by stating the principle that a railroad was a vital public enterprise which must be kept in operation; managers could not roundhouse their equipment nor workers stop trains when they wished. So much for the immediate crisis. Over the long pull the best safeguards against conflict between labor and capital were a community of interest and an esprit de corps. These the corporations had done little to cultivate. Retrospectively, but withal imaginatively, Adams thought the managers should have made employment on the railroads "a service, having, in case of good behavior, all the elements of permanence." The means to this end were a gradual increase of wages depending upon the length of service, protection against "arbitrary dismissal" by subordinate officials through "a hearing before a committee of the direction," and insurance against death and disability from sickness, accident, or old age. The corporation by providing these essential protections would wean employees away from a dependence upon the "benevolent" activities of trade unions. Meanwhile the strike of 1877 had collapsed. The historian of the engineers' organization dismissed it as "a grand dismal failure." [38]

Considerable as were Adams' accomplishments on the commission, neither his colleagues nor he had solved the railroad problem as he himself had defined it during the years he was learning about railroads. The heart of that problem was rates. In this matter the commission from first to last boasted it had no direct power. It could leave the determination of rates to the railroads themselves and hope that the natural laws of competition would keep rates from being excessive and discriminatory, or it could investigate and recommend legislation to the General Court. Adams spent a decade writing on this problem in what he called "the philosophical part" of the commission's annual report. He demonstrated that the natural laws of competition were no reliance, because competition between railroads was impossible. Railroads were a natural monopoly and they gravitated into agreements and combinations. If government chose to regulate their rates, it confronted the variety of business circumstances on the different roads. Rates which would enable one enterprise barely to survive would needlessly enrich another. Legislation and administrative decisions in the middle western states, particularly in Ohio and Illinois, had demonstrated the impossibility of meeting this dilemma, This "ignorance" of correct principles was Adams' real grudge against the legislation enacted in the Midwest in response to the demands of farmers organized in the Grange or Patrons of Husbandry. Adams was willing to grant the Granger acts were needed to bludgeon a sense of public obligation into the heads of managers who arrogantly regarded their enterprises as merely private business.[39]

In his own jurisdiction Adams was content to confine his first steps to compiling accurate information about costs. After this, what? To escape from the pincers Adams proposed to rejuvenate the competitive system through one governmentally owned and operated railroad; such a line would not enter into combinations and the inherent ineffectiveness of public management, about which Adams was very sure, would be avoided by comparison with the economies of private management. The experience of Belgium with a railroad system which mixed public and private roads held out the promise of success for Massachusetts. In spite of the opportunity offered by the Hoosac route, Adams was unable to prevail upon the Commonwealth to undertake the experiment. Even according to his own evidence, it was no cure-all. So Adams kept on writing. Meanwhile he held the state back from rate making except for a few attempts to lower passenger rates, usually on Boston commuting traffic. He also restrained as best he could the zeal of communities for subsidizing branch lines through town or municipal subscriptions: to restore competition by this means was unfeasible.[40]

Adams' analysis of the difficulty of statutory or administrative rate making was persuasive; nonetheless it was evidence that he failed to work out the problem. After a decade of erudition and pages of explanation, at the end he was still at the beginning. "Were there," he wrote in 1879, "in this country a great many more public investigations into alleged railroad abuses, and not nearly so many repressive laws, the condition of affairs would be greatly improved." [41] In the previous year, Adams' restatement of his experience and thought in *Railroads, Their Origin and Problems,* a vigorous summation of his commission years, could not conceal the fact that he had painted himself into a corner.

By visible standards Adams' position at the end of the 1870's had become exceedingly happy. He had able colleagues who acknowledged his leadership; irritating pinpricks from governor and General Court had ceased. But Adams' enthusiasm for the task had dimmed. Whereas when things had once been much less well arranged he did not wish to leave the commission unless he "could be a martyr," he was in 1878 writing, "How wearisome all this is! Can I ever get rid of this beastly Commissionership!" This exasperation and boredom might have stemmed from his failure to find an answer to the railroad problem; or from that lack of persistence which his father had deplored in him; or from the fact that the creative period which Adams liked had given way to the administrative phase he disliked. In any case it was time to let go — according to plan. The ten years of the railroad commission fulfilled "the self-allotted time I gave to that work. I declined a reappointment which was offered me."

Naturally, he wanted his successor to continue the Adams pattern. Eventually the star of destiny hovered over Judge Thomas Russell. In a patronage quarrel with General Butler over the Boston Custom House Russell had tried to run with both hare and hounds, but the knowledge of his double allegiance had not been general, and his departure from the Custom House made him appear a victim of Butler's malice. Furthermore Russell was a Harvard graduate, a south of Boston man, a person of wit and urbanity. Adams was willing to pass the torch to him. To carry it was a sacred cause in Adams' eyes. He had created and shaped the Railroad Commission; he had made it an "indisputable success."

The commission had indeed attained national prominence.

Partly this was due to Adams' skill as speaker and writer. He also left the impression that the Massachusetts commission was the first in existence and the only one in operation. On both these points he was misleading. But its procedures were original. It was the school master, not the constable. State after state copied it, and its influence upon the national regulatory movement was penetrating and pervasive.[42]

Even when the course of railroad regulation had later changed direction, Adams was still defending his true gospel against "the everlasting issuing of new legislative edicts in which the supposed popular will is crystallized and penalized. For myself, I don't believe in it. I never have believed in it; and for this reason, perhaps, have failed to be in sympathy with the sturdy champions of the 'Deer Peepul.' But, after all, such are but the old-time courtier, the sycophant and the parasite of the Tudor and Stuart periods thinly disguised and in a slightly different rôle; and the lot of the man who talks of Reason, Publicity and Patience now differs not greatly from the lot of him who three centuries ago questioned Divine Right, or gave open expression to a doubt as to the infallibility of the British Solomon."[43] In this burst of self-pity Adams deftly shifted an appraisal of the commission from impersonal to personal grounds. The world was always an arena in which Charles tested and appraised his own qualities. He felt later that during the commission years, "I showed tenacity, considerable sagacity, and, on the whole, a fair degree of judgment, though I fell into some mistakes, usually through want of tact and overeagerness which I do not like now to recall. I failed most in the element of courage, the thing for which the world gives me most credit but which I am in fact most wanting."[44]

Adams' resignation from the Massachusetts Railroad Commission confronted him with a dilemma. On the one hand, it offered him the chance to devote himself to his financial and literary interests; on the other hand he might bring his reputation and talents to bear upon a wider area than the railroads of Massachusetts. In short, he might guide the nation to a solution of its railroad problems. He confessed, "Things are very much mixed with me." [45] At that very moment developments in the relationships between the trunk lines had in fact already resolved his dilemmas.

In the mid-seventies Adams had announced a new theme, almost with trumpets, in the annual reports of the Massachusetts Railroad Commission and in his valedictory volume, *Railroads, Their Origins and Problems*. The major trunk lines connecting the midwestern shipping centers, in particular Chicago, with the Atlantic Coast ports of Boston, New York, Philadelphia, and Baltimore, in what was known as trunk-line territory, were seeking to still their competitive strife by agreeing upon common rates. Though most of their earlier understandings had broken down, these giant competitors had succeeded by 1877–1879 in establishing a joint executive committee for the trunk lines and their western connections. For its head as chairman they selected Albert Fink.

Fink was a railroad genius. Born in Germany and educated there as a civil engineer, he had migrated to the United States in 1850. He worked first on the Baltimore and Ohio and later on the Louisville and Nashville Railroad. On the latter, from a position in the general management, he had succeeded in imposing some harmony of policy among highly competitive roads in the southeast. For the trunk lines, he promised to be not only an organizer but a savior. On the joint executive committee the representatives of the roads set the rates at all important competitive shipping points; then to enforce these decisions they divided the traffic among the railroads upon agreed percentages. If the representatives on the joint executive committee could not agree, Fink's decision was to be final. There was the right of appeal to a board of arbitrators.[46]

All of this filled Adams with excited approval. Here was a

frank avowal to abandon competition by substituting cooperation. Responsibility succeeded irresponsibility; publicity succeeded secrecy. The result to be anticipated was stability, reason-
ableness, and order instead of anarchy. He did not underestimate the difficulties. "The greatest of all these combinations,
that of trunk-lines, is held together only by the personal influence and force of character of one man, — its commissioner,
Colonel Fink." [47]

The advantage of enlisting a man of Adams' stature and outlook in the trunk-line organization was apparent to Fink and
his associates. In late April 1879 they offered Adams an appointment as one of the three men constituting the general
board of arbitration. Returning to Quincy after a trip to New
York, Adams took a long walk through the Blue Hills. "It was
a mild, bright April day, the ground was full of water and the
air and landscape redolent of spring." After crossing a brook he
sat down on a rock — he later designated it his "decision stone"
— with his dog at his feet. He decided, fatefully as it turned
out, to continue his railroad career. He remained in the service
of the trunk lines for five years, as a member of the board and,
after a reorganization of 1882, as a single arbitrator for rates
and divisions.[48]

Whatever the detailed arrangements, Adams found the routine frustrating. He was constantly on the move to New York
and to western shipping centers; he attended hearings, shared
decisions, and wrote up awards. His fellow commissioners, who
not unexpectedly chose him as chairman of the board, furnished
the usual human friction. One, David A. Wells, was a friend
and an intellectual sharing Adams' viewpoints. But the third
commissioner, John A. Wright, a long-time director of the
Pennsylvania Railroad, proved "simply impossible," a "thick
witted lunkhead." [49]

In spite of Adams' many published encomiums of Fink, their
official relations were not always agreeable. In the organization

as a whole Adams found himself "playing a very second fiddle," a position he never enjoyed vis-à-vis anyone. Furthermore the procedures of the joint executive committee contained a built-in occasion of estrangement. Since the arbitrators acted on appeals from the chairman's decisions, Fink naturally regarded a different award as wrong and, as Adams complained, fought them "as usual." There were also times when Adams took the bit in his teeth, exceeded the limits of his assignments, and thus invaded Fink's preserves.[50]

More fundamental, the trunk-line agreement in the 1880's was running into heavy weather. Promoters were constantly building or assembling new competitors from existing enterprises. Since these were outside the pool and unfettered by its regulations, a slashing of rates ensued. Newcomers were eventually taken into the association, but the poison of bad faith and failure worked through the organization. Fink and his colleagues sought a cure in vain. In 1885, when he was no longer an arbitrator, Adams was informing some congressional investigators, "I have not seen the gentlemen responsible for the so-called trunk lines for several months. When I did see them last they were assembled in Mr. Fink's office. It struck me as a somewhat funereal gathering . . . Everything had been tried; and everything had failed. Mr. Fink's great and costly organization was all in ruins, and no one felt any faith in new experiments . . . They all reminded me of men in a boat in the swift water above the rapids of Niagara." [51]

Adams' experience on the trunk-line association, whether or not it had enhanced his reputation, had taught him something. Pools were not the way to attain the order and law which the new era of railroad combination required. Fink "was merely fighting the stars in their courses, — laboring through organization to defeat in its workings the great law of the survival of the fittest. As is usually the case with such efforts, by his interference he only made matters worse." Adams concluded elsewhere: "I have no faith in pools. There are too many parties. I had passed five of the best years of my life, in a vain struggle with the multiplication table, trying to get eight twenties out of a hundred . . . We had consequently, now to go on, in the old, hard way," until attrition and the mills of the gods ground down the number of participants to a feasible figure of perhaps five or six. But it had taken five years of much weariness and discouragement to learn this.[52]

Adams' disenchantment with pools contradicted the hopes he had entertained for them in the seventies. An observer charged he had also changed his opinions on other railroad matters since he "entered the service of the railroads," thereby increasing his salary from $4,000 to $10,000 a year. Adams acknowledged he had changed his opinions and would continue to do so. "Sticking for consistency's sake to a wrong opinion, after you have come to see it is wrong, is a kind of lying which is common enough; but I can't say I admire it . . . The fact is, however, that I am so far from wishing to have any 'employers' at all, or caring for their opinions, that there is but one possible position connected with the working out of this railroad problem which I covet. I should like for the next ten years to represent the United States officially in the discussion which ought to take place; just as during ten of the last twelve years, I represented Massachusetts. There would then be, as far as I, at least, should be concerned, no terrible grapple with a great monopoly, — no life-and-death struggle for popular liberty — nothing, I fancy, even remotely resembling that sort of thing. There would, though, be a good many tedious investigations — a great deal of rather intricate discussion — the gradual exposure of a large number of abuses; and, finally some very prosaic suggestions of laws calculated to correct them." [53]

In offering himself for a position not yet known to national law, Adams started his stretch drive too early. Congress did not pass the Act to Regulate Interstate Commerce until 1887. Nor did Adams think highly of those, of whom he was not one, then appointed to the Interstate Commerce Commission. "They are not the men for a Commission whose work should be to deal with a new economic and social force. They cannot begin to grasp the situation. They have no conception of the magnitude of the problem." The chairman of the commission, T. M. Cooley, "is a second-rate judge, somewhat past the prime of usefulness, and long and wholly past the period of growth. Judges are always canting about 'public policy' but they never have any conception of philosophic growth. They do not, — and from the bent of their professional training, rarely can turn their minds to the work of studying out the development of material and social forces . . . What asses officials of the second class are!" [54]

With tenacity, both a family and personal characteristic, Charles stuck by his conceptions of how the railroads should operate and the manner in which the government should regulate them. First of all the railroads were bound by the method of their creation, if in no other way, to serve the public. This insistence was perhaps more needed in his earlier years than in the twentieth century. The community could not rely upon natural competitive forces to ensure a proper public performance. Only large railroad systems acting in harmony had the resources and means to furnish the certainty, stability, and equality of treatment which the needs of modern business required. To attain these ends by a succession of legislative enactments, by constant tinkering, would introduce into railroad policy neither wisdom nor continuity. For the community to approach the railroads with excitement, hostility, and rhetoric was no way to reform. An informed and impartial agency, above the battle, should investigate abuses and attempt to persuade railroads and the public to accept its findings. Such an agency required punitive powers only to the extent that abuses multiplied and expanded and the railroads proved reluctant to adopt the recommendations of the spokesman for the public interest. Forty years or so after Massachusetts established the Railroad Commission, Adams observed that the nation had either disregarded the Adams vision of the railroad problem or else willfully discarded it through political caprice. He concluded that if any real progress had been made toward a satisfactory answer for so-called transportation abuses, "a knowledge of the fact has not reached me. Whatever improvement has been secured has been through the operation of natural influences and not as a result of legislative edict." [55]

❖ III ❖

MAKING A FORTUNE

1869-1890

IN an address in 1869 before the American Social Science
Association Adams found space to affirm: "If, however, Social
Science has one lesson to teach more emphatically than any
other it is that the accumulation of wealth is not the loftiest
end of human effort." [1] For the young and vigorous such judg-
ments are easy. The surprising thing about Adams was that he
wasted little time in ignoring his own maxim. For nearly a
quarter of a century after he had "caught the step" making
money took more of his effort, thought, and emotion than any
other single pursuit or interest.

At the start his resources were limited. When he moved to
Quincy with his young wife and lived in "the little house on
the Neponset road," "my income was a short $5,000, if indeed
it was quite as much." The wedding settlement of $3,000 a year
from his father clearly furnished the largest part of his income;
the rest came from small inheritances and probably from his
pre–Civil War ventures as part owner of certain Boston properties. But Adams came from a family with reputation and property, both assets when it came to borrowing money, and by
1869 with his appointment to the Railroad Commission he had
begun to make a name of his own. He became one of an
informal group of investors who gathered about Nathaniel

Thayer, eminent as the head of a great Boston banking house and as a steward of wealth. Dropping into Thayer's office he "saw all kinds of good things flying around loose" and left feeling "independent of the Commission and free and fearless to tell the whole truth." Nor were Adams' investments always made through the Thayer channel. After all Henry Lee Higginson, a partner in Lee Higginson Company, had been a fellow officer and confidant during the Civil War and in 1873 accompanied Adams to Vienna as one of the Massachusetts commissioners to the Vienna exposition. And occasionally Adams invested through New York firms.[2]

His involvements in manufacturing enterprises, except as auxiliaries to holdings of another kind, were limited. His admiration for the air brake led to an acquaintance with Westinghouse and eventually to investments in the Westinghouse Company which by the nineties was turning its attention in the direction of electrical equipment. By 1891 Adams had pushed up his holdings to $225,000.[3]

Mining was another destination of Adams' funds. For a brief interval in the seventies his along with other Boston dollars went westward into Calumet and Hecla, the leading Michigan copper producer. Though the dividends had been spectacular, his failure to sell out at the top of the market led him to reflect, "I have missed a great coup in Calumet. I feel bad." Still he made money out of it. Since the upper peninsula of Michigan was proving to be a storehouse of minerals, Adams invested in the Champion Iron Company, organized in 1869 to work a holding of magnetic ore in the Marquette iron range, the first of the Michigan–Lake Superior deposits to be exploited. The company's 1600 acres were by rail about thirty-three miles due west of Marquette, the ore port on Lake Superior. The symptoms of promise were all there. But the troubled times of the seventies stirred doubts in Adams, it was "a thing which ought to be clear but is not." In 1879, the year in which Adams was elected a director, the company passed its dividend. Actually in an underground operation, as was Champion's, the expense of working holdings always increased with the passage of time; furthermore the appearance of new Lake Superior ranges at Menominee and Gogebic in the 1880's and in the Mesabi in the 1890's was continually spawning competitors with lower costs.[4]

With the onset of the more prosperous 1880's Adams caught fire from the enthusiasm for silver mines, "an enormous speculative craze is setting in." As all eyes turned to Nevada he bought shares in the Chrysolite mine on Fryer Hill in Leadville. Within a short time he was "averaging down" by buying 500 shares more. Two months later when he visited Leadville to inspect the property he found the mine on fire. A year later Chrysolite declared a dividend and made "a very good showing." The next year the mine had "gone up." Undeterred by these treacherous vacillations in good and bad fortunes Adams at the end of 1881 "took a gamble" in Robinson Consolidated, "buying a 1000 shares @ $4.80." Disillusion and a sizable loss came at once. This experience Adams cheerfully accepted as "the price of my emancipation from all faith in mining stocks, or information concerning them or any man who deals in them, and also the close of my operations in stocks."[5]

With his experience, it was natural that Adams should invest in railroads. His integrity and sense of propriety were too powerful to permit investments in New England lines. Many of them were at that time well run and profitable, so it was not prudence which deterred him. Nor did the lines he chose elsewhere turn out very well. Michigan, booming with the development of its natural resources, mineral and timber, seemed to call for improved transportation. Following an inspection trip on behalf of Thayer to the upper peninsula in 1871, Adams apparently put $10,000 into a route building a little inland from the southern shore of Lake Superior and offering to carry ores to its ports and exchange commodities between enterprises. Through a consolidation these various small land-grant enterprises became the Marquette, Houghton, and Ontonagon Railroad, commonly known as the "mineral" or "peninsula" road. It was an act of faith, for prospects both superficial and fundamental dismayed Adams. On the first point the "cheerless" shores and "dismal" harbors of Lake Superior depressed him. Shortly the local management in the person of the road's president alarmed him. "The realities of these Western men fall so far short of the estimates." Be that as it may, Adams became a bondholder and a director, and, until the panic of 1873 closed in, a moderate optimist. But then the reports from the road proved so bad that Adams "thought all was up, and for once lay awake for hours, thinking, thinking, thinking." Two years later Adams' name disappeared from the directorate and the principal office and address of the corporation moved temporarily from State Street to Wall Street. The next year, however, Adams "slipped my neck once more into the Ontonagon noose to the tune of $20,000, but this time I feel safe." Nonetheless at the end of the decade a reorganization was necessary. Perhaps the fact that Adams had shared in it forestalled his repeating his earlier judgment on the M. H. and O., "another bitch-pup." As it turned out he escaped shortly with a profit.[6]

Long before this Adams turned toward the railroads in the lower peninsula of the same state. One road, the Detroit, Lansing and Lake Michigan (after 1876, the Detroit, Lansing, and Northern), ran west and north from Detroit — the place was "after all a one horse concern" — to Howard City, "a village of pine tree stumps and shanties in the midst of the wilderness." The other road, the Chicago and Michigan Lake Shore (Chicago and Western Michigan), perhaps encouraged by the fact that railroads in the East had succeeded in competing with waterways like the Hudson River, began at the Indiana state line at a junction with the New York Central lines and extended northward to Pentwater, a point half way up the east shore of Lake Michigan. It ran in large part "through a dismal forest, half burned over and wholly uninteresting." Both roads built extensions and branches and consolidated with other lines. Early in the seventies these companies were units in the group of railroads controlled by James F. Joy of Detroit, one of the most eminent of the satraps of Boston capital in the Midwest. Since these Michigan lines depended primarily upon the carriage of a wasting natural resource, lumber, neither of the roads had a particularly happy history. Soon after the panic of 1873 the Chicago and Michigan Lake Shore defaulted; a few years later it was reorganized. The Detroit, Lansing and Lake Michigan clung on until 1876, then went under. In both cases Adams had arrived just in time for the funeral; he joined such Boston stalwarts as Hunnewell, Merriam, Brooks, and Thayer in the direction of the first railroad in 1873 and of the second in 1876. By the end of the eighties Thayer was president of both these Michigan roads and Adams was still a director and general handyman.[7]

Though Adams was also in and out as investor in the Chicago, Burlington and Quincy, the Atchison, Topeka and Santa Fe, the Denver and Rio Grande — not to mention the Union Pacific — when he reviewed his investment career in 1888, twenty years after he had begun it, he concluded: "While railroads have been my work, all the money I have made has been in dealing in real estate in Kanzas [*sic*] City." This was a slight overstatement. The first move Adams and his associates made into Kansas City was in 1869. Adams later recalled the discouraging externals of the undertaking. "Before the war Kansas City did not exist. It was simply Westport-Landing — a forbidding spot on the southern bank of the Missouri consisting of a few warehouses, planters' dwellings, and negro shanties, scattered loosely along the river levee, with a tavern for its most permanent feature. A mere steamboat stopping-place, it was no more important than a dozen others up and down the stream and immeasurably less important than several. Insignificant, as it was, too, the place shone but with a borrowed light. Here persons and merchandise were landed to toil, or be painfully hauled, up through the steep ravines to the summit of the bluff before striking the old Santa Fé trail, which began six miles farther on at Westport." [8]

Already the quickening touch of the railroad had shattered this situation. In 1865 the Pacific Railroad after many vicissitudes had at last crossed Missouri from St. Louis to Kansas City. Two years earlier railroad builders had begun the construction of the Union Pacific, Eastern Division, later the Kansas Pacific, to run westward from Kansas City; the road reached Denver, Colorado, and Cheyenne, Wyoming, in 1871. Population began to fill up the Kansas City hinterland. In the Civil War decade the percentage of increase in the state of Kansas was 239.9, the third greatest for any state in the nation; in the seventies the percentage was 173.3, the fifth largest. The absolute figures of increase were in these decades between 200,000 and 600,000 people. Livestock competed with people. Enterprising Westerners were creating the cattle kingdom based largely on the free range of public lands in the Great Plains from Texas to Canada. The cattle were taken on a "long drive" to some destination on a transcontinental which would carry the animals to eastern slaughtering centers. Abilene, the first noted "cow town" where the long drive from Texas changed into a railroad journey, began operations in 1867 on the Kansas Pacific west of Kansas City. Kansas City, according to a commentator in the seventies, "located in the center of a district of country fully three hundred miles in diameter which, as an inevitable result of its unparalleled fertility and its immense yield of corn annually, must ever be a prolific hog country as well as a great cattle-feeding district." [9]

The Kansas City which Adams had described and in a way stigmatized, for he called it "southern," was the older settlement of Kansas City, Missouri. At that time the present site of Kansas City, Kansas, just to the west, was laid out in farms and small towns; in 1886 most of these settlements joined Kansas City, Kansas. Both cities were situated on high bluffs on the south side of the Missouri River at a point where that stream, coming down from the west and north, bends eastward to flow toward the Mississippi River, and at a point where the Kaw (or Kansas) River, rising far to the west, hooks north to empty into the Missouri. In this bistate area, easily accessible to the railroads which followed the valleys into it, were the stockyards. At first these were merely places of debarkation where animals were fed, watered, and rested before they continued their journey to the packing centers, notably Chicago. Railroads, or their officials, interested in carrying the livestock trade apparently introduced the first improvements. Thus in 1871 the president of the Kansas City Stockyards Company, J. M. Walker, was also president of the Chicago, Burlington and Quincy, and its general manager was president of another railroad. Apparently Adams and other Bostonians provided some of the capital. Adams owned 700 shares in the seventies. For a while he took satisfaction in the stable earnings of the enterprise, but eventually the personal devil appeared. At the end of 1873 Adams was writing, "Met J. M. Walker about the Kansas City cattle yards, — that man I do not like! — he's a bad fellow, I'll bet! — meeting very unsatisfactory, indeed, and money lost there, more money lost." He returned to Boston intent upon a reorganization and a new management. Apparently he interested Nat Thayer in the prospect, and in 1875 Adams became president and undertook to extend and rebuild the yards on a new scale of convenience.[10]

In 1879 Adams completed his organizational changes by appointing Charles F. Morse general manager. Morse was an exception to Adams' usual inability to find a competent on-the-ground manager for his far-flung activities. Morse was a Boston man, who had attended the Lawrence Scientific School at Harvard, walking ten miles round trip to attend its classes. He had served in the infantry during the Civil War and then secured employment on the railroads beyond the Mississippi. As a legacy to his children he left the advice: "Modest merit is often commended, but it does not lead to success in the world as it is and with human nature as we mostly find it." In sum Morse was hard-headed, industrious, and willing to accept responsibility.[11]

Geography, investment, and enterprise converted Kansas City into a terminal livestock market where shippers and purchasers gathered and where a packing business expanded to process the animals. The largest firm, Plankinton and Armour, dated from 1870 and represented through Philip D. Armour the packing dynasty of the Midwest. When Morse became general manager of the stockyard, its capitalization was $100,000 and it was grossing "perhaps" $20,000 a year. By the twentieth century its capitalization was above $10,000,000 and the gross annually was $1,200,000. It missed only a single quarterly dividend. It was the linchpin of the Adams fortune. The fear of catastrophe to his stake in that enterprise almost moved Charles, not one given to addressing the Deity, to this recourse: "Saw in the paper that Kanzas [sic] City is under water, — save the Cattle Yards!"[12]

Adams meanwhile had become interested in land purchases other than the stockyards. Though part of these acquisitions were on the southern outskirts of Kansas City, Missouri, the real novelty lay west of the Kaw in the area which was to become Kansas City, Kansas. Early in 1879 he was walking with Morse over the proposed purchases, projecting from bluff or other high spot the growth of the city, and buying farms at $150 to $200 an acre while land in Kansas City, Missouri —

"it seemed miles away" — was $1000 an acre. They put over $300,000 into land; chartered in 1880 the Kaw Valley Town Site and Bridge Company of which Adams became president; and built a steel bridge across the river to a connection with the older Kansas City. By the end of the year Adams was borrowing to pay for his purchases. There were occasions for alarm. "Telegram from Kansas City that my bridge was blown away. Was ever such luck, — or incompetence." It proved to be a different bridge. Meanwhile the full flood of the most remarkable land boom in the city's history carried the Adams Company to dazzling success. In the year ending June 1885 the concern paid 40 percent dividends and in 1886 paid twelve monthly dividends, each of 10 percent. By the time it was settled up in the twentieth century it had divided over 400 percent on its capital.[13]

Long before these successes materialized, Adams fell into the policy of buying land "at various promising centers and undeveloped terminal points — buying, selling, improving." He proposed to do in the West what the Astor family had done in New York "practically betting on the growth of the country." If he had had any reluctance, local boosters would do their best to dispel it, for every community wanted capital and growth. Adams had only to come to an ambitious city to be taken on the "usual drive" by the mayor; and in Fort Worth, Texas, where they did things in a big way, "a delegation of citizens in carriages" met the Adams party "and drove them about the town and out to the Stockyard" where there was a lunch with oysters and speeches.[14]

No precise or complete inventory of Adams' landholdings can be derived from accessible data; nor can acquisitions always be dated or the gains therefrom be ascertained. Investments in land are apt to yield income, if at all, over a very long period. But it seems certain that in the mid-eighties Adams undertook to repeat his Kansas City formula in Denver. He bought the stockyards and later, when he was on a buying spree and carried along in his team a real estate adviser or dealer, he purchased lands. The stockyards he later resold "at a large advance above its cost." Texas apparently impressed and charmed Adams. "We were astonished and delighted" by San Antonio, "it was Vienna in Texas"; and in 1889 he began buying city land. As for Houston, "Why the town grew up there 50 years ago is plain; why it continues is inexplicable." On the contrary the country around Fort Worth reminded him a little of the Kansas City hinterland, it "was very fine, wooded and watered, cotton and corn." On the same foray he enlarged holdings in Salt Lake City — "the town will develop to the south." [15]

With its "brilliant sky" and "old champagne atmosphere," the Northwest always exhilarated him. There investments ranged from safety in Portland and Seattle to chance — Helena, Spokane Falls ("boom in mines and doing business under canvas"), and Lewiston, Idaho, a major infatuation, located at the junction of the Snake and Clearwater Rivers, "the key to the railroad situation" in Washington. Though Adams was shrewd in his estimate of western Canadian cities — "Is Winnipeg destined to be the St. Paul of 1913? I judge it probable" — he does not reveal whether he followed up his hunches.[16]

For twenty years, beginning in 1870, he went West once every year and sometimes oftener, extending his range into the Mountain States in 1876, and in 1878 to the Pacific Coast. Occasionally these trips lasted months and covered well over ten thousand miles. At the end of the eighties he could use the comforts of the director's car of the Union Pacific, but he earlier relied upon the casualness of public transportation and the flea-ridden accommodations and poor food of small-town hotels. Though he usually had companions — either his brother John or Nat Thayer or Henry L. Higginson or F. L. Ames — the physical fatigue and boredom of these junkets was almost insufferable. Mint juleps with Nat Thayer in the evening, a game at the poker club of C. E. Perkins, "killed a lonely evening at a typical place of provincial amusement" in Detroit, a serenade by the local band ("a little humorous") at Iona, Michigan, an address on the race ground at Oshkosh, Wisconsin — "why did I do it" — were variations which hardly broke the deadly tedium. "Got off from the bewildering caravansery of the Palmer House . . . and passed the day in the C.B.& Q. cars running on a rainy day through monotonous Illinois, — newspapers, cigars, a glass of spirits now and again, talk, sleep, bad meals, and the Senate Report on transportation wore away the day." He knew the West at first hand but he detested it. "Chicago is a dismal place, the people all show they have no breeding, — no descent or education, — men and women are ordinary." The region as a whole was "that great, fat, uninteresting West." His departure he always gleefully celebrated by dispatching a bottle of champagne; he really began to be himself again when he "breathed freely of the salt air" even at New York City.[17]

As their forebears had, Charles and his brother John turned their eyes to real estate nearer home. For obvious reasons Charles had missed the great Back Bay speculation of Civil War days. In the mid-eighties the two Adams brothers bought land on the mill dam, fronting on the Charles River between Cottage Farm Bridge and the intersection of Commonwealth Avenue and Beacon Street; formed the Riverbank Improvement Company and the West End Land Company to manage these speculations; and, in the conventional fashion, resorted to the banks to provide the purchase funds of "over $726,000." [18]

Investment and speculation required money, and Charles started with little. He secured his means from the banks in Boston, particularly the Webster and Atlas, in Quincy, and elsewhere. The days following nearly every purchase of securities or when his notes fell due were always busy with "financiering," as Charles called it. In 1871, two years after the start toward his fortune, he had a floating debt of $50,000; a decade later he owed $200,000 "and more"; in the later eighties, as optimism swept him along, these sums mounted until he owed well over a million and was annually paying interest charges varying between $45,000 and $60,000. Of course if the nation's prosperity held and his individual judgment about enterprises was perceptive all went well, but a reduction in the volume of returns from the securities and lands he used as collateral compelled him to seek help. A month after the collapse of the boom in 1873 he "paid the penalty of carrying too much sail in money matters being compelled to pay 7% for 6 mos. on $16,000 notes, — not pleasant but wholesome, — my father endorsed my note and that is the last business transaction on my account I ever propose to have with him." Assistance from other members of the family Charles regarded as routine. Apparently when he described John as a "good figurehead" he was thinking of him as an endorser of notes; and Brooks's name signed to $26,000 of debt was one cause of friction between the brothers.[19]

Adams could not grow rich dangerously without extreme alternations of elation and fear. He was not a confident investor. The slightest tremor of misfortune sent him scurrying for comfort and calm to Thayer, Higginson, or other associates in seemingly threatened enterprises. Good resolutions and self-abasement were other means of meeting terror. In April 1874 he nailed to the mast this manifesto: "Here I stop! Cash or nothing." A decade later he was wearily acknowledging, "I can't get out of that old habit" of borrowing. Physical motion helped him to handle his frights: "Passed most of the day working off my nervous exhaustion and by evening had thought my problems out." Or he would defy or, more often, deny misfortune. Adams' interest in painting, for instance, was genuine. The American painter Francis D. Millet was one of Adams' most intimate friends and Adams purchased paintings by contemporaries lavishly. There was a marked correlation between his financial anxieties and his visits to art dealers and acquisition of expensive paintings.[20] It was as if he wanted to convince himself he had enough money to spend in this way or enough bravado to ignore his losses.

A deeper misgiving about his ways of money-getting must have haunted Adams. In his era no one else of importance had a greater detestation and contempt for Wall Street and expressed his feelings more consistently and harshly. Adams' youthful essay "A Chapter of Erie" is an indictment of Wall Street, of its men and methods; and charges against every detail of this institutionalized gambling run like a refrain through his diaries. He habitually characterized Wall Street men as "jockeys and gamblers," and their place of operations as a source of sinister contagion. "A man stands about the same chance there that a woman would stand in a brothel, — he or she will get out of the one locality or the other, and that right speedily, or stay there and become of it." [21] Yet it is hard to see how Adams' way of making a fortune greatly differed from that he censured. He borrowed and he gambled on the price of stocks, sometimes outrageously.

Perhaps he was blind to these disturbing similarities because Wall Street was in New York and he haunted Nat Thayer's office in Boston. They were gentlemen there, whereas those who followed the "New York style of doing business" were "monsters all!" Perhaps Adams thought he was superior because he invested rather than speculated. Usually he was prudent. In his mining ventures, for instance, he obtained advice from Clarence King, a personal friend and geologist, from Professor R. W. Raymond, one of the founders and long-time secretary of the American Institute of Mining Engineers, and from S. F. Emmons, the Harvard graduate who became an authority on Leadville geology. Unlike his fellow Bostonian T. Jefferson Coolidge, Adams did not flip a coin, while fortified by champagne cocktails, to decide whether he should invest in a silver mine. In the field of railroads Adams was of course his own expert. As for land purchases, he usually analyzed resources and potentialities, and ended up climbing to some high place — a bluff, a hill, a station cupola, a state capitol, or a reservoir site — to project in which direction the place would grow. With all his care, he or his agents sometimes dropped a stitch. When he rode out to his 900-acre tract at Spokane, on a western survey of his holdings in 1896, he "found to my utter amazement that it was a wholly different tract from the one I supposed and had intended to buy . . . It was not a pleasant surprise." [22]

Investments in land appealed to the countryman in Adams and rubbed traditional rural values to the surface. Land was safe, profitable, and "free from corporate entanglements." Also land enabled him to be the builder. At Kansas City he and his associates, sometimes at the prompting of the mayor, subsidized enterprises — packing plants, a fertilizer plant, the Kansas City Smelting and Refining Company — and consolidated, financed, operated, and improved the Metropolitan Street Railway. The sums involved in these enterprises were not mere auxiliaries to land purchases. Adams held more shares, 625, in the Metropolitan Street Railway than in the stockyards. Nor were lots, sticks, and stones everything; for an Adams the things of the spirit counted. Though he could never quite divest Kansas City of its Missourian character — not a compliment — he nonetheless rejoiced in the late eighties at "the evident increase of wealth and elevation of standards." Of Kansas City he boasted with pride in his autobiography, "*That,* I did." [23]

Let money accomplish what it could, it is still impossible to reconcile the contradiction between Adams' principles and practice. I am driven to believe that the violence of his epithets against Wall Street and speculation drugged a conscience outraged by departure from his own ideals. Once at least a flash of irony showed him what he was doing. After taking a flyer in the Denver and Rio Grande, he wrote, "a pure little gamble, by the way, wholly reprehensible, but pleasant — if it wins." [24]

On the whole he won handsomely and successfully. In the eighties the young man who started out with an income of $5000 was receiving an annual gross of around $125,000. The value of his assets hovered between $2,000,000 and $3,000,000. This was not the net figure, for his borrowings constituted about a third of his assets, and the interest charges on them of course diminished his income. Once, as a young husband, he had installed his own plumbing and upholstered his own furniture; he now had a seaside cottage at the Glades, a country estate at Quincy, and a town house on Commonwealth Avenue with a piece of La Farge stained glass. Year after year he chronicled as "most prosperous" or "immensely prosperous." In August 1887 he was writing, "I have all I want — and I want a great deal." [25]

At first a wish for independence from his family and from circumstances drove him to acquisition. His financial success pleased him because it was his own doing or the result of good luck; it did not come from funds inherited or received from a wealthy marriage. Relatively accurate the statement might be; there was something strident in its repetition. Meanwhile his experience with good fortune had given him a new motive for wealth. "They may say what they please, but today wealth is the $\pi o\hat{v}$ $\sigma\tau\hat{\omega}$ [literally, where I may stand; leverage ground] in America. Mere wealth will not enable a man to accomplish much; but it is a most powerful spring-board . . . [With wealth] I become a power to be considered. Whenever I choose to come forward, I am received with deference and listened to with acceptance; — I can dictate my own terms. It becomes a question of ability, emphasized by wealth. I could do more for my own success by getting rich than by slaving my life away in mere political action. This I failed to appreciate twenty years ago . . . I want wealth as the spring-board to influence, consideration, power, and enjoyment." [26]

Adams wrote this apologia a year after the close of the most remarkable and most vexatious episode in his career as a railroad man. In 1884 he had become the president of the Union Pacific Railway. A cluster of motives led him to accept that position, as we shall see in the next chapter; the desire to enlarge a fortune, already deemed adequate, was one though not the first of them.

THE UNION PACIFIC
FAILURE

1883-1890

IN the spring of 1884 Charles Francis Adams, Jr., assumed
the presidency of the Union Pacific Railroad; in the autumn
of 1890, against his will, he left it. The Union Pacific was an
exceptional railroad in its organization and history. As Adams
often lamented, he was the prisoner of both these factors.

Certainly until the 1880's the Union Pacific ranked with the
Pennsylvania or the New York Central as one of the largest
American corporations. The United States government had
granted it a charter in 1862 and in effect a second one in 1864.
The road was to be the eastern part of the first transcontinental;
the act of incorporation intended it to connect somewhere in
the western plains or mountains with the Central Pacific, running eastward from California. As it turned out, the wedding
of the rails of the two companies took place at Ogden, Utah, in
1869. To quiet the squabbles between Missouri River points
vying for the commercial advantage of being the eastern ter-
minus of the Union Pacific, the government had finally set the
spot on the Missouri at Omaha, Nebraska, and Council Bluffs,
Iowa. The main line of the road was a little over 1000 miles
long. Before Adams' presidency the Union Pacific had added

branches and had also consolidated with a threatening rival, the Kansas Pacific, running westward from Kansas City to Denver, and then bending north through a connection to the Union Pacific at Cheyenne, Wyoming.[1]

The voluminous literature of investigation clinging like a miasmic fog about the Union Pacific usually designated its main line as the "aided road." To build a road of such length through an unsettled country in anticipation of a traffic which did not yet exist was in the words of a hostile congressional investigation "visionary and perilous." Consequently the national government bestowed upon the Union Pacific a grant from the public lands along its route; this was a customary policy. The roads so aided usually issued bonds for which the lands were security. To dispel further uncertainties the government also loaned the Union Pacific thirty-year, 6-percent government bonds for each mile of construction. These bonds, constituting a second mortgage on the railroad's property and franchise, the Union Pacific bound itself to repay at maturity, principal and interest; before that final day the government was to retain one half of the payments for the transportation over the line of its personnel and property, for example troops or mail, and 5 percent of the company's net profits. Since this was to be a mixed enterprise, the government appointed five directors for the Union Pacific. These turned out to be perfunctory or honorific political appointees. Their oversight of the road's doings did not amount to much, nor did Congress, quite aware of their quality, pay attention to their frequent recommendations and reports.[2]

The specific explanation for the generosity and slackness of the government's backing was that it was necessary to tempt private capital into the enterprise. Consequently the incorporators turned to the eastern centers of capital — Philadelphia, New York, and Boston. Though groups from all three participated, capitalists from the last two came to predominate in the management. Indeed for a time in the course of the road's construction Massachusetts provided the titan who alone seemed able to handle the finances and organize construction, Oakes Ames. The mainstay of Ames's fortune and that of his family contemporaries and descendants was a shovel works in North Easton, Massachusetts. When the Union Pacific found it utterly impossible to sell its stock or even its first mortgage bonds except at ruinous discounts, Oakes Ames and others associated themselves in the Credit Mobilier, a company with a Pennsylvania charter, which entered into a contract with Oakes Ames to build the major portion of the Union Pacific lying unfinished across the Great Plains and the mountains. The members of the Credit Mobilier took the securities of the Union Pacific at various discounts from their face value, sold some to friends and associates, and used others as collateral upon which to borrow. In short they interposed their personal credit for that of the railroad; purchasers and lenders preferred an endorsement or recommendation from these capitalists to those proffered by the corporation.[3]

Later when Oakes Ames became financially embarrassed, he sold his Union Pacific holdings. They did not descend to his heirs, but Oliver Ames, his son, and F. L. Ames, his nephew, through repurchase or otherwise became powers in the Union Pacific. F. L. Ames was a friend and neighbor of Charles Francis Adams, Jr. The purchaser of Oakes Ames's holdings was Jay Gould of New York. Gould had been one of the villains in Adams' exposure of the Erie Railroad. In the 1870's a Boston "party" emerged; its most prominent members were Oliver Ames, F. L. Ames, Elisha Atkins, F. Gordon Dexter, and E. H. Baker. In the New York "party," Samuel J. Tilden was a large stockholder, but Gould, who held 100,000 shares, was the active policy maker and prime mover. Gould and associates sat on the board of directors: Sidney Dillon, the road's president, though disposed to harmonize faction, was Gould's man. Since the number of stockowners in the New York registry book bore the ratio of three to two in Boston and eastern New England, it is safe to speak of a Gould regime. In 1875 it inaugurated the payment of dividends at the rate of 8 percent; and a few years later manipulated the merger of the Kansas Pacific with the Union Pacific.[4]

Meanwhile the government had begun to repent of its bargain. A popular as well as an official opinion held that the railroad was failing to pay enough money to the government to enable the latter to meet the interest it was paying on the subsidy bonds it had loaned the railroad. While the railroad and government officials were bickering over this matter, a disagreement between stockholders in the Credit Mobilier dragged that device into the limelight during the peculiarly exciting presidential canvass of 1872. The builders of the Union Pacific, it was alleged, had violated the provisions of the acts of 1862 and 1864 and had made prodigious profits. Furthermore Oakes Ames had suborned several congressmen by selling them stock in the Credit Mobilier at prices that would enable them to make money. Behind these specific outrages lay the general anti-railroad hostility expressed through the Granger movement. Though the curling wave of railroad regulation had not yet crashed down on the states through which the Union Pacific ran, the Granger groundswell was tossing about the Old Northwest and Congress.[5]

In 1872–73 the House of Representatives authorized two investigations of the Credit Mobilier. One committee under the chairmanship of Luke P. Poland of Vermont focused on the alleged bribery of certain congressmen; the other under the chairmanship of J. M. Wilson of Indiana investigated the financing and construction of the Union Pacific. In view of the widespread impression that practically every member of Congress lined up for Credit Mobilier stock, the Poland Committee caught comparatively few victims in its net, and those were

84

more befuddled than corrupt. The Wilson Committee, however, drew a dark picture and reached very damaging conclusions. The chief charges were that the government had clothed the corporation with a "vast endowment"; the railroad corporation was not a "mere contractor" but a "trustee" for these gifts; the risk "was wholly that of the government" as the road "has been built chiefly with the resources of the Government." Seldom have the procedures and findings of congressional investigations been so sacrosanct for so long a time as these. After decades of acceptance by historians, it was only recently that an investigator using the tools of sophisticated modern analysis concluded simultaneously that "a precise determination of the profit of the promoters" was "impossible" and that "the upper limit of profit, $16,501,760.22," was more "justifiable" than the investigating committees thought.[6]

Considering the high cost of materials and labor in the post–Civil War era and the completion of the road six years in advance of expectation, Adams was apparently nearer right than the critics when he concluded that Oakes Ames was "a man of wonderful energy, he did a great work in the way natural to him; and, while doing it, he was concerned in transactions which called for a great deal of explanation, to say the least, both from himself and from others." This bland summary ignored an aftermath. A statute of March 3, 1873, directed the Secretary of the Treasury to withhold from the Union Pacific all payments for transporting government freight and personnel to an amount sufficient to pay the interest on the government subsidy bonds. Then to lock the door after the horse had been stolen, the statute declared that the Union Pacific could pay no dividend "but from actual net earnings," nor issue new stock or mortgages without congressional assent, and prohibited any director or officer of the road from being interested in any contract with it. In sum the government was to compel the road to operate "as required by law." To this end various contingent legal proceedings were to be undertaken. More important than these details were the general repercussions of the Credit Mobilier affair. Politicians are apt to resent any undertaking which has injured one of their guild; and of course they are sensitive to public opinion. After the Poland and Wilson investigations it probably took more courage to be fair to the Union Pacific than to be hostile to it. Besides the nation now had the railroad which in the emergency of the Civil War it so desperately needed.[7]

Pursuant to the act of 1873, certain proceedings came before the Supreme Court. Popular and congressional opinion to the contrary, the learned Justices in 1875 concluded that the government's contract with the Union Pacific did not compel the railroad to pay the principal of the government subsidy bonds until maturity — 1896 to 1899 — and that the railroad had from time to time to pay the interest on these bonds as it currently became due was "a pretty large inference." The words of the acts of 1862 and 1864 did not specify concurrent payment of interest. "The terms looked to ultimate security rather than immediate reimbursement." Three years later the Court in another series of suits reiterated the same point.[8]

In terms of popular opinion the invulnerability of the Union Pacific was infuriating. Here was a road scrupulously paying interest on its own bonds but refusing to pay interest on the government subsidy bonds; few other railroads in the country had the privilege of a loan of $27,000,000 with the payment of interest postponed thirty years. Furthermore Jay Gould, the archetype of "railroad wrecker" and "Wall Street speculator" controlled the road, which was paying 8 percent dividends to its stockholders at the very moment it was leaving the government, a creditor, to pick up the semiannual tab on the railroad's debt to it. All of this did not accord with ordinary business principles or practice. Even the Supreme Court granted that "since it [the Union Pacific] has grown to vigorous manhood, it may not have displayed the gratitude which so much care called for. If this be so, it is but another instance of the absence of human affections which is said to characterize all corporations." [9]

The failure to punish anyone in the corporation or to collect more money from it spurred those with anxieties, discontents, or personal interests to another try. Admittedly the situation was disturbing. Any citizen with a pencil and a knowledge of arithmetic could calculate that the postponement of interest payments to the middle of the 1890's meant that by then the sum of interest due might be larger than the sum of the principal. On large debts interest accumulates cruelly. Accordingly in 1878 Congress enacted the Thurman Act, bearing the name of Senator A. G. Thurman of Ohio, a conservative Democrat and a member of the Senate Judiciary Committee. The bill defined net earnings with care and then declared that the Union Pacific should pay annually to the government 25 percent of its net earnings. To compile this percentage the payments for carriage of government property and the 5 percent of earlier times were counted along with the necessary additional payments. If the Union Pacific defaulted on these payments, it could not declare dividends on its stock. For a divided Court, Chief Justice Waite wrote a majority opinion holding the Thurman Act was constitutional. To administer this policy with safety and precision Congress in an additional act authorized the appointment of a Commissioner of Railway Accounts, called after 1881 the Railroad Commissioner, to check the accounts of the trans-Missouri land-grant railroads. Of one proposal for this form of supervision Adams had written: "I can only say that if there is any single exploded feature of Granger Legislation which is not to be found in it, I do not know what it is . . . The position of 'Commissioner of Railway Affairs' would be the most valuable and certainly the most corrupt, in the gift of this government. The railroads would buy it . . .

I would if I had charge of the Pacific Roads (I should consider it my duty to my stock-holders to do so)." [10]

By the time Adams was thus spluttering he had inched somewhat nearer the center of Union Pacific affairs. He had first turned his attention to the Union Pacific during his course of self-education as railroad expert. At that time, in 1869, he had been repelled by the "curious mystery" hanging over "the financial arrangements of the concern"; however, he admired "the able and daring men who are with such splendid energy forcing it through to completion." Less than a decade later, in 1878, while traveling through the "dreary prairie states" and reading Mommsen and Hugo, he saw in the papers that he had been nominated as one of the five government directors. This was the doing of Carl Schurz, his friend and political alter ego. Adams telegraphed his refusal. A week later he reconsidered, for by this time he saw the position as a means of shaping the legislation for the Pacific railroads and perhaps a national railroad policy. He served a year and then with considerable wavering resigned. Nevertheless the experience had brought the Union Pacific within his sharper focus. Certain that "there was not a more valuable railroad property in existence or one with greater latent power of development," he bought 2500 shares for himself and additional shares for his various trustee accounts. His private correspondence discloses that he regarded the road as an exceedingly profitable speculation. On this basis a letter in the Boston *Advertiser* in 1882 urged others to invest in the Union Pacific, which along with the Chicago, Burlington and Quincy constituted "the Broadway or Washington Street of this continent," and expressed a hope that investors of New England would so act as to transfer the control of the Union Pacific from New York to Boston and from large stockholders to a dispersed ownership by small investors. On March 7, 1883, the stockholders elected him to the directorate.[11]

As Adams moved tentatively toward the realization of a

long-range plan, a specific crisis, as dark as those of 1873 and 1878, compelled more precipitate action. For one thing in 1883–1884 the net earnings of the Union Pacific declined catastrophically and thus revealed a fault built into the Thurman Act, for payments to the government, calculated as a percentage figure of earnings, declined also. Congressmen saw that the liquidation of the government claims was once more in jeopardy. At the same time the company and the government continued their decade of litigation with a dispute over the definition of net earnings and over the fair pay for the carriage of the mails. This suit was before the Court of Claims. The railroad thought its claims would diminish what it owed the government; the Commissioner of Railroad Accounts with his relentless arithmetic declared categorically that as of December 31, 1882, the Union Pacific owed $1,727,742.54 and "had not complied with the requirements" of the Thurman Act. Forthwith a measure passed the House of Representatives increasing the government's take to 55 percent of the net earnings. Whereas the debate over the Thurman Act in 1878 had been relatively sober and responsible, the debate over thus changing it was ignorant and impulsive. In the Union Pacific, asserted one representative, the government was dealing with a "wily enemy," "the stock-jobbers and financial gamblers of Wall Street, that financial Moloch whose demands are without limit and whose appetite is insatiable, the nursery of the 'predatory classes' of this Country who are sapping its foundation and fatally attacking the very life of our institutions." And one representative referred to another as "an enthusiast and I think a demagogue." In the Senate this bill was referred to the Judiciary Committee. During these economically and politically tumultuous days the stock of the Union Pacific sank from a February high of 84⅝ to a May low of 33¼.[12]

Of this accumulated distress, the "Washington business" was the only feature which conceivably was amenable to immediate handling. As a result of consultations among Ames and other interested parties, Adams went to Washington and got in touch with the Senate Judiciary Committee through the senior senator from Massachusetts, who was a committee member. The committee agreed to postpone any action until the end of December; the Union Pacific engaged not to declare any further dividends during 1884, to pay the government certain deposited sums, and to elect Charles Francis Adams, Jr., as president in place of Dillon, whose health was conveniently discovered to be "shattered." Boston thus displaced Wall Street. On June 24 the new man, with a characteristic touch of melodrama, "went on deck" at the Boston offices of the Union Pacific: "A regular turmoil all day." Though his plans for the future made no allowance for this fateful step — Adams always maintained he was "forced" into the presidency of the Union Pacific — he at once anticipated he would hold the office for two years.[13]

It was the fate of the new president to manage the railroad from four centers — Boston, New York, Washington, and Omaha. Each headquarters had its peculiar problems. According to the corporate or legal structure at that time, Boston was the financial agency of the Union Pacific. Though Adams was constitutionally inclined to magnify the faults of his associates, he found the Boston subordinates in general trustworthy and informed; he relied upon them for liaison with his outposts in Washington and Omaha and he frequently followed their advice. At Boston also were the banking houses — Kidder Peabody was the most important — to which Adams turned for financial assistance. The Boston *Advertiser* and Boston *Transcript,* some alleged, were the journalistic spokesmen or sycophants for the corporation. After the changeover of 1884 Bostonians constituted a third of the directory, not counting the government directors, and predominated on the executive committee.[14]

Adams seemed to have relied upon Ezra H. Baker, who held upwards of 10,000 shares, and upon F. Gordon Dexter, a Back Bay neighbor, with 6376. Elisha Atkins, in his seventies, occasionally bored Adams "nearly to extinction" with "the snarling criticisms of senility," but the president could neither ignore the extent of Atkins' investment — nearly 10,000 shares — nor his usefulness at critical times. With his approximately $5,000,-000 worth of bonds and shares, F. L. Ames sat at the head of the table. Like Atkins, he took a calmer view than Adams of the company's crises and his decisions often directed Adams' course. Beneath these leaders were the stockholders. Even before Adams' accession to the presidency their number had increased. In 1875 the Boston stock ledger listed only 95 holders; in 1884 there were 5712. In both Boston and New York there had been a fragmentation of large stockholdings. Adams with historic perception noted: "It was the usual course of events. The venturesome contractor made way for the speculative capitalist: he in due time sold out at his own price to the bona-fide investors . . . These are the stockholders I represent." These stockholders seem to have given Adams little trouble. Though he usually anticipated with terror annual meetings, they always turned out to be routine, albeit "sombre" affairs. Adams usually had his own way "unanimously." [15]

The general office of the road remained at Wall Street. The influence of the New York party, however, declined, for in 1885 directors Russell Sage and Jay Gould resigned. By sale Gould dispersed his once large block of stock. As he confessed, the Union Pacific "had tired me out . . . I had made up my mind that it was better for this property to have a large scattered ownership. As long as they said — the newspapers and everybody — that it was Jay Gould that controlled it, the property seemed to be handicapped, and I had made up my mind it was better to get a large number of investors, scattered around through the different States — rather than to have it said it was owned by one man." [16] If this sounded like Adams, it only proved the devil could quote scripture or make a better bargain.

Though Adams often talked as if he had broken sharply with

Gould and forcefully erased the New Yorker's infamous connection with the Union Pacific, his actions and his more circumstantial narrative showed that he followed quite the opposite policy. He hoped to conciliate his predecessors — within limits. After 1884, as before, he constantly traveled to New York and consulted Gould and his associates. Representatives of the old regime hung on. Of Sidney Dillon, who remained on the board of directors, Adams wrote "out of consideration for an old man and my predecessor in office, I didn't stir against the old thief." As for Gould, he "is an infernal scoundrel, a moral monstrosity, but he is astonishingly quick! But again, so was Napoleon." [17]

In retrospect Adams' decision to go along with Gould, rather than to "crush him" as "a man of the Bismarck or Wellington type" would have done, proved a misjudgment. As we shall see, the policy made neither a friend nor ally of Gould. Meanwhile it put Adams in an equivocal posture. Gould's competitors in the railroad arena of the West did not know whether or not they could count on Adams, and some congressmen and journalists suspected Adams was but "the mere nose of wax, the poor figurehead" for the Wall Street wrecker. Adams' denial — "I was not his choice" [18] — did not quiet them. Nor was the disavowal really necessary. The Adams temperament forbade him to play second fiddle in any organization.

From the West, whose territory the road traversed and whose people it served, there were on the board of directors three representatives. One was John Sharp of Salt Lake City, a Mormon ecclesiastic, called the "railroad bishop" because he had constructed some of the Utah lines projected and financed by his church. The second was General G. M. Dodge of Council Bluffs, distinguished as the alleged on-the-site builder of the Union Pacific. Adams admired him for his "natural hard sense, courage and directness," very much the same qualities which had once appealed to Adams in his fellow railroad commissioner Asa Briggs. The third western representative was the head officer in charge of operations at Omaha.[19]

Since Adams was fond of military analogies, perhaps we can call Omaha his field headquarters. There at least were the administrators and technicians and there were made, in the first instance, most decisions on rates, service, and finances. When Adams became president, S. H. H. Clark was general manager and one of the directors. Clark, a "henchman of Gould," was permitted to resign in the summer of 1884 ostensibly on account of ill-health. Adams had found him "tall, thin, dyspeptic with a long beard and a narrow forehead, he knows neither what a good railroad or a good man is"; or to put it briefly he was "the long-bearded conductor with the monkey head." Upon Clark's resignation S. R. Callaway, an official with experience on roads entering Chicago from the East, became second vice-president and general manager of the Union Pacific. Since the expenses of the road mounted, he lasted only a little more than a year; Ames was outraged by his lack of "nerve and backbone"; Adams constantly referred to him as "poor, feeble, cowardly Callaway." [20]

After a desperate canvass of possibilities, Adams in 1887 appointed Thomas J. Potter vice-president and general manager. Potter came to the Union Pacific from the Chicago, Burlington and Quincy on which he had been a protégé of its president, Charles Elliott Perkins, and general manager with particular responsibility for the portion of the system east of the Missouri. Within a year he died on his new job. Adams granted Potter was "experienced, quick, magnetic, a natural leader of men." Nonetheless "he was a good deal of a news-paper humbug" and though he somewhat sublimated his background of "a promoted brakeman" he was "subject to all a brakeman's limitations." He took too hasty decisions and was addicted to the bottle. Nevertheless his death moved Adams to remark "chaos is come again," and Potter had the unique distinction among

Adams' appointees of a memorial minute in the road's annual report. Adams now appointed as vice-president in charge of operations W. H. Holcomb, a tall, impressive westerner, and reconstituted the operations staff in such a fashion as to include as assistant to the general manager C. S. Mellen, formerly of the Boston and Lowell and later president of the New York, New Haven and Hartford. When Adams revealed this plan of organization to its participants, "I saw by their faces that I had it, and was once more top-dog. It was a great relief!" [21] Though he had consulted others, the promotion of Holcomb was primarily Adams' idea.

The relationship between Adams and Holcomb ran through a characteristic cycle. It began with elation at finding the right man, degenerated quickly into doubt, and ended in dismay and invective. Holcomb ran up expenses in the most perplexing way, and instead of analyzing the monthly returns from the road for a clue to the reasons, relapsed into a policy of drift. "As for poor, flabby, floundering Holcomb he reminds me . . . of nothing so much as a great, bewildered, old barn-yard hen, which goes flapping and fluttering about in abject terror." In the shorthand of Adams' abuse Holcomb became "Flabby-guts." [22]

Adams' subordinates necessarily seemed timid and weak to him since they failed to realize his larger program for the Union Pacific. In them "I found no vestige of statesmanship, — no observation, philosophy and patience. They were all uneducated strong men, — energetic, rough, and undisciplined, seeing what was immediately before them very clearly and nothing beyond. They were 'practical men': I was a 'theorist.' To preach the lessons of experience, — to point out the inevitable trend of events . . . to attempt anything of this sort — stamped you in their eyes as not a 'practical man.' Then how they do love cant! When from time to time I have come out and told them the truth in regard to their situation they have replied (1) that it was not so, and (2) that, if it was so, I ought not to say it." [23]

The remedy was clearly men of philosophy and education. Adams could not introduce these at once into the higher echelons, for such appointees were inexperienced, but placed in a "railroad kindergarten" they might acquire maturity and in time be moved up. The recurrent purges and shake-ups in the West gave Adams lots of chances to fill vacancies with "my kids" — usually easterners and Harvard men. All in all he sent out a dozen or so Harvard men "in the nature of a picket line, if not even of a forlorn hope." In his estimation three proved a success. The most promising was W. H. Baldwin, working, in 1890, on the northwest portion of the Union Pacific system. Adams found him a young fellow who "was working out his problems as problems, not wallowing and floundering about in a mire of uncertainties and surprises, bewildered at his situation and equally unable to say how he got there, or how he proposed to get out of it." Since Baldwin was too inexperienced for high administration, Adams was reduced once more to his recurrent moan: "All the tools I have found have bent or broken in my hand." [24]

Adams knew that these frequent shifts in command destroyed continuity of policy and were hence damaging to the road. But he seemed, on the other hand, rather surprised at the harm arising from the manner in which changes were made. The president of the road dismissed his high administrators as if they were adult delinquents. Very often they were put "savagely through the rolling mill." No doubt the reprimand was delivered in Adams' "wheezy way of speaking, more English than American." Callaway, after thus being handed his discharge papers, "whined about my interference and my not being 'practical.'" Adams may have put this down to faults of character in his subordinate, but Callaway and his predecessors and successors had followers, perhaps the recipients of favored treatment. Discharged officials told their dismal tale to them and to friendly editors; both fostered in localities where the railroad could ill afford a foe an image of the Union Pacific as an absentee corporation run by easterners of "classical educa-tion" who did not understand the needs of the West.[25]

For one man in management there were hundreds in the labor force. In his relations with employees Adams assumed the presidency under a handicap, for the previous administra-tion had just reduced wages and the local management ascribed this decision to eastern capitalists. Adams at once denied the East was responsible and promised for the present no further reductions in pay or in the number of workers. Unhappily the aim of Adams and Ames to effect immediate savings through abandoning certain activities auxiliary to the railroad and through discharges in the summer of 1884 weakened the com-fort of this presidential announcement.[26]

In any case Adams had gained time to formulate general principles of management-labor relations and to secure their adoption by the Union Pacific. In the 1870's he had become somewhat of an expert on these matters through the experience of the Massachusetts Railroad Commission. In 1886 he re-capitulated his ideas in a memorandum circulated to officials in the local management of the Union Pacific's lines, and three years later he reprinted this communication as an article in *Scribner's Magazine*. He started with the premise that a good share of the workers must be regarded as belonging to the "permanent service" of the railroad. Though such employees must be permitted to resign at will, they could not be arbi-trarily dismissed except for charges proved before a tribunal on which they were represented. Promotion was to be by sen-iority; as their service lengthened employees should be entitled to automatic pay increases. Furthermore the company and its employees should contribute to a fund which would provide "for hospital service, retiring provisions, sick pensions, and insurance against accident and death." Finally the railroad should underwrite "railroad educational institutions" which the children of employees could attend, and "the best of them would at the proper age be sent out upon the road to take their places in the shops, on the track, or at the brake." All this would increase employee loyalty and *esprit de corps*. To approach this program in the light of modern unionism would be to underestimate its daring and liberality. Even so intelligent a man as Charles Elliott Perkins believed workers should look after themselves without the help of the railroads.[27] Adams' army experience had convinced him of the importance of creating loyalty and morale; the town meeting had shown him the wisdom of a consensus of citizens in matters that concerned them.

Meanwhile labor turbulence on the railroads of the Middle and Far West gave urgency and point to Adams' reflections. The railroad labor crises of this period presented problems as boding and as complex as those clustering about 1877. Earlier the participants had been the brotherhoods of skilled train operators; now the Knights of Labor, whose appeal was mainly to shop mechanics, switchmen, and yardmen, was more likely to be involved. Leaders seemed to be more interested in agitation and the redress of particular grievances than in organizing an enduring union; labor outbreaks erupted spontaneously from local conditions considered oppressive. Though neither the extent of unionization nor the concepts of union leaders encouraged nationwide bargaining or agreements, strikers on a particular road hoped to enhance their coercive power by appealing to their fellows on other roads "to go out" in sympathy or, at the very least, to refuse to handle the cars of the struck railroad. Ill-defined embargoes and boycotts resulted. As a consequence the labor turmoil was as apt to confront Adams in the guise of a strike on another line as on his.

In 1885, a short time after Adams assumed charge of the Union Pacific, a strike broke out on the Missouri Pacific, one of the Gould lines. Although the Knights won a complete victory, it satisfied neither them nor, of course, the management. As a consequence both parties anticipated the resumption of the power struggle; it occurred in March 1886. This time Gould and his officers sat out the stoppage of traffic and the violence and with the backing of public opinion won. Reverberations of this famous Southwest strike stirred up the Knights on the Union Pacific, and a strike of brakemen, repudiated by the central officers of the brotherhood, broke out on that road. The management concentrated armed guards at Cheyenne and the uprising collapsed. Simultaneously Adams wearily informed his stockholders: "We are passing through an epidemic of strikes and an employer has only to say booh and his men get up and quit." The same annual report promised that the road would try to spread the work through the winter and would not discharge, if it could help it, those with seniority.[28]

In 1888 a strike on the Chicago, Burlington and Quincy convinced him that relations between railroad employees and railroad companies were still "unsatisfactory." In this great strike the brotherhoods of locomotive engineers and of firemen, both conservative organizations, decided to try conclusions with one of the most powerful and conservatively managed roads in the Midwest. Its president, Charles Elliott Perkins, was one of the ablest and most relentlessly logical of railroad executives. He had little use for labor organizations, for their strikes interfered with managerial decisions and with loyalty to the company. This outlook prevented a sympathetic hearing of the engineers' grievances over pay and promotion. The strikers planned that members of the brotherhoods on other roads would refuse to handle the cars of the Burlington. Though Adams currently had grievances on other matters against Perkins, he resolutely announced that the Union Pacific was bound by its charter and by the Interstate Commerce Act to interchange traffic with the Burlington and that it would continue to do so. He instructed his Omaha officials to inform Union Pacific employees "it would be no more illegal for them to call upon us to burn the C.B.& Q. freight house and murder its officials" than to make the demand that the Union Pacific cease to interchange freight, and concluded his communication, "Be in this matter very considerate of the men, but absolutely firm." When a partial boycott spread to the Union Pacific, operating officials were less eager for a showdown than their president and their policy was less forceful. Ironically it was the Burlington which sought an injunction against the Union Pacific engineers to compel the latter to handle its cars.[29] Both strike and boycott failed.

These affrays left a residue of unrest on the Union Pacific, for Adams eventually discovered that "Flabby-guts" Holcomb had run up expenses by making concessions to the men, a policy that heightened his wrath against this most unsatisfactory of general managers. "To buy peace" "at company expense" was calamitous. "Concessions to employees also are final. Once made, they cannot be recalled." As far as practical measures during these years of turmoil were concerned, Adams had been forced to remain largely on the sidelines, where he formulated presumably correct general principles in private — always a congenial occupation — and rejoiced as other managers, notably Perkins, triumphed over offending labor organizations.[30]

At Washington the affairs of the Union Pacific seemed entangled with every branch of the national government. On a single trip to the capital Adams was likely to call on the Attorney General to discuss the many railroad or government suits before the Supreme Court or the Court of Claims; on the Secretary of the Treasury to whom the railroad made its payments; on the Secretary of the Interior in whose department was the General Land Office which handled the railroad's land grants; on the railroad commissioner who kept the books on the subsidized roads; on a government director or two, if they were available;[31] and finally on the President who appointed the government directors and could direct cabinet officials and make recommendations to Congress.

At the other end of Pennsylvania Avenue sat "that incapable and mischievous body, the U.S. Congress," ready at any moment to interfere by legislation in almost any phase of management that stirred its interest. The introduction into the House or Senate of no less than twenty-six bills or resolutions involving the Union Pacific railroad during the session of 1885 to 1886 demonstrated how widespread that interest was. With officials in the executive department Adams' eminence and ability and, on occasion, even his aloofness from parties made him a persuasive spokesman for his corporation. For instance the election of Cleveland, whom Adams as a mugwump had supported, promised some advantage. "At U.P. the election of Cleveland brings me to the point and Gould takes a back seat." In the rough-and-tumble Congress party loyalties were fiercer and representatives from the West, less impressed by hallowed New England names, were more mindful of grievances inflicted on their constituents by an absentee corporation. During the feverish days when the Boston party was jockeying to get Adams into the presidency of the Union Pacific and assuage congressional demands for action, a Senator from Nebraska had served notice that there were "bunko men of Boston" too, that "the same crowd of gamblers" as before were behind Charles Francis Adams, and that the people wanted "a better guarantee than the mere respectability of the head of the concern." [32]

To handle politicians who talked like this, Adams recognized the need for a "somewhat unscrupulous man possessed of infinite tact and skill in the manipulation of men. Not I." Consequently he had the sense to call on General Dodge when it came to dealing with western congressmen. He was not equally acute in the choice of his year-round representative in Washington, Moorfield Storey. Like Adams, Storey was a Boston Brahmin and a political independent with the expected touch of self-righteousness. So Adams resorted unwillingly to a substratum of lobbyists, like E. W. Ayres and David T. Littler, both of the West. These men attached themselves to the Union Pacific payroll as "agents" to do the hard and dirty work of persuasion which, if they were lucky, did not get into the newspapers. If good deeds counted more than lobbyists, the fact that the Union Pacific never fell behind on its payments to the government during the Adams administration should have been counted to his credit.[33]

Tired of hand-to-mouth adjustments, the Adams administration and many Federal administrators wanted a final, long-term solution of relations between the government and the Union Pacific. The directors realized that if only the debt owed the government were out of the way the corporation could manage its own business affairs. "I think it is this constant introduction of troublesome bills in Congress that has the effect to keep the matter in constant agitation in the minds of the public, so that a great many people will not touch the securities of the Union Pacific for that very reason. They say, 'We do not know what Congress is going to do next winter,' and every winter, as certain as winter comes, somebody introduces some bill for the regulation of the Union Pacific, and it must be investigated." [34] Furthermore the failure to pay the debt limited the freedom to declare dividends and along with the Thurman Act circumscribed the Union Pacific's flexibility in spending its money. Adams and others of like mind wanted, therefore, to handle the emergency as a private corporation would have handled it in the private money market. They wanted to fund the debt by issuing new securities running at low rates of interest over a long period and to pay to the government annual fixed sums, the accumulation of which would in the end discharge the indebtedness, principal and interest, owed the government by the road.

In 1886 Joseph H. Outhwaite, a Democratic representative from Ohio, reported such a bill to the House of Representatives with the unanimous approval of the Committee on Pacific

Railways, and George F. Hoar, a Republican from Massachusetts, did the same, but without unanimity, for the Committee on the Judiciary in the Senate. These bills arranged for ascertaining the "present worth" of the indebtedness and postponed the final payment on this sum until 1921. Meanwhile the new sum was to bear 3¼ percent interest and the railroad was to discharge the principal and interest in semiannual payments. Outhwaite estimated that the present value of the debt was $52,897,885.55 and that each semiannual payment would be $903,617.03. The Outhwaite bill postponed the deadline for the Union Pacific and lowered the rate of interest as compared with the original loan; on the other hand, its provisions for initiating payments some ten years earlier than the courts had said they were due and for substituting fixed payments for those based on a percentage of fluctuating net earnings were certainly to the advantage of the government. The bill so caught by surprise its likely opponents, largely Democrats from the trans-Mississippi states, that Outhwaite complained during the debate: "Everybody seems to be talking at the same time, and nobody seems to be asking me to yield to him, but all have taken possession of the floor." Those opposed to the bill were moderately ill informed about the history of the Pacific railroads and incapable of distinguishing the present situation from the past. Perhaps it did not matter, for Henley of California and Weaver, an "antimonopolist" from Iowa, hoped to utilize the occasion to have the government foreclose its second mortgage, pay off the first mortgage bondholders, and run the road. This vision shocked Outhwaite: "The most injurious thing which could happen to this government would be for it to go into the railroad business." [35]

Adams surmised that "a large majority" of the House of Representatives was favorable to the funding bill, and the proceedings in the House confirm that impression. Nonetheless the opposition succeeded in putting over a decision to the next session. Meanwhile the idea of again investigating the Pacific railroads promised to slow the momentum behind the funding bill — investigation should precede rather than accompany or follow legislation — and perhaps stir suspicion, if the Union Pacific objected, that the road had something to conceal. Though Adams protested that the road was already under the continuous surveillance of many government officials and that it "has been more frequently and thoroughly investigated than any other business corporation on earth," he promised to cooperate. Senator Edmunds of Vermont, now chairman of the Senate Committee on the Judiciary, agreed that further investigation was a substitute for inaction and consequently attached to the enabling resolution a section declaring that beginning with July 1887 the Pacific roads should pay not 25 percent but 40 percent of their net earnings to the government. Adams was alarmed at this stab from the Senate committee and no doubt stung when one senator lampooned him for the reformist company he kept. He was "in the mugwumpian attitude where Mr. George William Curtis and Mr. Carl Schurz are supposed to be riding sideways, because there is not one among them masculine enough to ride astraddle." He took heart, however, when the Senate dropped the net earnings provision. Furthermore the friends of funding apparently felt an investigation might refute the objections against their proposal. Consequently Congress authorized the President to appoint three commissioners to "investigate the books, accounts, and methods of the Pacific railroads." [36]

If some of the congressional verbiage were to be believed, the United States Pacific Railroad Commission, as it came to be called, was to be composed of "able men, able financiers, able lawyers" whose character was to checkmate scandal, blackmail, intrigue, and "the harpies of the New York stock market" from whom Mr. Adams had already rescued the Union Pacific. Since gods were apparently to walk the earth again, Adams at once bestirred himself to make sure they would hearken to the right prayers. The prospects were alluring. For Adams to see Cleveland about these appointments was natural and innocent enough; to entertain some of the hopes he did seemed to indicate that political reformers could mix the material with naïveté. It would "be a very great thing for us to get some man put on that Commission familiar with Congressional ways and Congressional action, and who might possibly, after the service on the commission was done, enter our employ as our agent at Washington. He would then be familiar with the whole question, and able to press it forward much more effectively." [37]

Adams anticipated Cleveland might appoint some one of the eminence and experience of Schurz or of Thurman; the commissioners the President chose — Robert E. Pattison of Pennsylvania, E. Ellery Anderson of New York, and David T. Littler of Illinois — were distinctly anticlimactic. They were all "deserving Democrats." Pattison had the distinction of being the only Democratic governor of Pennsylvania between the Civil War and the 1930's. Anderson was a corporation lawyer in New York City, and Littler was a member of a law firm in Springfield, Illinois, and had served in the state Senate. The commission elected Pattison chairman and appointed a staff of accountants. Their most significant minor appointment was that of John Norris, news editor of the Philadelphia *Record*, a penny paper that had forged ahead by a muted sensationalism and the promotion of Pattison's political aspirations. Eventually this journalist proceeded "to prepare statistics, tables and other detailed evidence." The suspicious concluded he was actually a sleuth, crusader, and private adviser for Governor Pattison. Adams had a word for him: "a reptile." [38]

The commission held hearings in New York and Boston at which most of the road's officers and large investors testified *in extenso*. Adams made three formal statements, submitted letters and exhibits, and also participated informally when others were being questioned. He thought the Boston hearings revealed that the "ignorance of our judges is something appalling." His impatience and exasperation mounted as he accompanied the commission on a month's tour of the road's territory from Kansas City to Ogden. In view of their mandate the commission had no choice but to take testimony locally from shippers, city officials, politicians, and journalists. Nonetheless the jaunt was a fishing expedition for unsupported charges. To answer these "bores, schemers, etc.," Adams had continuously to explain how and why a railroad functioned as it did; he had to run a "railroad kindergarten." At last at Ogden the "repulsive journey" was over and he passed the commissioners over to the Central Pacific with a sigh of "deliverance." [39]

No matter how derogatory his opinion of the commission as a whole, Adams did not refrain from trying privately to influence them as individuals. Even before the hearings began he was at work upon Anderson with the aid of Dillon and later through the mediation of a government director. He tried to please Pattison by a speech at the centennial celebration of the Constitution in Philadelphia and to find out what made him tick by inquiries from the governor's intimates. The desire of David T. Littler to be of service to Adams and the Union Pacific was something of a windfall. He was soon keeping Adams informed of what went on on the commission and acting as a go-between with the "inquisition." After the commissioners had transmitted their reports to Cleveland came the "first suggestion of corruption from Littler, — a bad taste in my mouth." A year later the importunities for money from this "striker" were intolerable. [40]

No investigation can rise above the level of its procedures and the evidence thereby collected. The Pacific Railroad Commission heard voluminous testimony but, as two members charged, a good deal of it was hearsay and would not stand up in a court of law. The commission also refused to go behind the testimony and findings of earlier investigations. As Anderson brusquely informed one witness: "We know how the road was built from 1867 to 1869 . . . There is no necessity of going over that. It is all in other reports made by other committees." While such impatience is understandable, the decision to accept the Poland and Wilson investigations as infallible and nonpartisan put error at compound interest.[41]

Even before their excursion to the West was completed, a rift appeared among the commissioners. Littler and Anderson were in agreement, but in Littler's words, "God only knows what that other fellow will do." Eventually on December 1, 1887, the majority of Littler and Anderson presented one report and R. E. Pattison another. The majority and minority did come to one common conclusion. As Governor Pattison put it, the best policy was "to withdraw the government from further connection with private enterprises"; as the majority wrote, "The sovereign should not be mated with the subject." Over the path to this objective, however, there was complete disagreement. The majority preferred some form of the current proposals for funding the debt owed to the government. On his part, Pattison recommended that the government begin judicial proceedings to forfeit the charters of the roads and subsequently appoint a receiver "to provide for the immediate settlement of the government debt." After stages, more blurred than clear in his telling, a new company whose capital stock and bonded indebtedness was to be no greater than the cost of reproducing the properties was to take over. "The purchasing company . . . should be forbidden, directly or indirectly, to invest" in the securities of parallel or competing railroads. "A mere money recovery is the least of benefits" the government should consider. To extend the debt would "condone" the past misdeeds of the Union Pacific and "place a mortgage upon the earnings and upon the products of the people of Kansas, Nebraska, and Colorado, not only of this but of succeeding generations."[42]

Pattison's report was both visionary and vindictive. His proposal would have involved complicated and endless litigation; and an outcome favoring the government, in the light of existing Supreme Court decisions, was exceedingly dubious. The majority preferred a less punitive policy. A new day had come with Adams' administration: "We are satisfied that this administration has devoted itself honestly and intelligently to the herculean task of rescuing the Union Pacific Railway from the insolvency which seriously threatened it at the inception of its work; that it has devoted itself by rigid economy, by intelligent management, and by an application of every dollar of the earning capacity of the system to its improvement and betterment, to place the company on a sound and enduring financial foundation." To Pattison, Adams was a surrogate for Jay Gould, and the policies of both "showed an entire disregard of sound principles of trade," and revealed "the incapacity of its officers to deal with such great matters." [43] Pattison, to paraphrase a political slogan of that day, "waved the bloody Credit Mobilier." His report was an invitation to the old demagoguery and delay.

Adams, promptly informed about "new entanglements" on the commission, rushed to Washington to see Cleveland, sought "to pull wires," and essayed an answer to Pattison's report, "the dyspeptic utterance of an untruthful, dishonest, political crank." The reply did not come easily. Meanwhile Cleveland had submitted to Congress the two reports with a covering message. He rejected any program placing the roads "in the possession and control of the government," warned against indulging in irritation and indignation, suggested the application of the "well devised" plan of the majority to roads which would accept and meet its conditions, and concluded "the public interest urges prompt and efficient action." [44] In this cautious fashion the President met the dilemma of dissent between commissioners of his own choosing.

In any case Adams judged he had sufficient support within

the government to justify a strong push for a settlement. He mobilized his customary lobby of Storey and Ayres, considered and put to one side the possibility of "additional" employments to aid in the passage of the bill, and rejected "point blank" the suggestion of Littler "to start bribing." Probably the judicious distribution of favors did not fall within this rubric. He thought, for example, that he could persuade Senator Dawes of Massachusetts and Senator Butler of South Carolina, both of whom held key positions on committees dealing with Indian Affairs, and President Cleveland to favor organizing the Oklahoma Territory into a state in case two representatives from Iowa, who wanted that measure, proved less hostile to the program of the Union Pacific. Adams himself went to Washington to lobby. All his effort and scheming availed nothing, however. Anderson of Iowa engineered a "fiasco" by securing the postponement of the Outhwaite bill and instead introducing one for the control and regulation of railroads acquired by the United States under judicial foreclosure or forfeiture.[45]

In the next session of Congress the scene shifted to the Senate, where a Special Committee on the President's Message relating to the Pacific Railroad fathered a measure essentially similar to the Outhwaite bill. The chairman of the Special Committee was Senator Frye of Maine. Adams apparently decided this time to leave little to chance. The presidential campaign of 1888 presented opportunities, since the chairmen of both national committees, W. H. Barnum for the Democrats and Matthew Quay for the Republicans, were willing to be of service. Ames and Adams decided to give each $50,000, $20,000 immediately and the remainder when the Union Pacific got its bill. Barnum assured Adams about the House: "I can get your bill passed if any man can, and you can rest assured, if I can't get it passed, it cannot be passed." [46]

Adams also tried to sway individuals. While he was sure that most public men though "commonplace and 'ornery' " were "very honest," he was equally certain that he needed to dislodge from his path two of the most influential congressmen. One obstacle was Senator P. B. Plumb of Kansas. A veteran of the struggle to make Kansas a free state and of the Civil War, Plumb served three consecutive senatorial terms after 1877 as a Republican. The scholar who contributed a sketch of Plumb's life to the *Dictionary of American Biography* wrote: "His whole career was marked by strenuous effort, untiring industry, and wholesome enthusiasm." Be that as it may, Adams found him an adroit master at delaying the Union Pacific's funding bill. Adams first tried to please Plumb's constituents by building a station at Lawrence and leasing them a local railroad. Though Plumb did not rise to this bait and neither Adams nor Storey "had any means of coping with Western men," Adams was determined to find out what Plumb wanted. The truth left him "speechless." Plumb wanted $50,000 and the assurance he would not have to vote for the bill nor be forbidden to propose amendments as long as they were "meaningless." Adams capitulated: "I was willing enough . . . to fling the dirty dog his bone, provided I could do so in safety" and after the bill was passed.[47]

Each depth a lower depth concealed. Adams consigned to that nethermost of regions George F. Edmunds, a senator from Vermont for twenty-five years, who became one of the most venerated elder statesmen of the post–Civil War era. As almost permanent chairman of the Senate Committee on the Judiciary, he was in a position to "bushwhack" legislation affecting the Union Pacific. Adams described him as "the most thoroughly corrupt and dishonest, and the most insidiously dangerous man, when balked of his bribes, that there is today in Washington." He was a "thorough-going hypocrite . . . he never allows a direct bribe to reach him, but he only takes retainers." Gould, Huntington, and Villard told Adams they retained Edmunds to represent them in the courts, and he incidentally looked after their interests in the Senate. The Union Pacific had once earned his enmity by not hiring him. Of course in the Adams version he was also "fond of his whiskey bottle." His biographer in the *Dictionary of American Biography* salutes Edmunds for a "political morality . . . unsmirched" at a time of low standards and the papers on his retirement praised his "integrity," but Adams snarled "Moll [*sic*] Tearsheet's virtue." [48]

It should be said in defense of these gentlemen that the evidence for "Plumb's pabulum" is circumstantial and inconclusive, and he never got the $50,000. As for "the sea-green immaculate from Vermont" there is no need to probe for the secret of his opposition. He had been the joint and really the chief author of the Thurman Act and logically preferred a decade later the stiffening of that statute as a means of handling the Union Pacific's debt to the government. The real curiosity in this affair is how Adams, with the principles and scruples of a political reformer, persuaded himself to participate in what he admitted was a "most extraordinary and discreditable negotiation" and which he confided to his diary only that "some future historical use be made" of it. One justification was his duty to the stockholders. If he would not bribe Plumb "it was questionable whether I had any right to retain my place as President." In the case of his campaign contributions to both parties, Adams pictured Ames and himself as white-coated technicians conducting a laboratory experiment in political science. "We would soon in this way learn what political influence money could buy." Unhappily for the Union Pacific it bought nothing; in February 1889, as in the previous July, the funding bill was "thrown out." [49]

After that defeat Adams took a different tack. Thenceforth as far as Washington was concerned, Adams' policy was one of "quiet observation." The spectacle of Congress denying realism in order to punish the wrong people and shape policy from wishful thinking perplexed Adams. It must have been his fault.

In one of the most piteous statements he ever penned, he blamed the outcome on his defects as a corruptionist. He could have bought Plumb and Edmunds. "I simply didn't know how to go to work. Not that I am above it; I'm not. I would have bought Plumb, just as I would have bought a horse or a hog, and there would to me have been a perfect and intense satisfaction in slipping the dollars into the greedy hands of the Vermont immaculate; but simply it wasn't in me to do it. And I knew it and they knew it, and they despised and hated me accordingly." Adams was capable of sounder analysis than this perverse abasement. "The fact is that in Washington unless there is some great popular demand for a given measure, so small an amount of obstruction suffices to complicate the wheels that it seems almost hopeless to do anything." Strangely he did not see the fatal incongruity in pressing for "the liberation of the company and its business, as far as possible, from the control of the United States and its officers and from all interference" at the precise moment when Congress through the Interstate Commerce Act was at last moving to restrain railroad abuses in general. Finally the proposal to fund aroused the hostility of the road's rivals. The opposition of the Central Pacific and of other bond-aided roads was another reason for the defeat of the bill in 1889. The position of Charles E. Perkins and the Chicago, Burlington and Quincy left Adams "mad all the way through all the time." Perkins stated his point simply: "It seems outrageous to supply one Road with 3 per cent money while the rest must do the best they can, but I am very much afraid the bill will go through. There is nothing like character to carry through jobs!" [50] One of the cardinal points in Adams' policy when he assumed the presidency was to separate the Union Pacific and the government. This he had failed to achieve.

In the course of operating the road, Adams faced the problem of competition. In a measure this was a new problem for that corporation. A government director had once written the Union Pacific "was a perfect and absolute monopoly," and Adams prophesied in 1882 that other lines "will be to the Union Pacific only what Third and Sixth Avenues are to Broadway." Some of the investors thought Congress intended this state of affairs, but the evidence points in the other direction. That body, contemporaneously with the chartering of the Union Pacific, chartered the Northern Pacific Railway to run from some point on Lake Superior to the West Coast at Puget Sound and, by a branch down the Columbia River, to Portland. The line was to lie mainly north of the 45th degree of latitude. Congress at almost the same time reactivated the pre–Civil War proposals for transcontinentals coinciding roughly with parallels of latitude, one along the 32nd and another along the 35th.[51] None of these companies reached its destination under its own name. The 32nd parallel became a part of the Southern Pacific from the coast to St. Louis and New Orleans; the 35th parallel became the route by which the Atchison, Topeka and Santa Fe reached California. The Northern Pacific reached Portland by connecting with the Oregon Railway and Navigation Company, an aggregate of coastal and river boat lines and of short railways in the Pacific Northwest. The Northern Pacific's direct line to Puget Sound was not completed until 1887–1888.

For the business talents and morals of the titans associated with these transcontinentals, Adams had pointed estimates. The overlord of the Northwest was Henry Villard, an immigrant from Germany, whose success as railroad strategist and conservator gave him access to German investment capital. When Villard had worsted him in some maneuver, Adams habitually called him a "vagabond German and charlatan adventurer"; when their relations were more serene, Adams reverted to an estimate more appropriate for one who, after all, had been a fellow member of the American Social Science Association. Villard was "the only man who can take an idea and work persistently to it," "the biggest man of the crowd." On the Southern Pacific the real driving force in the eighties was C. P. Huntington, in Adams' words "shrewd, wily, vulgar, and unscrupulous." "He uses words with a good deal of skill to conceal thought. He is a bad lot." The Atchison, Topeka and Santa Fe was a Boston enterprise and William B. Strong, the president, who made the road a power, was a New Englander. Adams thought him "narrow-minded, logical in a small way, — a bargainer by nature and training, and cold-blooded to the last possible degree in all matters of business." [52]

These contestants not only faced each other, they also faced water competition, for sailing vessels interchanged goods around Cape Horn at rates which made this all-water route seem to the transcontinentals "the worst of the whole crowd"; and the Pacific Mail Steamship Company, operating steam vessels from both coasts and transshipping by the Panama Railway across the Isthmus, was so menacing a rival that the transcontinentals gave it subsidies to hamstring its full force. Some of the rivals had distinct advantages over the Union-Central line. The Atchison, Topeka and Santa Fe, for instance, built eastward to Chicago in the late eighties, thus securing a direct connection with the eastern trunklines. More damaging was the creation of the great "Sunset Route," a "Morgan line" of steamers from Atlantic ports to New Orleans and thence over the Southern Pacific. It is striking that shortly before Adams became president the transcontinental business of the Union Pacific contributed only $7\frac{1}{2}$ percent of the net earnings of its freight business.[53]

Meanwhile railroads inappropriately denominated local were encroaching upon the trans-Mississippi traffic. Before the Civil War lines began to fan out westward from Chicago to the Mississippi, to cross the river, and to penetrate the first tier of states beyond. One of these, the Chicago, Burlington and Quincy, after reaching the Mississippi River at Burlington pushed westward beyond a mere connection with the Union Pacific at Council Bluffs and in 1882 reached Denver. The Burlington was a Boston road; its *éminence grise* was John Murray Forbes, a Saturday Club associate, congenial to Adams and a neighbor in Milton, adjacent to Quincy. The road's man on the job was Charles Elliott Perkins. Perkins was reflective and competent enough to elicit Adams' admiration, but Adams detected limitations. He was "the typical head of a small, independent state. The very idea of central authority and obedience to natural law is repugnant to him. He would jealously retain his petty independence and always go in earnestly for peace and two thirds of the traffic." Other local roads were the Rock Island and the Chicago and Northwestern. Throughout the mid-eighties the Rock Island under R. R. Cable, "aggressive, outspoken, and western," and the Chicago and Northwestern, in which there was Vanderbilt money, were content, after crossing Illinois and Iowa from Chicago, to stop at the Omaha–Council Bluffs gateway.[54]

In the trans-Mississippi West, as elsewhere, the multiplication of competing lines led to a constant reduction in fares and rates and also to other railroad practices more likely to stir discontent. One such practice was the rebate given to powerful, favored shippers. Another was the comparatively lower rate for a long haul than for a short one. Also railroads had constantly to promote a favorable climate of opinion; a lobby in the state legislature, cultivation of the local press, and free passes to state officials, shippers, editors, and other leaders of public opinion were commonplace examples of the procedure. If a road curtailed "the privilege of riding free," "the newspapers would lose no opportunity to assail it; it would be denounced everywhere as 'illiberal', 'stingy', 'aristocratic and autocratic' . . . it would, in short, have no 'friends.' "[55] Indeed, he who would understand policy made at Washington for the Union Pacific should study first the opinion and attitudes of the localities.

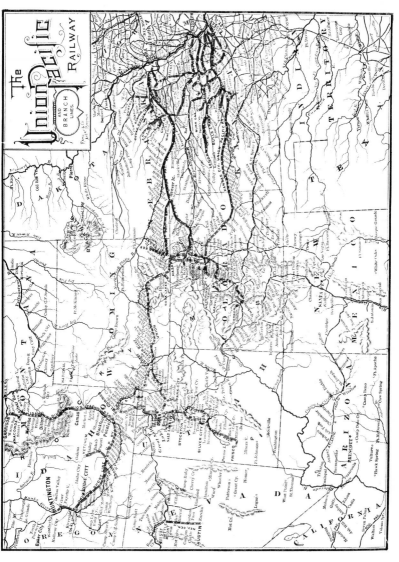

The Union Pacific Railway and Branch Lines

The house on President's Hill. "In the morning went up to the house with Minnie and

Ironically Adams had excoriated these local railroad abuses as a Massachusetts railroad reformer. When he went West, his opinion did not change, but he learned there were limitations on his decisions and accomplishments. He had to surrender the responsibility for day-to-day operations to local officials and he could not police their violations of general policy. Also, he had to consider security holders reluctant to have their investments jeopardized by changes from customary practices. "I cannot undertake to reform the whole world, or to attend to all of its details, at least not in a day. If, when I became president of the Union Pacific, I had said, 'I must have certain reforms go on, regardless of consequences, and make them', I should have had the railroad bankrupted on my hands at a very early day . . . A man who today undertook to manage a railroad on wholly correct principles would be much in the position of Don Quixote when he ran his tilt muck with the windmill." [56] As it was, he nibbled at reform just enough to frustrate and puzzle his subordinates and to gain the reputation of being a "theorist" rather than a "practical" man.

There were areas, however, where Adams had both freedom and the willingness to maneuver. He had been and he was to remain the apostle of publicity as one cure for the railroad's ills. "It is no use for me to slaughter the interests of the company intrusted to my hands. If I am playing a game of chance, and show my hand where nobody else in the game does, the effect is not long to be waited for." But publicity about the railroad's general course rather than details was another matter. Publicity bludgeoned railroads into correct actions, and by discarding concealment dispelled suspicion. "Railroad men . . . wish to make their lines popular." It was an article of deep faith with Adams that railroads must be sensitive to the opinions and interests of shippers and communities. "I do not believe that the Pennsylvania would be managed in direct opposition to the public opinion of Pennsylvania; or the New York Central in opposition to the public opinion of the State of New York; or the Boston and Albany in opposition to the public opinion of the State of Massachusetts. In regard to the last I know from experience that this would be impossible." Certainly on the score of publicity the Boston office and not local agencies had the initiative and power; it made out the annual report. That watchman of Wall Street, the *Commercial and Financial Chronicle*, was at first somewhat captious about Adams' performance and feared he was not shaking loose from the precedents of his predecessors, but at the end of 1884 it bestowed a commendation: "The rights of security holders have never received so much consideration at the hands of those in control as now." Soon the railroad's reports were running to two hundred pages, handsomely printed with a map in color of the system, and the *Commercial and Financial Chronicle* was saluting that of 1885 as "one of the most complete railroad reports ever issued." [57]

"We have," said Adams, "some forty organizations of which I am president, I think." He had largely inherited this structure from his predecessors. Once, as railroad commissioner of Massachusetts, he had been censorious about the irrational eagerness of railroad executives to build extensions to any beckoning traffic and of the ambition of communities to be on the line of more than one railroad. Adams' attitude toward competitive expansion in the West, where population was flowing in, might well have been different, for he was ready to admit that Massachusetts problems and solutions were not universal. Still, when he became president in 1884 the financial and political circumstances of the Union Pacific did not encourage a building program. Adams consequently expressed reservations about Gould's "large schemes. His theory, which I think was a correct theory for that time, was for the Union Pacific to be developed into a complete system, starting from Missouri River points between Kansas City and Omaha, and serving the country west of the river." [58] Although the Union Pacific had some "agricultural" branches, its Kansas and Nebraska network, for example, did not equal that of the Chicago, Burlington and Quincy.

When the road reached eastern Colorado, the pattern changed. Denver was the nucleus of a Union Pacific network. South and west of that city Gould had acquired a road which ran among the peaks of the Rockies, in two places at altitudes of 10,000 feet and at one of 15,000. Its chief revenue came from "carrying men and material into Colorado to dig holes in the ground called mines, and until it was discovered there was nothing in those mines the business was immense." Adams concluded: "there are few regions in the world where more acts of costly folly, in the way of railroad building, have been permitted than in Colorado." [59]

The aspect was more cheering in the next center of Union Pacific strength, Salt Lake City. The Utah and Northern Railway Company, constructed on "religious principles" by the Mormons with Brigham Young as engineer, ran north from Ogden, which was on the Union Pacific, and terminated "practically at Butte which is now the largest and most active mining camp in the world." The road, with an "immense business" in the carriage of copper and coal, "was the most important and valuable of the Union Pacific's auxiliary lines." [60]

The Utah and Northern had been completed on the premise that the difficulties of the promoters and financiers of the Northern Pacific were so immense that their line pushing westward from Duluth could not successfully cross the northernmost tier of American states. This surmise appealed to Adams, who preferred on general principles to stake out a territory without provoking a rival. Since Henry Villard, the transportation overlord of the Northwest, felt much the same way, he had proposed to Gould in the late 1870's that Villard's Oregon Railroad and Navigation Company should build eastward along the south bank of the Columbia and thence southward to Huntington near the Oregon-Idaho border along the Snake, where it would join with a line built northwestward by the Union Pacific from the Salt Lake region. Although Gould's and Dillon's enthusiasm for this proposed transcontinental cooled, Congress chartered the so-called Oregon Short Line in 1881. Several months after Adams became president of the Union Pacific the Short Line was completed. For it Adams cherished an excessive ardor: "I regard Idaho as the most promising field of development — undeveloped field — that the Union Pacific now has," he testified in 1887. All it needed was water! [61]

Adams was a great defender of the branch line system. These pieces fell into his general strategy. The Union Pacific, having reached "a stage of active development," should move into undeveloped country "on the west side of the continental divide in the direction of the valleys of western Colorado . . . Further West I would also develop vigorously in western Idaho and southeastern Oregon . . . So far as the country east of Cheyenne and Denver is concerned I should there build only as much as was necessary to protect existing business. We do not have a sufficient haul on traffic from that country to enable us to hold our own as against a line running to Chicago." [62]

The branches also gave the management of the Union Pacific a measure of freedom. Their charters came from the states rather than the national government. Since the courts held Congress could legislate only for the aided mileage of the Union Pacific, the branches could finance and combine pretty much as they pleased; and they had no government bond subsidy. Toward the end of his presidency Adams sought to combine these many roads into independent systems. They would be so valuable that by offering to include them in the security for the government subsidy he could tempt the government into a settlement along the lines of the funding bill, or he could use them as a basis for a huge loan in the private market to raise funds to buy out the government. A prosperous railroad system gave the government greater security than the Thurman Act;

the government could not have both. Disinterested business opinion agreed with him. To those convinced that the Union Pacific was always seeking a way to deprive the government of its due, the branch lines seemed a trickery, and many feared the railroad would make a system of them on which the government would have no claim. Suspicions of this extravagant sort became so commonplace that the government directors in 1889 specifically asserted: "There is no evidence of any purpose on the part of the company to surrender that portion of the road on which the government has a statutory lien." [63]

The Adams policy of active development and expansion was hard to reconcile with his traditional exposition of the advantages of railroad peace. In December 1888 an opportunity for the application of that gospel opened. J. P. Morgan called a conference at his home. Seated around the dining room table were the representatives of the powerful banking houses of Drexel, Morgan and Company, Brown Brothers, and Kidder Peabody, and about a dozen presidents of the chief western roads, including Perkins, Cable, Hughitt, Strong, Gould, and Adams. On the first day Adams kept quiet, but on the second "I spoke the truth that was in me." Agreements about rates and traffic were ropes of sand because they lacked executive force or enforcement. Law and order must be imposed from a source outside the roads, either from the bankers or from the government. On this occasion Adams recommended the recently established Interstate Commerce Commission. The railroads should form an agreement consonant with the provisions of the Interstate Commerce Act, and the commission should assent to this accord in advance. Strong and Perkins hung back; Cable and Hughitt were favorable; Gould "picked up the idea instantly and in his characteristic way went straight to the point"; Morgan said they must have a plan, paying attention "to the prevailing sensitiveness of public opinion." [64]

Adams was appointed to head the inevitable subcommittee.

His attempt to confer with Cooley and Morrison of the commission under agreeable circumstances — dinner at the Union Club and talk afterwards — was wrecked by the railroad commissioners' lack of social sophistication. "Our country is just about half civilized, and the average public man belongs to the uncivilized portion. The idea of combining dinner with business was beyond the mental grasp of Col. W. R. Morrison of Illinois." Morrison perhaps sensed the political imprudence of regulators dining with the regulated. Nonetheless Cooley, "only half emerged from the primitive man," gave the grand design a measure of approval.[65]

Such were the preliminaries to the formation of the Interstate Commerce Railway Association. "On this occasion I feel that I did naturally and easily come to the front. I assumed leadership naturally and by common consent. All this was gratifying, very gratifying." Details remained to be perfected and to win acceptance. Since the "weak brothers" like the Burlington had to be conciliated rather than coerced, Adams early in 1889 felt the plan was being whittled away and impatiently left a Chicago meeting summoned to patch it up. "I failed at the pinch." Nonetheless an association of sorts did come into being and in a fashion regulated rates and shipments for almost six months. Then the aggressiveness of the individual roads, including the Union Pacific, led to its collapse.[66]

During these months while he vacillated between pride and elation on the one hand and "dissatisfied reflections" on the other, Adams kept turning over in his mind the way out of the competitive jungle. Perhaps the best route was a reduction in the number of contestants; perhaps the consolidation of all railroads into a single system, dangerous as were the implications, might be the only answer. In the here and now "a railroad Bismarck is needed." Fink had failed, Adams had failed. "Will Pierpont Morgan develop the needed force? Possibly. He has many of the elements of power needed. It remains to be seen if he is an organizer." The alternative was to let the law of competition and of the survival of the fittest or "might makes right" work out its destined way. "Might certainly does not make right, but natural law works in many ways, and it very often works extreme hardship and cruelty to individuals." Meanwhile his own proposals for pooling and agreement were but "makeshifts" to check the operation of these laws.[67]

Adams gave the impression that as a philosopher on railroads he was waiting for an answer to turn up. As an administrator he soon found that to move forward was as dangerous as to stand still. The extension of the Union Pacific to the Pacific Northwest threw the road into a competitive cockpit. The Central Pacific under Huntington built north from California and made a bid to carry the trade of the Northwest to the East over the Southern Pacific. Adams in general managed to get along with this threat. Relations with Henry Villard varied. In spite of his power and the complex structure of his corporate control, Villard did not have a continuous, firm control of the Northern Pacific; rival interests within it allied themselves with the railroad ambitions of different communities in the Northwest — "the hyenas are eating each other up" [68] — and Adams tried to pick his way among these numerous factions. Sometimes Villard and he were allies, sometimes not. Construction of branches into the nominally acknowledged preserves of others continually upset alliances and agreements.

In the course of these competitive frays, the Union Pacific first leased the Oregon Railway and Navigation Company and then in 1889, discontented at the terms, purchased 120,027 shares of Oregon Railway stock, a majority holding. During his struggles in the Northwest Adams came to rely upon the potential influence of the Great Northern, which J. J. Hill — "Hill's methods of discussion are simply bewildering" — was by the early 1890's pushing to completion as another transcontinental.[69] Meanwhile General G. M. Dodge, once builder of the Union Pacific and now a director, had been trying to interest Adams in an agreement with a road running from Denver to Galveston on the Gulf of Mexico — which meant it ran from Denver to Fort Worth. Early in 1890 Adams merged this and other lines in Colorado and beyond into the Union Pacific, Denver and Gulf Railway Company.

All the while Adams had been conscious of the Union Pacific's inferior status east of Omaha. While the roads from Chicago and elsewhere were extending westward into its territory in the plains states, or threatening to do so, the Union Pacific had no reliable Chicago connection. Since construction was expensive and bound to stir bitter retaliation, Adams in October 1889 executed an alliance with the Chicago and Northwestern under which the eastbound traffic of the Union Pacific would flow as far as possible over the lines of the Chicago and Northwestern, and the westbound traffic of the latter over the lines of the Union Pacific. As Adams wrote, "the two companies become in all essential through traffic respects one company. They will protect and sustain each other, and, in case of attack, make common cause." This alliance also gave the Union Pacific connections to Duluth, St. Paul, and Minneapolis. Six months later, perhaps to placate roads angered by this agreement, Adams entered into a contract permitting the Rock Island, once content to stop at the Missouri, and the Chicago, Milwaukee and St. Paul to use the Union Pacific's bridge and trackage at Omaha, and thus move their traffic more easily into the trans-Missouri area.[70]

The expansion of its mileage and the favoring connections forged with other roads alarmed the former managers of the Union Pacific. Jay Gould was the most sensitive, for he had put together a system of railroads reaching from St. Louis and Kansas City into the Southwest as far as the Rio Grande; and through the Missouri Pacific, starting at St. Louis, across Kansas into central Colorado. Gould had forged a link between these systems and the eastern trunklines through the Wabash Railroad, terminating at Toledo. Adams' alliances with the Chicago and Northwestern and the contracts with the Rock Island and the Chicago, Milwaukee and St. Paul seemed to Gould a direct threat, particularly to his linchpin, the Missouri Pacific. The expansionist policy of the Union Pacific farther west also made him uneasy. One of Gould's associates had once jocosely said of him, "You know he always claims all the territory there is within 1,000 miles of his road." The obvious countermove was to regain control of the Union Pacific and thus reverse its policy. Adams was defiant and cocksure. In April 1890 he noted, "Rumors that Gould is making a drive at me — let him drive!" and in November he was publicly asserting that to get control of the stock of the Union Pacific "would be a task of enormous proportions even for Gould," for of the $60,000,000 stock one third was held in New England and one third abroad.[71]

Adams' bravado ignored the financial vulnerability of the Union Pacific. Early in his administration, Adams' willingness to avoid expansion, his prudent administration, and the sale of securities in other roads by the Union Pacific had enabled him to handle the road's floating debt. On August 24, 1886, he "went into town and paid off the last U.P. note and gave clerks a half holiday . . . Today was memorable. The work I went into the U.P. to do is accomplished." Later he allowed the directors "to talk me" into the creation of a new debt. "I was not equal to the position," he added. To finance a policy of expansion, in this instance the purchase of the Oregon Railway and Navigation stock, put strains upon the Union Pacific that other railroads would not have had to face. Summarizing the restrictions Congress had imposed by the fundamental acts and later enactments, Adams said: "We stand in the position of a tradesman whose creditor holds his arms while his competitor robs his till. The Government says we shall not borrow; we shall not lease; we shall not guarantee except within very narrow limits." [72]

In essence the Union Pacific was compelled to take the bonds and stock of branches and extensions; observe due care to retain in its treasury at least enough stock to ensure voting control of its acquisitions; and raise the essential cash upon the remaining assets through borrowing from the banks on short-term loans. When the Union Pacific wished to escape the suspense and expense inherent in constantly renewing such loans and paying interest on them, it would lump together a bunch of securities and upon them issue collateral trust bonds and attempt their sale. Whether these bonds could be sold depended upon the confidence of the market, a willingness and ability to buy by those already heavily committed to the enterprise, and general business conditions. Though the phrase "undigested securities" seems to have been associated for the first time with the panic of 1893, the condition it described overhung the Union Pacific long before.

When Adams took command in 1884, the net floating debt of the road had been $6,900,178. Though he had paid it off, the release was not enduring. In the fall of 1890 Adams calculated the road's indebtedness: "We were carrying $14,000,000 stock we had bought on short term loans; we had sold about half the bonds [of the Oregon Railroad and Navigation] but the poor returns spoiled our market. It had a floating debt of $10,000,000. I had failed to market $6,000,000 of O.R.& N. Co. advances and $3,000,000 of equipment bonds and I had failed to secure the $2,000,000 of new money which would have enabled me to sell the bonds. My budget was askew. It fell like a house of cards." [73] There was a good deal of duplication as well as exaggeration in these desperate gross sums.

The ability of a railroad officer to keep these items in air largely depended upon the returns from operations. "This is the only thing in U.P. that I, and no other man, can stand up against, — ruinous traffic returns mean downfall." Adams consequently regarded the monthly traffic returns "as all in all"; when they were large he had blue skies and serenity and when they were small one of his Union Pacific *"cui bono* days" ensued.[74] In the summer of 1890 Adams found Holcomb was running up expenses in a mysterious fashion and the surplus he was counting upon shrank or disappeared. The road confronted bankruptcy and Adams, as an investor, staggering personal losses. Unable to stand the suspense he went to the West in October 1890.

From then on it was Götterdämmerung — self-consciously arranged. "As we pulled out from Omaha and I crossed the Missouri, I looked back on the city, — its smoke rising against the glowing Western sky, and in my bones I felt it was the last time. I was nearing the end." Where could he get money to stave off a showdown? Usually when in straits he had turned to Kidder, Peabody, who would get a loan from the Barings by selling sterling. The cost was high — 1 percent a month — but the money was forthcoming. This time the Boston firm engaged to furnish $4,000,000; since the Barings were on the brink of failure through losses in the Argentine, the possibility evaporated. The Adams management turned to Morgan without success. The Chicago and Northwestern refused to help, as the Vanderbilt interests did not wish to undertake financial involvements beyond Chicago. Ames, Adams, and members of his family moved on to New York for the final curtain. "Bought engraving of Meissonier's '1814', it being suggestive of my recent and present experience." The only escape from Adams' dilemma was Gould, who had been buying Union Pacific stock and had matured a scheme of stalling off the Union Pacific's creditors. Ames and Adams by appointment met the "little wizard" in his office. Adams told Gould, "quiet, small, furtive, inscrutable . . . my credit, position, and responsibility have been undermined and I could no longer carry the load and he must carry it. He assented. After telling him I would call a meeting of the Directors on the 27th and turn the company over to him . . . There being nothing more for me to do there, I got up to go . . . Gould showed me out. As we formally shook hands, the little man seemed to look smaller, meaner, more haggard and livid in the face and more shrivelled up and ashamed of himself than usual; — his clothes seemed too big for him, and, his eyes did not seek mine, but were fixed on the upper buttonhole of my waist-coat. I felt as if in my hour of defeat, I was overawing him, — and, as if he felt so, too." [75]

Adams was as prompt as his promise. On November 26, 1890, he noted in his diary, "Today ceased to be Pres't of Union Pacific and so ended my life of rail-road work . . . Gould, Sage, and the pirate band were scrambling on deck at 10." Once again Sidney Dillon became president and S. H. H. Clark managing vice-president.[76] Gould remained a director until his death in 1892; the following year the decline in earnings on the Union Pacific, its floating debt, and the onset of a general financial panic compelled the road to seek a receivership.

To say that Adams was uninterested in this aftermath would be untrue. His chief anxiety, however, remained his own presidency. This had been a failure. He realized it; the public knew it. He had failed to fulfill his program to separate the railroad from the government, to resume dividends, and to recruit a competent leadership in the West. He had taken over a water-logged craft; he left it still water-logged. His own phrase for his presidency — "this everlasting rowing against wind and tide" — was accurate. Things happened, little was solved. Finally there was the humiliation of being brushed aside by Gould and not being able to prevent it. Since he had "to meditate the fact of failure," he luckily knew the proper role. "The only true course is to bow like a gentleman, quietly pass in your chips, and leave the table. The man, who under such circumstances hangs round the table, proving to others how it ought to have resulted otherwise, is a bore, as well as an ass." [77] But the failure which had dogged his life had now overtaken him, and it hurt so deeply that he recurred constantly to its circumstances and provided explanation after explanation for it.

He felt it was all his fault. The usual emotional tone of these outbursts did not entirely preclude a fairly accurate appraisal of his qualities as a railroad executive. The fault was not planning but character. "My mind was active enough, and my plan of operations and scheme of development was well devised, well thought out, and wholly practicable." "My ideas were right but I did not hold to them . . . I was weak of will." In a calmer moment midway in his presidency he had written: "The fact is I lack combativeness. I get into a fight easily enough: but, being in it, I lack desperate courage . . . I fail because I cannot make up my mind on the instant and my reserves are not at my command." A more palatable way of diluting his guilt was to strike childishly the sacrificial pose. The history of the Union Pacific had been one of so many misdeeds and mistakes that "we would have fallen anyway." "The original sin has got to be expiated." [78]

The compulsive explanations for his failure gave far more space to the faults of his subordinates. These narratives included that long lexicon of epithets from "cowardly Callaway" to "Flabby guts" Holcomb. If this litany of censure ever paused, it voiced a regret for the young men of education and philosophy whom Adams had appointed to official positions as a matter of policy. Now they were vulnerable to reprisals from his successors. Worse, "In railroads I was the typical college man, — my success would have been the success of my class, my failure is now regarded as the failure of my class . . . Today so far as the management of railroads is concerned, I am the most discredited man in America, and my class is discredited through me, and that hurts." [79]

There is one curious hiatus in the flow of Adams' abuse. He did not accuse his Boston associates of letting him down. To be sure, with the wound from his Union Pacific failure still unhealed, he penned in his *Autobiography* that classic indictment of businessmen so often cited as a generalized judgment. "I have known, and known tolerably well, a good many 'successful' men — 'big' financially — men famous during the last half-century; and a less interesting crowd I do not care to encounter. Not one that I have ever known would I care to meet again, either in this world or the next; nor is one of them associated in my mind with the idea of humor, thought, or refinement. A set of mere money-getters and traders; they were essentially unattractive and uninteresting." Free as he was with suspicion and epithets, he never stigmatized his Boston associates as double dealers. Yet tangential touches in his "dethronement" from the Union Pacific are suggestive. Adams sent Atkins to New York in advance to sound out Gould; Gould was "gentle and persuasive." After the shattering final interview with Gould, Gould showed Adams to the door, but Ames stayed on; he "said he would meet me at the cars." And Ames, Atkins, and Dexter remained on the directorate after Adams was forced out. But in spite of these straws in the wind, in view of Adams' long intimacy with Ames and the friendship of the two families, betrayal is not plausible.[80]

A certain ambiguity even surrounds the relationship between Adams and Gould. Gould had plotted Adams' downfall; and Gould's decision had brought it about — this was undeniable. The operation had long been planned and had been skillfully executed. Gould "was gunning for me; and he had dropped me." Behind this campaign lay Gould's "long memory." Adams hints at the possibility that Gould was seeking revenge because Adams had dismissed him from the directorate of the Union Pacific in 1885, or perhaps for writing "A Chapter of Erie" sixteen years earlier. In view of Adams' tendency to personal melodrama, it would take more than a random sentence or a vagrant adjective to substantiate this surmise. Years later, in connection with another enterprise, Adams more correctly stated the explanation for his loss of the presidency. "Expansion and debt; my Union Pacific over again." [81]

Adams naturally reflected — but not in tranquillity — whether

his Union Pacific experience had been for him a sheer wasteland. He concluded it had not. "I have seen much of life and
affairs, — mixed largely with men and events; — travelled much,
and taken my full share in the great game." [82] Also the Union
Pacific presidency gave to Adams' thought and style, and hence
to his personality a more realistic tone. After his failure he was
less ready to fall back upon abstractions and general morali-
ties. Some of that practicality which he so much derided in
others rubbed off on him.

The new note was reflected in his response to the advice of
Charles W. Eliot. The president of Harvard felt Adams could
not afford to sit down under the "stigma of failure," but must
go back and "vindicate" himself "by results." While acknowledging his respect for Eliot's correctness of judgment and hard
candor of speech, Adams turned his back on this advice; "Not
if I understand myself!" [83]

Adams' scheme of values and range of inclinations had already provided an alternative to the pursuit for vindication.
In spite of his daily presence in a Boston office — that of the
Railroad Commission or the one he occupied with John at
23 Court Street or that of the Union Pacific — in spite of a
pattern of journeying that took him to New York, Washington,
Omaha, or "Kanzas City," Adams had built his life all along
into the village of Quincy. He thought of himself as a countryman — albeit with a difference.

❖ V ❖

THE HOUSE ON PRESIDENT'S HILL

1870-1893

IN Charles' words, Quincy was the "race-place" of the family. The first Adams had settled about 1636 in the "north precinct" of Braintree, a portion of the town in 1792 set off as Quincy. Four generations later his descendant John Adams, who had married a granddaughter of John Quincy, the family after whom the new town was named, bought the Vassall house, built by a West Indian sugar planter who had come to Massachusetts. During his presidency John Adams enlarged the house and successive generations made their additions. Old furniture, some of it from the White House — for the occupants once had to provide their own furnishings — old silver, and oil portraits ornamented the rooms. Whether occupied all the year round, as in John Adams' days, or during the long summer from May to November, as more commonly later, this place of elegance and charm was "the old house." It is now a national historic site. It drew the Adamses like a magnet. Even when Charles had his own home, he was always "going down" to the "old house." Though he had a wife and children, those in residence at the "old house" were always "the family." Like as not Sumner, Holmes, or some other Boston worthy was calling there, and a long conversation on history, literature, or politics, presided over by an Adams, was in progress. At the "old house" an Adams, like Antaeus, could feel the solid ground under his feet, and from it he drew strength.[1]

Even when they lived in Boston, the "governor" and his family spent the summers in Quincy. To Charles it was a place of escape and delight. "Quincy was associated in my mind with spring and summer — bright skies, open windows, green fields, singing birds, the blue bay with white sails dotting it, and a distant view over a country rolling into great whale-back hills." After the Civil War, the return of their father from England, and their own marriages, John Quincy Adams, 2nd, and Charles left Mount Vernon Street behind and established their year-round homes at Quincy. By 1873 John had set up as a "gentleman farmer" on Mount Wollaston, a low eminence a stone's throw from the sea. Charles began his Quincy career humbly. By 1870, however, he thought he could afford a house of his own. He chose a site on a rough, rocky slope, now called President's Hill, which rose sharply across Adams Street from the old house, and commissioned a fashionable and expensive architect. In spite of its size, the new building, with its mansard roof, when dressed with the awnings of summer seemed gay, almost airy.[2]

His place originally contained a trifle over seventeen acres. These Charles proceeded to transform into an estate. Every spring the hill top hummed with activity. Shipments of saplings poured in from nurseries in the West, from England, or from Scotland; oaks, grown from acorns gathered by his children and planted in his own plantations, were transplanted; trees were brought over from John's; extra help was taken on; derricks creaked under the burdens of forestation; carts arrived with seaweed to mulch the trees. Charles stayed away from his Boston office or his books to take charge, and perchance to dig "like a fool." By the end of the season in May or June the scores of accomplishment were astronomical. In 1877 Adams set out 5000 trees, including larch, maples, oaks, elms, and firs. Always he was among his trees, pruning, cutting, transplanting, watering. These activities he enjoyed to the full. After a day of treeplanting in 1875 he wrote, "What a good time — this is worth living for." His dedication to trees rather than to the more prosaic aspects of farming — Adams did not "take much stock in potato planting" — continued a deep family tradition. His grandfather had once commissioned a personal seal displaying a cluster of oak leaves and an acorn and words from a Latin quotation which read as a whole: "Serit arbores quae alteri seculo prosint" (he plants trees for the benefit of later generations).[3]

Later generations were very much on Adams' mind. His first child, a daughter, had been born before the move to Quincy; the next two children were also girls. Charles gritted his teeth to stifle the disappointment at his failure to perpetuate the family name through male children. However, on July 17, 1875, on a hint from his wife Charles "cleared the house for action," summoned a physician, and scoured Boston and Cambridge for a nurse. "Felt bad, did not dare go home for fear of hearing of 'another daughter', — set my teeth and out at 1.45 [train]; walked up my hill feeling sick, and Lizzie Ogden met me to announce twins — boys! Oh! the relief — it completely swamped my surprise . . . Rest of the day at home, — very happy." [4]

With home, descent, and fortune assured, Charles, as country gentleman, followed the way of his forebears and lived with the seasons. Summer was a time to worry about hay and drought; autumn — "I can't express how I dislike this season of the year — the fall of the leaf and the approach of winter, — it is almost morbid." The "things of winter" meant double windows, stoking the furnace, a house full of coughing children, "iron roads," icy blasts. When at last the ice went out of the Neponset and filled the harbor, spring was at hand. Charles never knew "what the spring was" until he went to Quincy. It meant dining with open windows. It meant "Spring" or "Blossom Sunday" when he went walking with John or the children in the fields, or a May day, "the most perfect and joyous of all days in the year — the air fragrant, the trees white with blossoms and the young leaves glittering in the sun." [5]

Charles always chafed at his physical limitations. He was "muscle-slow." Until he took up bicycle riding in the nineties, his chief outdoor pleasures were those naturally growing out of a rural life. In addition to planting trees he walked the countryside south of Boston; nor did Quincy's distance of eight or ten miles from Boston, depending upon the route, deter him from walking both ways on holiday or Sunday to see how "the family" on Mount Vernon Street was doing. The pace was frequently a strenuous four miles an hour. In the eighties horseback riding took the place of walking. These were "the rare moments worth living for . . . No epicure could have rolled a sweet morsel under their tongue with more gusto than I drank in and lingered out those moments of enjoyment in which my horse was my only companion." [6]

Both John Quincy and Charles sailed boats, sloops, or schooners from thirty to forty-five feet at the waterline, around Boston Bay with a destination at some favorite resort or to an island where they could make a chowder. Longer trips caried them to Cape Cod or Cape Ann or occasionally down-east to Maine. These were days "saved." "I can count on the fingers of my two hands the days I have passed in my boat on the bay there. In those only do I seem to have lived." But his favorite exercise was swimming. From the Lido on the Adriatic to the Pacific at Monterey, from Lake Michigan to the Yosemite Valley, he never missed an opportunity to take "one of my headers." [7]

Though the Quincy shoreline gave opportunity for these aquatic activities, it was not immediately accessible to the Adams properties. Accordingly in 1880 Charles bought into a group of associates who owned and were developing for themselves a seaside community at the Glades, north of Scituate. To the east the place faced the open sea and the "last land" of Minot's Ledge and Light; the seaway was alive with the sails of vessels coming from or going to the coast south of Boston. Inland from the Glades were marshes and marsh grass and a land of winding roads and gray weather-beaten houses. It was like a world that had gone to sleep. One could drive to the Old Colony station at Cohasset, but it was feasible to sail thither and, if the wind served, go on to Quincy or even to commute to Boston. And there was surf swimming at the bathing "rocks for the men and at the rafts for the women." At the Glades the individual associates owned cottages but ate in the big house and gathered there for Sunday services and other occasions. It was a place for parents and children. The associates in 1880 included John Quincy Adams, 2nd, F. L. Ames, and assorted Codmans, Sturgises, and Lorings. Though Charles had his moments of boredom and disillusion with the Glades, the time there was generally time won. Sailing back to Quincy in 1883, he wrote, "Another blessed and fortunate noon-day summer is over! The past at least is secure." [8]

There was often a purposefulness and system about these physical activities which raises the suspicion they were not happiness. Whenever he could Adams approached the water with a bathometer. One year at least he numbered each swim in his diary and recorded the temperature of the water. Similarly he kept accounts of his rides and the number of hours in the saddle. Were he thrown from his horse, he analyzed the affair with the detail and precision he applied to a railroad accident in Massachusetts. This tendency to the self-conscious in pleasure reached its limit in a treatise on the comparative qualities of bathing water — its buoyancy, crispness, and the like — in different places. After surveying the fresh and sea waters he had tried on two continents, he concluded the water off the bathing rocks at the Glades was the best. In short, self-discipline and doggedness drove him to exercise more often than enjoyment tempted him to it. Rides were apt to be "medical rides" made "for the record"; September swims were tests of courage; even when a gale or squall spoiled an "ideal sail," "It had paid, there was health and excitement in it." Then suddenly a sensuous, even a poetic note broke through these dutiful overtones: "Last evening I rode through the Braintree woods amid soft, falling snow." The last swims at the Glades in 1891 included "a noble bath — in water cool and clear and crisp, — while great rolling, kindly breakers broke over us and seemed to caress us . . . We had thirteen bathers on the rocks at once. It seemed like the old times; and it did my heart good to see the straight, muscular figures of these boys and young men as they laugh and sport in the breakers, and generally enjoy a closeness to nature. It is good after books!" [9]

This mention of books was not an afterthought for the Adams pattern meant books. Both the presidents had large personal libraries. In 1815, before these attained their maximum size, the combined total was greater than that of the Library of Congress, at the time not a very flattering comparison, or that of Thomas Jefferson, one of the most learned men in America. Though these collections were moved about among depositories and frequently fragmented, the signatures and bookplates in individual items reveal that at least three generations of Adamses read certain of the volumes. In time Charles came to censure these accumulations. His grandfather, John Quincy Adams, "showed no judgement at all in collecting . . . There are not 500 really valuable books in the whole lot. I doubt, if there are 100." As for the library of the "governor," Charles, Jr., appraising it after his father's death, thought it "old fashioned," "a very dreary object of contemplation." [10] Be that as it may, books with the Adamses were not, as Emerson had written, "for the scholar's idle times." They were life. The Adamses were persistent and systematic readers. They did not read books; they studied them. The breadth and depth of the taste of these early generations was impressive. They were equally at ease with works in Latin and Greek and in many modern languages.

Though Charles, Jr., sometimes derided a life spent in libraries and among books, he followed the ancestral example. He read days and he read nights; he read to himself and he read aloud to his wife; he read weekdays and he noted with amazement one October Sunday when he "didn't touch a book the day long." He read at home and he read on trains and on ships. On one of his western trips when he missed a boat connection at Marquette, he passed "an idle day" pleasantly on the shores of the lake under the pines reading "that nasty wretch, Swinburne." When he changed residences it was a gamble whether he first moved his wines or his books; the books usually took precedence. Nevertheless with Charles came a sharp break in the pattern of family erudition. Greek he always avoided, Latin usually. Though he did not speak French or German nor understand them when others did, and his awkwardness in reading German wasted into disuse, he was an enthusiastic but selective reader of French literature. Among contemporaries, he found Balzac difficult to accept; surprisingly Zola impressed him favorably. As for the past, "I am not familiar with Moliere, I know little, & care even less for Rabelais . . . but I am a constant reader and great admirer of Montaigne." Since he bought a bust of him for his bookcase, Voltaire also must have passed the Adams test.[11]

The fact was, as he once wrote Henry, he had given up German and new books generally until he read Milton and Shakespeare. Charles' literary fare was English. It included drama, poetry, and novels. Though he often had reservations about Browning's opaqueness, he found the poet's very "obscurity tickles me," and whether reading him alone on shipboard or in the more formalized gathering of "a Browning seance," Adams enjoyed puzzling out the poet's meaning. Of the novelists, Walter Scott was "a clumsy artist"; Trollope "good but very stupid," "spreads his butter very thin"; Fielding "good reading, but clumsy work compared to Thackeray's." In truth all paled before Thackeray, whose *Pendennis* once gave Charles "the most intense pleasure." Thackeray's "wonderful English" moved Charles to despair: "I never shall know how to write." In nonfiction, Adams read historians and the solid English classics. Early in 1870 he "discovered for the first time the greatness of Edmund Burke," and six months later he was reading Burke in order to improve his own style.[12]

Edward Gibbon's *History of the Decline and Fall of the Roman Empire* had the greatest influence upon Adams' personal and literary style. It took him a year to read it, and to it he returned again and again. Gibbon was "an orb of the first order" and his work was the "most delightful of all books." In its pages Adams found a quotation, the translation of a memorial discovered in the closet of the Caliph Abdahrahman, by which to measure the values of his own life. "I have now reigned above fifty years in victory or peace, dreaded by my enemies, beloved by my subjects and respected by my allies. Riches and honors, power and pleasure have waited on my call, nor does any earthly blessing appear wanting to my felicity. In this situation I have carefully considered all the days of pure and genuine happiness which have fallen to my lot: they amount to fourteen. O man! Place not thy confidence in things of this present world!"[13] The pursuit of days of happinesss became a persistent note in Adams' writing and action; it was his lodestar, his ambition, his half-raised standard of revolt against family values.

"For myself," Adams once wrote, "I can freely say that it has required thirty years of incessant and intelligent practice, with eye and ear and tongue and pen, to give me that ready mastery of the English language which enables me thoroughly to appreciate the more subtle beauties of the English literature." Reading was not, then, the only school. The emphasis upon "ear" and "tongue" reveals that talk was a supplementary system of education. Truly Adams more than most in his generation made a science of talk. Early in 1883 he was invited to become a member of the Saturday Club, that assemblage of authors, statesmen, scholars, and others with intellectual interests of Boston, Cambridge, and Concord which met at Parker's at two o'clock Saturday to dine, drink champagne, and talk. Adams found his first dinner "very pleasant." By the end of his life there was not a metropolis along the Atlantic seaboard that did not provide Adams a somewhat similar opportunity, from the Round Table at the Century Club in New York to one of the same name in Washington at which Herbert Putnam, head of the Congressional Library, presided. If there was no talking club available, Adams was ready to found one.[14]

However eminent the roster of these groups or strong their traditions, they frequently did not operate to Adams' satisfaction. In his own home he could control things better. At any rate he could reverse "the decadence of the dinner table" becoming prevalent in the 1890's, when hosts or hostesses were getting up at the end of a meal, going to a "fresh room" where the guests had coffee and proceeded to break up into small groups and were soon "whispering together in couples." Adams "made a study" of the problem of keeping conversation going and of preventing "bores" from talking. The ideal number at dinner was eight. The silver candelabra on the tables were elevated on blocks of ebony so conversation could flow around them and, as a host, he tried "to make a ball of the conversation, throwing it across the table and then catching it at the rebound, and throwing it again. To do this . . . I found it necessary to violate the rules by sitting at the side, and not at the head of the table and putting the guest of honor, not on my right but opposite me. I can then control the conversation and get him talking to the table and not to me." Gatherings, which thus resembled an examination for the doctorate more than dinner parties, had to be moderated. If the conversation strayed, Adams interfered "by a funny little preliminary grinding in his throat like an old-fashioned clock in damp weather." [15] Admittedly conversation as literary training is a two-edged sword. Talk can become talkativeness; and some of Adams' longer papers sound to the reader as if the garrulous author were simply thinking out loud. But, given direction, talk between peers encourages originality, precision, incisiveness; it is the nurse of epigram. With Adams talk honed the style.

Books, among other reasons, explained why Adams departed from the family pattern of religious belief and personal piety. The break was sharp. Gifts from President John Adams, "a church-going animal" for seventy-six years, had aided financially the building in the Grecian mode of a "stone temple," sometimes called "the Adams Temple," now the most beautiful public building in Quincy. Charles' grandfather, John Quincy Adams, read through the Bible several times; and the "governor" spent nearly all Sunday in church and put his boys through additional religious services at home.[16] But Charles continued neither this temper nor habit. When he and his wife first moved to Quincy, they often started for church but seldom got there. Soon he settled down to attendance at church or parish meetings only when some issue of importance arose: such as trying out a new minister, listening to eulogies and funeral sermons when a death occurred in the Adams family, or perhaps giving a commemorative historical address.

There are several plausible explanations for this departure from family, and village, ways. Charles himself on occasion asserted that the tradition of Quincy had been one of religious nonconformists. At another time he ascribed his religious emancipation to reading. While in England in 1865 he happened upon John Stuart Mill's essay on Auguste Comte. "That essay of Mill's revolutionized in a single morning my whole mental attitude. I emerged from the theological stage in which I had been nurtured, — and passed into the scientific. I had up to that time never even heard of Darwin." [17]

Probably an acquaintance with Darwin's thought first reached him through Spencer or John Fiske, for Charles did not read the *Origin of Species* until the 1880's. Then with a shout he fell upon the "generalization," not as a basis for social Darwinism, though there were traces of it in Adams' thought, but as a religious event. "On the first day of October, 1859," the day of the publication of *The Origin of Species*, "the Mosaic cosmogony finally gave place to the Darwinian theory of evolution." Like others, Adams saw "the English naturalist and observer quietly rise up, and looking back across more than thirty centuries, confront the Hebrew prophet and law-giver, while he maintained for his thesis that man was an evolution from the ape, and not the immediate creation of Jehovah." [18]

These seeds fell upon a receptive mind. The turn of Charles' thinking was to the secular and concrete. The "Phenomena," which Comte emphasized, were more congenial than metaphysics. Attempting to read metaphysics one Sunday evening Adams responded by "being immeasurably amused at my absolute inability to understand a single paragraph of what I read." He could only pity or censure Jonathan Edwards and John Witherspoon for trying to handle "intellectual impossibilities." [19] With Adams, religion had evolved into an occasional ceremonial.

The twin influence of a family of note and of an attachment to an American small town gave Adams attitudes and values which were sure to set him apart from an America which after the Civil War was tending toward urbanism and business dominance. He was bound to be restless at these trends and to measure "progress" by a different test than most of his contemporaries. That he thought and acted with the fastidious detachment of the patrician only increased his alienation. Paradoxically he carried the banner of Thomas Jefferson into the late nineteenth century — the Jefferson who was the associate and rival of John Adams in the days of the Revolution and the young Republic. From his forebears he also inherited a tradition of public service and the expectation that an Adams should lead and dominate. But how were these great expectations to be realized in a post–Civil War America by a man who, like Charles, could write: "I don't associate with the laborers on my place, nor would the association be agreeable to either of us. Their customs, language, habits and conventionalities differ from mine; as do those of their children . . . I believe in the equality of men before the law; but social equality, whether for man or child, is altogether another thing." [20] This aggregate of thought, feeling, and experience was to shape, not always happily, a career of national importance.

Meanwhile his attitudes and abilities found an outlet in the smaller theater of Quincy. When he moved there the town had a little less than 7000 inhabitants. Luckily geography still maintained it as a place apart from Boston for the estuary of the Neponset River, Quincy's northern boundary, formed a moat against the spread of the metropolis, and the waters of Quincy Bay were too shallow to encourage a commercial development along the shorefront. History had given Quincy a distinctive flavor. Pilgrim influences diluted Puritanism. In the first party of white men to visit Quincy shores were Miles Standish, William Bradford, and Edward Winslow. And thither came those whom Boston either would not admit or expelled. It was on Mount Wollaston, or Merrymount, in Quincy that Thomas Morton, "an ingrained Bohemian and sportsman," set up a maypole, presided over "a sort of saturnalia," and sought to combine making money, drinking beer, and playing with "Indian lassies." Later the heretical supporters of Anne Hutchinson and her favored pastor, John Wheelwright, lived in Quincy. In addition to providing two American presidents, it was the birthplace of John Hancock whose signature stands out from every facsimile of the Declaration of Independence as it did from the original. Around Quincy clustered other Yankee towns, Milton, Dedham, Braintree, Weymouth, Randolph. Though varied in size, history, and source of income, these communities were in the nineteenth century much the same in their political and social features. It is especially noteworthy that their inhabitants were predominately native-born; in only one instance did the percentage of foreign-born exceeed twenty-five.[21]

As he looked east from the "gallery" of his house on President's Hill Adams could forget the small granite quarries opened on the hills some distance behind him or the "Catholic village" where the stone workers lived. The Old Colony Railroad, with its station only five minutes' walk away, ran too close to the east slope of "my hill" to spoil the view. Beyond the railroad lay the graveyard where the two presidents had first been laid to rest, and beyond that the granite town hall and the Adams Temple. Somewhat more distant but clearly visible was John's farm on Mount Wollaston. After a scatter of islands and the land spit of Nantasket came the open sea. It was a prospect dear to Adams; he was never able to erase it from his heart or mind.

Still, like most prospects it did not wholly please. When Charles and his brother John took up residence in their ancestral village, they proposed a program of civic rejuvenation. To their minds the system of government which worked well enough when Quincy was a village of a few voters was proving ill-adapted to the larger and more modern town. The community's growing needs in the areas of education, roads, and public health had led to an increase in the size of annual appropriations and of the town debt and to a rising rate of taxation. These burdens the town attempted to handle through the town meeting: "A large hall the floor of which, sprinkled with sawdust and foul with tobacco-juice, was thronged by a mass of noisy men, standing in groups or moving incessantly to and fro, and in and out. There were no rows of seats in the room . . . The men all wore their hats, and many of them had pipes and cigars in their mouths; while the air reeked with odors, tobacco-smoke being the least objectionable. Quite a number of those present had plainly been drinking." For introducing and running a reformed order of things the Adams brothers had distinctive talents. John was the most personable, social, and charming of the Adamses, "remarkably handsome," with a sense of humor and imagination, fanatically devoted to Quincy. Charles, who correctly diagnosed himself as incapable of winning popularity, had ability and talent as an administrator. Significantly their program returned for many of its devices to the golden age of Quincy in the first half of the nineteenth century when a member of the "gentry," Thomas Greenleaf, ran the town. Like Greenleaf and like his own grandfather, John Quincy Adams, John "by common consent" became moderator of the town meeting. Charles with equal fitness became a committee man and floor manager.[22]

The first step in a return to the old and correct methods was to divide the town meeting into two parts. At the first the voters elected town officers and referred the business articles to a large "committee on the warrant" which recommended to a later meeting the policy to be followed. Charles was usually a member of the warrant committee and his diary is full of self-satisfaction at "getting my articles by." Perhaps the cogency of his arguments carried the day. He could also turn forensic savagery upon those who questioned the beneficence of government by the best people. According to the local reporter, on one of these occasions Adams "hopped to his feet and with an eye of a hawk and the voice of an eagle, commenced picking the beautiful feathers from his assailant. And he did not leave him . . . until he appeared much like a young game cock, half dressed for market." All this was in a greater than American tradition, for, as Charles once wrote, "Demosthenes and Cicero . . . were town-meeting orators." [23]

Having rehabilitated the town meeting, the Adamses planned to strip the partisan label from the election of town officers. This end was furthered by the fact that John was a Democrat and Charles a Republican, mugwump variety. Also fundamental to their program was economy, for however lavish his habits of personal expenditure, Charles believed in thrift in the civic sector. Appropriations were carefully made and officers were required to keep within them; deficiencies were met by special appropriations rather than overdrawing, and exceptional outlays were distributed over a series of years. For the past debt a sinking fund was established. Nor was government by the gentry purely negative; town services were extended and bettered. On this count revitalization of the committees upon which the town had habitually depended and an element of good luck enabled Charles to attain a large measure of the success so dear to him.[24]

In 1872 he became a member of the town's school committee, on which his brother had served and continued to serve, and he was soon caught up in the round of duties expected of it: visits to the schools, the choice of teachers, and the testing of the school year's work by oral examinations of the pupils. In spite of these routines, Adams relished the job: "The work has interested me greatly and is one worth doing." Adamses were always interested in education, particularly their own; Charles had also been reading Horace Mann, and he had begun pressing down in the examination of pupils, "slaughtering divers classes in grammar" which "I took for my province." What he found appalled him. The pupils were gifted enough at reading what they had read frequently but they could not manage a strange book at sight; they could parse and construe a piece of prose but they could not write even an ordinary letter. He concluded that the methods of instruction had not changed during decades of "immobility." "It was in a word, all smatter, veneering, and cram." This was a waste of taxpayers' money. He judged the Quincy schools "were neither much better nor worse than those of the surrounding towns." [25]

Since the school committee did not possess the expertness to bring about a reformation or the audacity to ask for increased appropriations for more teachers, it decided to establish the office of superintendent and appoint a man who could give it his consistent attention. The superintendent would have to teach teachers new ways. Through the "merest chance" the committee was able in 1875 to employ Francis W. Parker. Parker was largely self-educated, had taught school in New Hampshire and in the Midwest, served as an officer in the Civil War, and visited Germany to view its educational changes. Candid and courageous, in debate and exposition he possessed a "sweet dogmatism" and the ability to attract attention. In short he was a man after the heart of Charles Francis Adams, Jr., if not a facsimile of him.[26] The "new departure" in the public schools of Quincy began with Parker's appointment in 1875.

The school committee and their superintendent decided to reduce the number of subjects studied and to concentrate on the three R's, convinced as they were that children should learn to use the tools of reading, writing, and arithmetic. Children were taught to read by learning whole words rather than the alphabet and syllabification; grammar was subordinated; and every subject was to be an occasion for learning to write. Instruction was individualized through small groups. There was also a greater use of blackboards, object lessons, and modeling. Throughout there was an emphasis on flexibility and experi-

ment in methods. Furthermore under the new system the cost
of educating each Quincy child declined. According to Adams,
Parker was the architect of the "new departure"; according to
many educationalists, the unflinching support of the school
board, the members of which were customarily re-elected and
who gave Parker responsibility and left him alone, was an in-
spiring example for other communities who wanted to improve
their schools.[27]

Changes in the schools usually engender friction. Teachers
are dismissed; parents are bewildered and angered by the demands upon their children. It was so in Quincy. In 1875 a town
meeting whose looks alarmed Adams turned into "an Irish
field day" and he "was elected on school committee by the skin
of my teeth." Individuals whom Adams wanted as associates on
the committee the voters frequently rejected, and sometimes his
fellow committeemen proved trying. One of them became convinced that Parker was a "libertine," and even "poor John"
at one committee meeting "made a fool of himself by flying
into a causeless passion with Superintendent Parker." In 1880
the town meeting threatened to balk at a motion for printing
at town expense Adams' report on the town school system.
Opponents of the system derisively favored the appropriation
so "that all should have an opportunity to learn of its [the
committee's] fancies strange, of its methods nowhere else revealed, and of assumed facts . . . probably overlooked and
forever lost." Adams had his defenders; and on this occasion
he could take care of himself. They were successful in repelling
the indignity.[28]

Adams saw to it that the light from Quincy shone widely.
In the spring of 1879 he appeared before the Association of
School Committees and Superintendents of Norfolk County
and gave them the true gospel in his *The New Departure in
the Common Schools of Quincy*. The next year he journeyed
to Chautauqua and before the National Educational Associa-

Entry hall in the house on President's Hill. "My engagement day . . .
I gave Minnie a Venus de Milo in bronze & myself a frame for my
da Vinci & we passed the evening very pleasantly putting them in
place." (*Diary*)

Dining room in the house on President's Hill. "My oak dining room."
(*Memorabilia*)

The Glades. "I have been in the habit of daily going there, and at all stages of the tide, plunging into the surf; . . . nor do I believe there is any other water so pure, so fresh, so invigorating." (*Memorabilia*)

tion delivered "a declaration of war" on the same theme. Somewhat later this pungent address had a reprise in an article in *Harper's Magazine*. Meanwhile newspapers and periodicals in New York, Boston, and Chicago were reporting the Quincy experiment enthusiastically. Charles wrote some of these articles, and he grew so bewildered by the number of his addresses and statements that he sometimes achieved the feat of quoting himself in his own behalf.[29]

When the controversy aroused by the "Quincy system" relied upon evidence it usually resorted to an examination of the Norfolk County schools made by George A. Walton, an agent of the Massachusetts Board of Education. The board printed this report, along with facsimiles of letters and themes written by pupils in the various schools. Though the report identified schools only as "A.B.C. etc.," Adams and his partisans often cited it as support for the effectiveness of the Quincy schools, the designation for which was "C," or for their indictment of the general level of schooling in Massachusetts and elsewhere in the country. At any rate visitors flooded the Quincy schools in such numbers as to constitute a nuisance.[30]

This flood of documentation was highly characteristic of Adams, for his fingers, like those of his forebears, were "inkstained." He was always writing, and he was, as in this case, frequently repeating himself. Usually he also raised his voice. Likewise characteristic were the methods of argument: an overstatement of existing conditions, usually "appalling"; an instinctive preference for an assertion that would make two enemies instead of one; the prescription of an effective and unique path to salvation; and a profusion of words chosen to inflict pain. Thus, it might have been judicious to pacify a local constituency by asserting that its schools were no worse than others, but it was hardly flattering to the pride of Massachusetts; and to infer that if Massachusetts went astray, a "highly unsatisfactory condition of affairs . . . will be found to exist pretty much everywhere else" was certain to ignite antagonisms. Nor were superintendents pleased by being called "drill sergeants" and by having the schools they organized and directed described as "a combination of the cotton mill and the railroad with the model State-prison." Adams then enlarged the indictment: "There is a science of law, and schools and professors to teach it . . . There is a science of mining, and institutes of technology in which it is taught. It is even claimed there is a science of divinity." Yet "We . . . turn over our children to those whom we would never dream of entrusting with our potato patch." [31]

However excited were the claims, pro and con, the new departure was an achievement — albeit an uneven one. Innovations in methods and emphasis were very successful in teaching reading and writing; their effect was negligible upon subjects like arithmetic, where a "strict regard to formulas patiently learned" was essential. Apparently the morale of the school children was excellent. They found school interesting, and the problem of truancy fell away. Still the "Quincy System" was not as unique as Adams claimed. It was a period of widespread educational ferment and change in Massachusetts and Connecticut; St. Louis, Cincinnati, and Cleveland were also making new departures. Parker was not the only reform superintendent; W. T. Harris and E. A. Sheldon were also pioneers. In any case like all periods of experiment, this one came to an end. Parker left Quincy in 1880 for the Boston schools, the next step in a career which was to take him to the University of Chicago where he was briefly an associate of John Dewey.[32] Also Adams resigned from the school committee before his third term ran out in 1881.

Meanwhile Adams' activity in Quincy and his self-advertising had given him a reputation as an educational reformer, if not in the nation at least within Massachusetts. In 1880 Governor Long appointed him a member of the state Board of Education.

Those prone to detect a conspiracy scented trouble. Adams "belongs to the highest class of American society, the class of ancestry, of wealth, and of culture." There was something sinister in his constant preference for the phrase "common school." His emphasis on utility in studies was undemocratic and "mediaeval." "Here the least liberal portion of the aristocracy and the illiterates join hands and fight under the same flag . . . Mr. Adams seems to have assumed command of the American division of this army . . . One of his lieutenants [Brooks Adams], who is a rising *litterateur*, having two years ago been elected a member of the Boston School Committee, has already made some progress, aided by the late superintendent, in carrying that city . . . In the mean time the chief having been appointed a member of the State Board of Education, it is presumed that he will now remove his headquarters from the rural town of Quincy to the Capitol on Beacon Hill, whence future orders may be expected, bearing the stamp of the State seal . . . For my part I take my stand under the opposing ensign, bearing no such miserable device as '*Three R's only for the children of the masses*', but that other motto, dear to the hearts of the American people, '*The public free school, made good enough for the best and free to all.*' " [33]

In spite of its demagoguery, this statement contained a measure of acumen. Its detection of a conspiracy, however, proved ludicrous almost at once. The secretary of the state Board of Education was, as Horace Mann had demonstrated, a powerful officer in the Commonwealth; the present incumbent was John W. Dickenson. Early in 1881 Adams recorded a "disagreeable talk with Dickenson . . . He is an old woman: and it is time thrown away for me to try to get anything attempted if he is to organize it." Indeed a few weeks earlier Dickenson had concluded that the Massachusetts schools "measured by an absolute standard, are more or less imperfect; relatively we believe they have . . . no superiors, considered as intellectual institutions." [34] In 1881 Adams resigned from the state board five years before his term expired.

In Quincy, in the meantime, Adams furthered other means of education. His great-grandfather, John Adams, moved by his affection for the community, had bequeathed resources to establish a private classical school. Charles served on the board of managers for this Adams Academy for many years. With patience he attended graduation and declamations, plays, and outdoor games, and strove, we may surmise, to make the Academy as unlike as possible the Boston Latin School which he hated. The headmaster of the Academy also provided an intellectual companion in a village which otherwise furnished few of them. But on the whole Adams' interest in the Academy was secondary.

Adams really put his shoulder to the wheel for the free public library — "one of those institutions, undreamed of in former times, which may without exaggeration be called the universities of the poor." The origin of this institution was also a gift from John Adams, for in 1822 he presented "the fragments of my library" to the Academy. These were housed at the start in the town building and later in the Adams Academy building. As Charles correctly asserted, "for popular use the collection was almost ludicrously inappropriate." If the people of Quincy were to have a means of "self-culture," an end Charles endorsed, the nature of the collection should be changed and it should be properly housed. In 1871 the town meeting appropriated $2500 for a public library provided an equal sum be raised by private subscription. The condition was met by the end of the year. Not surprisingly the town elected Charles one of the trustees, a position he held by frequent reelection until the end of his Quincy sojourn. Though he had able and devoted associates, it could be said of Charles' use of the phrase "library trustees," as it had been about those on the school committee, it was "a modest euphemism, probably, for the pronoun 'I.' " He initiated his career by giving the library 1650 volumes of congressional and other documents and bound newspapers [35] — almost as inappropriate as the original gift of his great-grandfather.

After cleansing his own bookshelves, Charles was soon stating a larger policy. He realized that books in the library must appeal to the reading tastes of its users, that the library should be integrated with the schools, and that, if it were to serve as a means of self-education, it must provide catalogues which, through their notes and selection of volumes, were really guides to the study of heavy or serious subjects. Charles plunged personally into the deadly routine of preparing such catalogues and soon encountered the customary factor of human friction in the person of Miss Merriam, a "most accomplished cataloguer" employed by the library. Evidently she did not subscribe to the Adams creed: "Quincy, c'est moi." Adams had a "tall, old time" with her — "the woman is crazy and lit right out, the fur flew lively until I sent her home." The next day Charles "amused myself by astonishing Miss Merriam into politeness by the airy courtesy of my address." He dragged on through the summer with his "hairshirt." When the *Nation* said the published catalogue was better than the one at Harvard or the Boston Public Library Adams insisted that Miss Merriam's contribution to it be acknowledged. This generous public acknowledgment accompanied a private misgiving, for by this time Adams felt his own "work on it had been a waste of force." [36]

Perhaps responding to a hint in the annual report of the library trustees, a representative of the Crane family, once associated with Quincy but no longer resident there, approached Adams to see if a gift of money for a library building would be accepted. Charles plunged into the task with his customary thoroughness and ardor. He secured the incorporation of the Thomas R. Crane Memorial Library and turned over its design and landscaping to the talents of a pair then in high favor in Boston and its suburbs — the architect H. H. Richardson and the landscaper F. L. Olmsted. Charles "kept his countenance" when the cornerstone was laid with "masonic ceremonies" — "all very droll mummery for grown up men." When the library was opened in 1882 he made the dedicatory address and subsequently gave a large luncheon. There were other more homely Adams touches all along the line. Trees from Charles' nurseries on the hill were set out in the library grounds. And with a like-minded fellow committee man, he sneaked down to the building and removed from the box beneath the cornerstone volumes written by a third member of the board of trustees. They scrupulously returned these to the library. Though his work with the library never made the national stir that the new departure in the schools had, Adams justly deserved the encomium of "master builder" conferred on him by the trustees of the library when he resigned this, his last public office in Quincy.[37]

Though Charles fretted over the fact that he was doing too many things, early in 1881 he conceived the idea of giving a park to Quincy if the town would accept it. "If anything comes of this I shall be a benefactor indeed to the town." By conference and communication he was soon "cooking up" the project. The town meeting was of a divided and vacillating mind. But Adams' patience, persistence, and generosity prevailed. In 1885 Adams proffered to the town Merrymount Park, an area of eighty-nine acres along the northern and western bank of one of the town's creeks; the gift was accepted. Adams refused to serve as park commissioner.[38]

Since his efforts had helped to extend and visibly improve the town's public services while reducing, if not virtually extinguishing the debt, Charles was entitled to a measure of self-congratulation. In the mid-1880's he was writing: "There is also a stability and permanence in the town which in America is not always seen. It adheres to the ancient ways. The inhabitants yet meet in their own hall and manage their own affairs as their fathers for generations before. And just as, a century and a half ago, John Quincy by common consent presided over each town-meeting that was held, so now does a descendant [John Quincy Adams, 2nd] five generations removed but still bearing his name. Never in the history of the town were those meetings more orderly, more intelligent, or more prone to do right." This was the public record. Privately Charles was appraising his relationship to it. In his Diary of 1888 he stated his judgment on "my service as a town officer. I am rather proud of my record. I did not know it was so good . . . Since May 1871 I have been a candidate on one or both tickets 15 times and have not once been defeated, — at least three times won the largest number of votes passed for any candidate. For a man far from popular, the above is, I think, not a bad record. My municipal service is, I fancy, about over." [39]

This dejected note followed a traumatic experience at the town meeting of 1888. Actually other personal factors had already begun to fray his connections with Quincy. As his three daughters grew up, Boston offered advantages, including a more formally organized and more acceptable society. The "little boys" were also attending school in Boston and later the Groton School. "All our children have ceased to be little." Perhaps, also, his election to the presidency of the Union Pacific required facilities for entertaining that Quincy did not have. So he moved to the Back Bay where proper Bostonians, business and professional leaders, were rearing an island upon the land, a Bostonian "West End." Toward the close of 1884 the Charles Adamses rented a house at 21 Fairfield Street — "after 16 years of all the year round life at Quincy — the best years I shall ever have." They continued to rent while they built on the corner of Gloucester Street and Commonwealth Avenue, at 20 Gloucester Street, an immense three-story brick house with a fourth story within a sloping roof; a turret, capped by a candle snuffer, looked up and down the avenue, and huge chimneys rose from the first floor through the roof line. Adams' friends admired it and he admitted, "it *is* very handsome." In 1887 the Adamses moved into their Boston town house.[40] As with his forebears Quincy remained a spring and fall residence; the Glades took care of the late summer.

Even as Charles was making the transfer, further cracks appeared in the Quincy scheme of things. The country activities, once so vital, had lost their savor. "Began my spring planting. I am very sorry to say that for the first time it wholly fails to interest me — things are dropping off." The cherished routes for walks and rides were vanishing. "Found that the development fiend in guise of a telegraph company had devastated ruthlessly the beautiful wood-road by Braintree Great Pond — more evidence that our days in Quincy are numbered." After his mother's death in 1889 even the "old house" was closed — albeit temporarily. "John Adams moved into it in May 1789 — one century of consequitive [*sic*] family life closes." [41]

Finally aliens laid impious hands upon the ancient ways of doing town business. There had always been restiveness, particularly over economy measures; in 1887 the dikes broke. "The methods of doing business which John and I inaugurated . . . and which worked so admirably, broke down under the pressure of the labor and communistic elements. The town-meeting passed completely out of the control of reasoning men and into the hands of those who, for example, fixed by vote that all town laborers were to work nine hours a day and be paid $2 therefor . . . The efforts of the old leaders to control things were simply ludicrous." The next year the deluge came. "The hall was filled with a restless throng of men of noticeably low type, — young, vulgar, badly dressed, of the hoodlum type." They took over, electioneered, and forced Adams to stand in line to cast his vote. "John and I thought it was high time for us to haul out." [42]

Adams was too perceptive not to realize the fundamental forces behind these dissatisfactions. The town had changed. When Adams had moved there the population was less than 7000; by 1885 it had increased to 12,145. This crowding in filled up the open spaces, threatened historic buildings, obliterated wild country walks, and caused the loss of old trees; it meant also wider paved streets and larger schools. These improvements cost money and compelled an increase in taxes. No sooner had his house on the hill been built than Charles was scuffling with town officials over its appraised value. In 1890–1891 another quarrel flared in the course of which Charles issued an ultimatum that if his taxes were increased, he would leave town; he moved among his tree plantations moaning, "the place must soon go — no child of mine inherit." [43]

The Old Colony Railroad, opened to Quincy in 1846, and the streetcar lines, arriving in the 1880's, brought in the newcomers whom the Neponset had once held back or turned aside. New occupations gave them employment. As in other towns south of Boston artisans and merchants organized shops and started small factories to make shoes. More distinctive was quarrying. The Bunker Hill Monument, dedicated in 1825, was built of Quincy granite. The proximity of the quarries to sea transportation led to the construction of the famous Granite Railway, one of the earliest railroads in the nation. Quincy granite enjoyed a tremendous vogue for public buildings in Boston and elsewhere until the Great Boston Fire of 1872 demonstrated that it turned brittle under heat and shattered under streams of water. Then Quincy turned to the monument trade. Quarries and derricks spread over the hills, and the shops for finishing the stone multiplied. [44]

Adams found flaws in those who labored in these trades. The shoemaker was "apt to be round-shouldered and hollow-chested, thin and long limbed." "In politics he was inclined to admire what he called 'smartness' rather than grasp, and though he would not vote for a convicted knave, he felt a good deal of inner kindness for the successful rascal, and an absolute contempt for the well-intentioned dolt." At first the quarrymen were transient workers predominantly from New Hampshire, "noisy, muscular, hard-living native Americans with small reverence." The Irish Catholics, coming later to the quarries, "instinctively sided against all settled political traditions." Charles, a grandson of an Adams who had once celebrated Irish freedom in an epic poem and had appealed to the Irish vote, on most occasions now relapsed into a mild nativism. He emphasized the English blood of the Adamses and of other Quincy families like the Cranes. And in his biography of "the governor" he asserted that "race characteristics went with him in the blood," and detected an "instinctive Irish dislike to the essentially Anglo-Saxon." [45]

As if bent upon inflicting pain upon himself, if no one else, Charles lashed out against the land sharks who were dividing up the old properties, cutting down trees, and building tenements and villas. To him Quincy had become "a 'go-ahead' suburban city, the retiring room, the sleeping apartment of the Boston counting-house." But the great enemy was granite, the "ugliest stone"; its quarries were cutting the hills to pieces. Quincy was "a mining camp," "cursed with the stone industry, much as California on a larger scale was cursed with gold." "And we were proud of it! Quincy granite! Pah!" From the western part of the town the enemy pushed closer and closer. The stone cutters regarded "my place as a park and a pleasure ground; but me they look upon as an aristocrat and the old homestead about which all my pleasant memories center, as a mere hindrance to growth." While the final indictment had pathos, the step-by-step decline into disapproval and despair was more poignant. "January 5, 1885. J. Quincy and Sigourney Butler dined with me and we discussed the city government for Quincy. Their central idea is that they want to get a machinery under which they can enter upon a course of so-called improvements involving a large municipal debt and heavy increased taxation." "June 11, 1888. Quincy today accepted a city charter and they actually rang bells and rejoiced at closing out a great political system which had worked well for 250 years." "January 7, 1889. Could not get to Q. to attend inauguration of city government." [46]

In the happier days of the previous decade, the auspices seemed to forecast for the Adams family a larger stage in politics than Quincy or the Commonwealth. The "governor," who had attained the position of an elder statesman, was always being mentioned for this or that office, and in 1872 was appointed as the American member of the tribunal which was arbitrating the Alabama and other claims arising from British policy and action during the Civil War. The choice pleased Charles. "No higher compliment was ever paid to an American citizen." Of the sons, Henry, according to a critic with a sharp pen was clearly unfitted for the political hurly-burly. "Mr. Henry has altogether too much of the English supercilious character which belongs to 'the New-York Nation' School." John Quincy Adams, 2nd, who had signalized his distaste for radical reconstruction by "ratting to the Copperheads," according to his Harvard necrology "held an almost unique position among the radical Democrats." The party nominated him for the governorship in 1868 and repeated the experiment three successive times; in 1879 the anti-Butler or "Faneuil Hall Democrats" nominated him. John's record was distinctive; he always lost and his popular vote always declined. In 1879 it was minuscule and humiliating. He did, however, represent the town in the legislature four times. An attempt at re-election in 1875 failed because of "Irish Catholic treachery" according to Charles.[47]

Charles, aside from an occasional twinge of family duty and ambition, clung to his own diagnosis of himself as incapacitated by character and temperament for elective office. Though personally apart from politics while on the Railroad Commission, his concern with the railroad problem was still a concern with politics in a wider sense. As he told his readers in 1871, the railroad system of the country was materially a success, but this fact could not submerge the "moral and political" aspects of the railroad problem. With a documentation somewhat fragmentary and not always persuasive, he stigmatized railroad corporations as privileged, as harmful to their own stockholders, and as "a disturbing and degrading influence in our politics." [48] Politics thus came in at the back door. Adams also felt keenly that it was the inescapable obligation of an American citizen to be interested in politics and of the "sophists" to provide guidance in this area for the general public. In practice, he did not go beyond being a Republican party member in Quincy and attending state conventions, where his facility at expression often secured him a position on the platform committee.

Fundamentally he had neither the temperament nor philosophy of the party regular. There were many times he was perfectly willing to go it alone; to "belong," as Thoreau once put it, "to the party of one." Since Adams thought somewhat more concretely than most of his reformist colleagues, he realized the desirability of common action to formulate and promote definite programs, and to provide for the like-minded minority a means of self assurance and mutual admiration. It was at a gathering of this sort, the general meeting of the American Social Science Association at Albany in 1869, that Adams first disclosed his estimate of the political needs of his time and his suggestion for coping with them. His essay "The Protection of the Ballot in National Elections" was dashed off with considerable haste — "very imperfect and superficial" — in the intervals between his railroad articles.[49] He started with the axiom that the United States for good or ill had embarked upon a system of government by "the enumeration of noses" and that this was the accepted panacea for all political evils.

Since the nation had chosen majority rule, it might as well be a real or honest majority. One great barrier to such an attainment was the electoral college which conceals the wishes of the real majority. The candidate who carried a few pivotal states, for example New York, Indiana, and Pennsylvania, even by a narrow margin could amass a disproportionately successful majority in the electoral college. The presence of this opportunity appeals to manipulators who concentrate upon the critical states their arts of false registration and ballot-box stuffing. Statutes cannot legislate morality in individual voters but they can remove the inducement to immorality on the part of politicians. Otherwise the time will come when some one will "be cheated into the Presidential Chair" by the electoral college.

The second phenomenon of the time was the appearance, with the growth of wealth and cities, of a proletariat. So far only New York City had one. "The essence of a proletariat is to seek the political control of a community through a close combination of vice, ignorance, and brute force, wholly inaccessible to reason or to the dictates of public virtue." The contemporary agitation for woman suffrage, though logical enough, would increase the weight in the electorate "of the more voluble, demonstrative and impulsive female element." Though "excitable natures rarely strengthen free institutions," the country will probably have to enfranchise women in time. The extension of suffrage to Africans was a "portentous experiment." "The Anglo-Saxon was not educated to his efforts at self-government . . . by two centuries of Slavery superimposed on unnumbered centuries of barbarism." Liberal naturalization laws were another dangerous means of swamping the country with ignorant votes. The country survived the evil results of Celtic immigration; it "has resulted in deterioration, not in catastrophe." But the multitudes of incoming Chinese are neither Christian nor "in any way akin to us . . . or intellectually approachable by us." In sum, universal suffrage "means a European, and especially Celtic proletariat on the Atlantic coast, an African proletariat on the shores of the Gulf, and a Chinese proletariat on the Pacific." The country cannot escape by imposing a property test on voters, for that is "unworthy in itself" and "impossible," for here "poverty is a vulgar virtue." "Education then only remains. A knowledge of the language of our laws and the faculty of informing oneself without aid of their provisions, would in itself constitute a test, if rigorously enforced, incompatible with the existence of a proletariat." [50]

The American Social Science Association, which Adams was thus addressing, had been founded in Boston in 1865 by professional reformers like Wendell Phillips and W. L. Garrison, philanthropists like S. G. Howe, and scholars like Benjamin Peirce and James Russell Lowell. The chairman of the New York branch was E. L. Godkin, editor of the *Nation*. The metropolitan membership included William C. Bryant, Horace Greeley, and William M. Evarts. The national officers were mostly Bostonians; Adams himself was treasurer and member of the executive committee. In fact the application of Adams' proposed educational qualification would not have deprived a single member of the association of the ballot. According to its constitution, the group was to ascertain scientifically "the laws of Education, of Public Health, and Social Economy" and when these were "fully ascertained, the laws of the land should recognize and define them all." [51]

The 1870's whittled down the zeal and size of this organization, Charles F. Adams, Jr., and Henry remained members of an informal group which turned more single-mindedly to the attainment of a consensus on the concrete political problems of their day. Adams was forever rushing to New York to attend some conference where there was, as he put it delightedly, "no end of talk." On one occasion, a gathering lasting until midnight, the Adamses prevailed: "Henry and I had clearer ideas of what was wanted than any one else and finally shaped the course of events." The participants at these seminars included editors and journalists: E. L. Godkin; Samuel Bowles, the fiercely independent and censorious editor of the Springfield *Republican*; Charles Nordhoff, onetime editor of the New York *Post* and Washington correspondent of the New York *Herald*; Murat Halstead of the Cincinnati *Commercial*; and Horace White, the correspondent on financial and economic affairs for the *Nation* and the New York *Post*. Some of these men, like Nordhoff and White, were scholars; some, for instance Francis Walker, economist and president of Massachusetts Institute of Technology, made a living from scholarship. Politicians like W. M. Evarts and Carl Schurz also attended. David A. Wells was usually present and sometimes arranged these gatherings. The platform of these independents generally favored the "true faith" of free trade, hard money, and civil service reform.[52] To the last cause they showed exceptionally fervent devotion, for it gave them a choice between recognized good and evil, between individual honesty and corruption. This reform also furnished those who could agree on little else a unifying moral issue.

In national politics, Charles was at first thoroughly committed to the Republican party and its leader Grant. He was after all the son of one of the builders of Republican principles and success; he himself had "deposited his virgin vote for Fremont." As a soldier he had admired Grant at first hand and as a veteran could not entirely shake off the "intense political feeling of the rebellion and the fever of excitement which followed it." With Charles the momentum of such allegiances was not likely to endure. The election of 1872 presented him with a tangle of problems. The liberal Republican wing had resolved upon the experiment of going it alone and they summoned a convention at Cincinnati to organize the break and to make nominations. Among the most prominent names mentioned for their presidential choice was Charles Francis Adams.

The prospect of yet another Adams being president swept the sons into the excitement. They talked, hoped, speculated, and grew "cross" with one another on this subject. The "governor" did not share this youthful excitement; the Liberal Republican movement left him unmoved and his letters and aloofness did little to further his candidacy.[53]

The attitude of the elder Adams together with convention maneuvers resulted in the surprise nomination of Horace Greeley, the erratic Republican editor of the New York *Tribune*. The diary of Charles voiced an incredulity shared by others then and since. "Greeley nominated!!! Words fail to do justice to my disgust & surprise, — for us free traders all is lost, including honor! I must say that my heart was heavy within me all day." When the Democratic national convention later chose as its nominee their onetime Republican foe Greeley, the topsy-turvy character of the campaign was complete. "The governor" and John decided to support Greeley, but Charles, Jr., could not align himself with "John's political bummers." Deciding to remain a regular, perhaps an obscurantist one, on one occasion he "delivered my mind of cant to my Republican fellow citizens . . . though my audience didn't know what to make of it." As early elections pointed to Grant's success, Adams wrote: "I must confess to intense satisfaction both in public and private point of view as charlatans are down, men of convictions go up." A little later Adams feared the Republicans might "have too much success,"[54] and Grant's second term convinced him that his misgivings were correct.

In 1876 along with other independents he moved in mid-May to call a conference in New York City in advance of the national conventions. About one hundred and seventy, mostly Republicans, attended. According to one reporter, the delegates were "men of intelligence and sobriety" and the Fifth Avenue Hotel bar was comparatively deserted. The presiding officer at the conference was President Woolsey of Yale. Adams apparently made the speech which most stirred the delegates. "It hit the mark square and hard so that for a few hours I enjoyed the intoxication of oratory, — meeting a great success." He felt that the Independents should support the Republicans if they nominated B. H. Bristow, Grant's Secretary of the Treasury who had reorganized his department and had, spectacularly and on the whole successfully, just broken the Whiskey Ring of corrupt distillers who were evading taxes. If the Republicans did not heed this hint, and the Democrats nominated Governor Samuel J. Tilden of New York, the Independents should support the latter. If Republicans and Democrats both failed to respond, the Independents should nominate their own candidate. The convention favored the wait-and-see policy and issued an address asserting the supreme issue of the campaign was to establish the "moral character of our government." [55]

When the major parties nominated Rutherford B. Hayes and Tilden, Adams followed his own advice in supporting the latter. "Though he has paddled in dirty water all his life, [and] belongs to a set which I thoroughly despise," he was a shrewd, skillful, and firm leader. Hayes on the other hand is "a man of the calibre of Pierce on a meaningless platform." "If the Republican party will not act, it must be beaten." After he had somewhat edited these private reactions, Adams repeated them in an airy article in the *North American Review* — that is, if forty pages can be characterized as "airy." In any case the author, after declaring that "every campaign discussion may be decomposed" into "rubbish, formalities, and essence," assigned to the last rubric the superior political experience of Tilden and his greater grasp of the facts of politics. "My political manifesto seems to have made a roar and burst the N. American." [56]

The disputed election of 1876, in which Tilden had a majority of the popular vote and initially an electoral majority, though this became an electoral majority of one for Hayes through the creation and manipulation of returning boards in three Southern states, deeply disturbed Adams. It reinforced his dislike of the electoral college. A dishonest and inefficient way of "counting noses," as he had foreseen, had now "cheated" a candidate into the presidency. Nor could he tolerate the proposed congressional solutions for solving the current dispute. In the restlessness brought on by the "political tempest" Adams called for a new election for which he thought there was both time and constitutional warrant. At other times he buzzed about in an effort to induce Martin Brimmer, a Massachusetts elector of reformist temperament, to cast his vote so as to throw the election into the House. In the end these stratagems and suggestions did not prevent Congress from establishing an Electoral Commission which decided the count in favor of Hayes. "The great Centennial political fraud" filled Adams with amazement. His incredulity mounted when Carl Schurz, with whom Adams had managed the Independents' conference in May, accepted appointment as Secretary of the Interior in Hayes's cabinet. "As I now see it, Mr. Hayes' and your (through him) success will go far to establish in the great, vague, loose-reasoning public mind an abiding conviction that it isn't of much consequence how political power is secured by a party provided a good use is made of it by individuals." [57]

This bruising experience left Adams, like Othello, "perplexed in the extreme," and he drew back for a time from political exertion. "Speech is silver and with me has been demonetized." Four years later, however, he took heart from the election of Garfield because it was "apparently decisive" and the closeness of the popular vote "forcibly illustrates the power of the Independent vote." The independent voter "thus occupies the centre of the tilting-board. He can send either end up or down." In 1884, along with other Bostonian reformers, he was "hot about Blaine" — he did not mean enthusiastic — but his own election to the presidency of the Union Pacific in the same year convinced him he must abstain from political activity. Nonetheless he much preferred Cleveland, and the latter's election, as it turned out, had advantages for both Adams and the railroad. By 1892, after Adams' tour of duty with the Union Pacific was over, his admiration for Cleveland had so mounted that he was able to take an avowed position in the campaign. "I did this out of pure public spirit, for the course Cleveland has pursued in steadily preferring to be right rather than to be President, deserved and should receive whatever recognition it is in the power of an individual placed as I am to render." Adams went further than this. Admitting that Cleveland's policy on tariff, civil service, currency, and pensions coincided with his own, he added, "If the published utterances of ex-President Cleveland upon all the leading issues of the day constitute what is now Democracy, then I and those who feel as I do must for the time being submit . . . to be accounted Democrats." [58] There for the moment Adams' evolution from Republicanism through independency to Democracy came to rest.

For Massachusetts reformers of the Adams type, most controversies on local issues in the Commonwealth during the 1870's and 1880's boiled down to one overriding issue — Benjamin F. Butler. A Lowell lawyer, a man of wealth, of flamboyant taste and great rhetorical prowess, Butler had started his political career as a Democrat. At the national convention of that party in 1860 he cast fifty-one times the only vote for the nomination of Jefferson Davis to the Union presidency. When the Civil War broke out Butler became the most colorful of a horde of "political" generals, an impromptu emancipator of the slaves, and the "beast" of New Orleans where he commanded the occupying Federal forces. After the war he joined the radical Republicans and, elected to Congress, was a leader in the impeachment of Johnson, a crony of General Grant, and, most fatefully of all, a convert to the Greenback gospel. Though he remained in Congress until 1875, he had a persistent desire to be governor of

Massachusetts, and since the state had annual elections he was always running for something.[59]

The general, Charles Francis Adams, Jr., once observed, was wont to disregard "all rule and usage," and campaigns in which he participated "could be counted upon to be unusually animated." Toward the end of the seventies he left the Republican party when it "deserted its founders the laboring men," and from then on he tried driving a tandem. The Butler wing — the largest wing — of the Massachusetts Democratic party emphasized the most palatable reforms of the era: abolition of the poll tax, a secret ballot, shorter workday; whereas the Greenback or Labor party, on whose ticket Butler also ran, voiced the easy money philosophy in its most varied and extreme forms. The issue of greenbacks would ease the "people's Burdens." A career so footloose naturally raised questions as to its integrity, which the extravagance of Butler's rhetoric and the irrelevance of his charges did little to mend. He had a certain consistency for he always wanted office. He also correctly appraised the core of opposition to him. He described it in surely one of the most extraordinary platform planks ever written. The Independent Democrats in 1879 "put the seal of condemnation upon that growing spirit of 'Bourbonism' and 'caste' which conceals itself under the pretentious title of the 'better element', which sets itself upon a high pedestal of preëminent right to dictate and to control the people because of its alleged superior public virtue." [60]

Adams' dislike of Butler went back to the Civil War and the military inertia of General Butler which prolonged the drive against Richmond in 1864. "As I remember that awful campaign and those months passed in front of Petersburg, I entertain a very bitter feeling toward Major-General Benjamin F. Butler." Nor did he see any reason to change his opinion in 1868. In that year an element in the Republican party nominated R. H. Dana, Adams' former mentor in the law, to challenge Butler for his congressional seat. "In this species of warfare General Butler was not to be excelled, and his references to his opponent's personal habits and peculiarities, his ancestry and his supposed aristocratic tendencies, his equipage, his gloves, and his apparel, were no less numerous than, as the result showed, they were telling." Two years later when the Republican convention refused to nominate Butler for the governorship Adams felt, "It was a great deliverance and we drew a long breath of relief." When Butler caromed out of the Republican party, Adams' direct responsibility for checkmating him evaporated. It did not, however, diminish his hostility or fear. In November 1882 he "woke up to find Ben Butler Governor of Massachusetts — a good deal of an earthquake." Although Butler failed to repeat his success the following year, Adams feared his election was "ominous for the future." [61] This proved a false prophecy; Butler had passed his peak.

Less than a decade later, in 1891, the ascendancy of Cleveland and the realignment of factions led Adams to invite to dinner "the rising lights among the young democratic politicians," as well as Moorfield Storey, young R. H. Dana, and Charles W. Eliot, president of Harvard. It was a gesture only an Adams could conceive or bring off. Luckily the guests did not realize their host was "sizing" them and would subsequently confide to his diary who were "somewhat light weight" or who "will go some distance." [62] A representative of the "better element" not present on this occasion was deploring the "combination" in Massachusetts politics "of Harvard and the slums of Boston." This gathering ought to have reassured him; those present were all Harvard men with the exception of Mayor Matthews.

The Civil War closed out the slavery issue; no longer polarized around a single theme, reformers thereafter differed from one another in objectives, methods, and tone. The national program which Adams favored was generally a return to the prewar status — the tariff and the currency were examples — and perhaps to conditions even more remote. Though he took pains to disparage the Jefferson tradition — "not a vestige of his theories remains in the practice of the government" — the statement has a *pro-forma* ring. On the state level Adams thought woman suffrage theoretically undesirable but inevitable and approved of the Australian ballot, the regulation of railroads, and the reform of public education; the remaining clamor did not interest him. The one overriding issue everywhere was an elevation of moral tone and professional competence in government. Here Adams along with his fellows apparently felt they had achieved some success. There was much less drunkenness and corruption among public men in Washington in the 1890's than in the "coarse, vulgar *regime* of Grant's second term." [63]

Adams' pilgrimage as a political reformer had been long and earnest. He moved from the Republican party, the one of "our youth and devotion," into mugwumpery and then came to rest in the conservative wing of the Democracy. Along the way he had received an education in political action and some insight into the moods and methods of his fellow reformers. The last left him disillusioned. Sumner, whom he had once ardently admired, turned out "to be in the first rank of the extremists, wholly failing to realize the inevitable trend of events." Wendell Phillips, Adams regarded with a touch of amusement until he took up with General Butler. Then Adams saluted Phillips derisively as "our great mentor." "Now, Wendell Phillips has no faith in your man of formulas and inductions, who would reason on that in regard to which inspiration should be our guide. He *knows* what is right, and does not need to investigate it." [64] In Adams' estimation the ideal reformer should not be extravagant, rhetorical, intuitive, or self-seeking. Reform should arrive at the front door in a horse and carriage; preferably he should wear a frock coat and have his name in the Quinquennial Catalogue.

In the circumstances how could "the sifted grain" among

reformers hope for success? Adams saw, "It is all a question of organization, and of that we have none." At other times he argued that the independents held the balance of power and could thus swing the decision, as in Garfield's case. A hard-headed observer pointed out to Adams that "Garfield owes his success to the votes of *all* his supporters — just as much to the vote purchased for a dollar as to that of a civil service reformer." In the end Adams fell back upon influence in high places and his own importance. As he wrote to Schurz in 1903, "Considering who you and I are, and the fact that our names are not unknown to the community in which we live and of which he is the chief official, I feel that he [Roosevelt] has treated us with scant courtesy." [65]

Surveying from the threshold of the early 1890's the eleven presidential campaigns he had known, Adams confessed: "I feel myself forced to the conclusion that in the course of them I have been through a great deal of most unnecessary anxiety and witnessed the expenditure of a vast amount of energy and enthusiasm with very inadequate returns; because, though generally I have been on the winning side, and so at the moment seen my country saved from what appeared to be imminent peril, yet now, looking back over the lines of that country's development and the political battle-fields which marked and more or less deflected those lines, I cannot help feeling that so far as the country as a whole is concerned, the grand result would in the long run have been about the same whether at any particular election" — with the exception of 1864 — "the party I sympathized with had won the day or whether the other party had won it." Reluctantly Adams had become convinced that current politics had no place for men of his type. The 1890's was "the golden period of the light weight politician and manager." Since the voters were convinced "that everything was going to turn out all right without any very active exertion on the part of any one," "our appeals to principles fell on indifferent ears." He was not only disillusioned with politics, he was disillusioned with any effort in their direction. Consenting to attend a conference proposed by Moorfield Storey and some younger idealists, Adams wearily wrote, "I have been to many such before." [66]

For all his attention to trends, Adams could not foresee that a tidal wave of economic misfortune was to hit the country and set the "immobile parties" traveling in new directions under new political leaders — McKinley, Bryan, and Roosevelt. These unexpected events challenged Adams' deepest convictions, jeopardized his fortune, and stirred his personal aversions. They also raised the question whether a dedicated "sophist" could rise above the mere complaint and captious commentary of the past to a position of effective leadership in the future.

❖ VI ❖

AN AVERSION
TO REFORMERS OF THE
WRONG SORT

1890-1915

LOOKING back over 1892, Adams noted: "Physically it was distinctly a year of climax passed. I saw that in ways unmistakable. The tissues were relaxing, the muscles laid waste, the virile force was abated, the furnace gave out no surplus heat. I didn't need Dr. White to tell me this." [1] He was fifty-seven. Entirely aside from his severance from the Union Pacific, he was also passing through a cluster of crises which conjoined to make the early 1890's a genuine watershed in his career.

For one thing he had broken with Quincy. Though he had long anticipated and carefully considered the step, he persisted in picturing it as impulsive and melodramatic. Thus in May 1893 he impetuously purchased a place in Lincoln, a suburban town a little west of Boston. Six months later, "Early one Monday morning in the latter part of November, 1893, I mounted my horse at the door of my house on the hill at Quincy — the sun being hardly above the horizon of the distant sea-line in the nipping atmosphere — and rode over to Lincoln. I have not passed a night at Quincy since." [2]

His new estate, Birnham Wood, with its 320 acres along

Fairhaven Bay, where the Sudbury River spread out, had all he "wanted — view, water, trees, grounds, house, outbuildings." Here he could "feel and smell and taste the country, the sunshine, the stillness, the unbroken view." In short, it had everything but associations, and his nostalgic planting of acorns from his Quincy pin oak was not the equivalent of the full grown trees he had started years ago any more than the Sudbury was the sea. According to the record, every return to Quincy on errand or chore filled him with revulsion and left "a bad taste" in his mouth. When he saw the plans for the development of his Quincy real estate, he screamed with pain: "My God! it was bitter! Roads run through my lawn, my plantations rooted up, my view annihilated — and I powerless to prevent. Oh! the bitter dreggs [*sic*] in the cup!" [3]

Since he had broken physically and forever with "family traditions," "boyhood surroundings," and "the graves of my forbears," he worried about both Quincy and himself. "Nonetheless all Adamses out of Quincy, does seem a bit out of place. We shall see." "It remains to be seen whether the tree will bear transplanting." Conceivably the resolution of these doubts involved further movement. Charles' diary now more frequently records a sweeping condemnation of New England weather and scenery; and on his return from a European trip in 1897 he asked and answered the rhetorical question "Lives there a man with soul so dead?" — "Well — just now, me decidedly, — yes." Earlier he had described the trip as "a sort of semi-exile." In the end, however, the satisfactions of Lincoln, the sale of the Boston house, and the purchase of a winter home in Washington united with his constant ferrying across the Atlantic to prevent him from becoming expatriate.[4]

Changes in Massachusetts residences did not explain entirely Adams' distress in the early 1890's. A prolonged and mysterious illness had seized his wife. There were alternations of attacks and convalescence, but at the end of 1892 the illness reached a climax in appendicitis, the treatment of which, as was common before the modern operation, entailed the lancing of an abscess, the insertion of drains, and an incision which did not heal for months. "I seem to remember only those awful, sickening days of June and July and August 1893, when I came home frightened and restless and had to keep a quiet exterior in order not to disturb Minnie. So I would sit with her for a little while and then crawl over to that hateful Annex in order to be alone with my fright and restless misery, as a dog licks his wounds in the kennel. It was simply a terror." Though at the end of the year Minnie was well enough to go to Europe, the "ugly symptoms" recurred in Madrid; and when the Adamses reached Venice, they consulted Dr. Cabot. The doctor "crushed out hope." Fear rode in the gondola with Adams; it walked by his side as he paced the Piazza San Marco; it crawled into the bath house at the Lido whither he retreated "like a sick dog into its hiding place." Again and again there ran through his mind the lines of Tennyson:

> O Love, what hours were thine and mine
> In lands of palm and southern pine.
> O Love, we two shall go no longer
> To lands of summer beyond the sea.

Then when he reached London, he was handed a cablegram telling of John's death. "I never knew life without John." After the return from Europe Minnie's health took a turn for the better, and in 1895, after three years of invalidism, she rode out in the saddle again.[5]

In this time of misery, when Adams was always having to "pull myself together" and "brace myself up," one of his hardest tasks in self-control was to postpone telling Minnie of his financial anxieties. For the depression of the first half of the 1890's struck his fortunes in other ways than the collapse of the Barings. Aside from that blow, Adams thought 1890 had been "another good year." His net income had been $167,000; the market value of his assets over liabilities was $1,795,495.16, a sum which did not include Minnie's property. Then the shrinkage set in. By 1893 the financial record was "perilous." His joint income with Minnie was $63,000; his valuation was $1,500,000. A period of holding on ensued. The year 1895 was "not marked by any calamity or particular success; but nothing was achieved nor was anything lost." Income was $70,000; the value of his inventory was $775,000, of Minnie's $600,000.[6]

However varied his holdings and his estimates of their worth, the pattern of the dangers confronting Adams during the nineties was simple. The mainstay of his fortune was investment in land. From Kansas City to Portland, from Lewiston to Denver, he valued his holdings in 1892 at $1,500,000. Nearer home, Charles and his brother John held for speculative purposes a Boston area extending along the Charles River between the intersection of Commonwealth Avenue and Beacon Street (now Kenmore Square) and the Cottage Farm Bridge. Since the Riverbank Land Company and the West End Land Company had signally failed to dispose of this property over a period of twenty years, these holdings were "the real millstone around our necks." The message from every quarter was the same: land did not move.[7]

Adams depended, therefore, upon returns from securities to support a far from modest way of life and to meet interest payments on his borrowings. In a time of vast business disaster such returns were uncertain or nonexistent. Through inertia or doggedness he still held onto "those wretched lumber railroads," the Chicago and Western Michigan and the Detroit, Lansing and Northern. By 1895 they were either paying tiny dividends or none and had defaulted the interest on their bonds. Larger and more ominous was the cloud over the Union Pacific. "During that last crazy year in the U.P." he had in his folly allowed himself to be loaded with $500,000 in securities of the Oregon Railway and Navigation Company. In addition he probably owned $300,000 in Union Pacific securities. Much as he desired Gould, Dillon, and Clark to fail in the management they had seized in 1890, he wanted the road to hold together until he got his money out. So he began "taking in sail" on the Oregon Railway by trading the stock for that in other corporations; sometimes in his eagerness he "tumbled overboard." Still at the end of 1891 he was rejoicing that he was nearly out of the Union Pacific. "Lo! how brightly breaks the evening." [8]

To develop Kansas City Adams had put large sums into the stockyards, packing plants, the Kansas City Smelting and Refining Company, a cement works, and the Metropolitan Street Railways. By the summer of 1890 clear signals of a recession were flying. A few months later the cement works "was a corpse," the iron works "a funeral." By 1895 even the real estate had become "a burden and a heavy one." The next year, when Adams visited the city, he found the country round about "singularly unchanged and Missourian — a very low type of development. First impressions far from encouraging: signs everywhere of deep-seated trouble — 40 cent wheat and 25 cent corn." [9]

A novelty in the Adams financial picture was the Westinghouse Electric Company. Adams had first become acquainted with George Westinghouse when he was inventing and manufacturing the air brake for railroad operation; later Westinghouse induced Adams to invest in his enlarged operations, and by 1891 Adams had $225,000 in the company. He had become a member of the board of directors and of its executive committee and acted as a liaison officer for this enterprise in its financial appeals to Boston bankers. To be "in it again" at first did something to restore a self-esteem injured by his Union Pacific failure, but soon all sorts of parallels filled him with despair. Whether in railroads or electrical equipment, there was a "flabby guts" Holcomb, the symbol of slackness, and Adams'

New York associates soon revealed they could play "the usual Wall Street game." "They were neither able nor strong of will. They are mostly crafty, selfish, secretive and false, one never can tell what they are after." George Westinghouse, however, was a personality for which there had been no parallel on the Union Pacific. This "curious man" defied Adams' analysis. "He reminds me in a way of John Adams, — in essentials a really great man but cursed with a vanity which limits him in every direction." [10]

Personalities aside, the position of the producers of electrical equipment was not a happy one. Sales of heavy installations for light and power required capital expenditures which the depression discouraged; the possession of patents by rival producers hampered the efficient utilization of the best devices and spurred litigation. Not surprisingly, in view of his railroad philosophy, Adams' solution was a consolidation. The idea had occurred to others, among them the Boston capitalists F. L. Ames, Henry L. Higginson, and Jefferson Coolidge, but the company they helped found in 1892, General Electric, did not include Westinghouse. In March 1896 these two giants signed an agreement for the joint use of patents on a royalty basis. From time to time Adams allowed himself the consolation that Westinghouse stocks had appreciated. The comfort was temporary.[11]

At the root of Adams' difficulties was the dependence of his fortune on short-term loans. When the panic shrank the value of his assets, his collateral brought less at the bank; when the panic put everything in jeopardy, including confidence, he could not get loans, or, if he did, paid a high interest on them. When he left the Union Pacific in November 1890, he had $500,000 in notes maturing within the month. By financiering he scraped enough money to "get through, January 20th." His fortune, nevertheless, continued to hang on hazards of this sort. His net interest account for 1890 was $52,000. At the end of

1893, the worst year of the depression, his debts stood at $2,100,000; the valuation of his property was not sufficient to meet this; his interest account stood at $70,000. "I am running behind fast," he concluded, and then added, "interest is eating me up." [12]

Only desperate expedients saved him. In June 1893 he faced up to the fact that in August he had "notes of $300,000 to meet, wholly unsecured." Scourged by the financial agony, he resolved to ask F. L. Ames to stand behind his credit. "As frightened a man as walked," he journeyed to North Easton; when Ames asked him how much he needed, Adams replied $900,000. "He immediately said he would let me have it." At the time Adams regarded this as "an awful experience." Their understanding seemed to involve an appraisal of Adams' assets, the shattering possibility of the sale of the "old house," and the lodgment of certain securities with Ames. Even with Ames' backing, Adams had to pay 10 percent interest on his August loans. The next month Ames was dead of apoplexy. As money eased throughout the rest of the year, Adams was able to borrow and at lower rates. But the Ames interposition "enabled me to go through, — if indeed I yet am through." With the country, as with Adams, August 1893 marked the depth of the depression; but his interest account at the end of 1894 still stood at $98,000. Two years later Adams summarized 1896 as "the stormiest and least 'propitious' I ever passed." [13]

In spite of his despair on matters of detail and occasional forecasts of total disaster, Adams fundamentally was optimistic. Though he often exhorted himself "to take in sail," he did not do it consistently. The basis for his rather genial attitude toward the depression was, "these things take care of themselves. My theory is that the world is not going to come to an end just at present; that the United States will continue to prosper and grow; and that the wheels of business will in time get in motion." [14] In the circumstances the correct financial axiom was

"Patience and shuffle the cards." He repeated it over and over again as he sought successfully to transfer his money from weak to sounder securities.

Meanwhile events were always assailing his underlying confidence; eventually they grew powerful enough to shatter it and convince Adams that a new order of things had supplanted the old. "No courage or staying power could have made up for the Barings." The next two crises, those of 1893 and 1896, were connected in some uncertain way with the national currency. Originally Charles attributed the steady erosion of values and the fall in prices attending the depression to the overproduction which followed improvements in manufacturing and transportation. Others, however, felt the crises of these years were due to gold monometallism. From the West, where lay so many of his interests, there rose a cry for inflation through the free and unlimited coinage of silver at the ratio of sixteen to one. In 1893 Cleveland secured the repeal of the Sherman Silver Purchase Act which had once compromised this issue by permitting a limited coinage; and in July 1896 the silverites had captured the Democratic party and nominated William Jennings Bryan for the presidency. In the intervening years there had been a gold drain to foreign countries and the Treasury had been hard pressed to stay on gold and keep off silver. Nor were agrarians the only apostles of a bimetallic standard. Charles was always listening to arguments on its behalf from Henry and Brooks. In 1893 he could not feel "so completely cocksure" as his brothers; their case was too simple. He was, however, ready to grant that the demonetization of silver might have been a contributory factor in the present crisis.[15]

A year or so later he cast aside this moderate interpretation. There had been a conspiracy of the banking classes, particularly in England, to collect their debts in currency of high value. "The measure of value should have increased in the same proportion as for commodities . . . There wouldn't have been a fall in prices for values would have kept the same relation to the cost of production. If things had been left alone, it would have been alright. They weren't. Silver was demonetized and gold was hoarded in every war chest and bank reserve of the civilized world . . . Today the treasury of the United States which under our wretched, maddening fiscal system either directly affects or wholly controls every financial and industrial interest in the country has been turned over to the Rothschilds and Morgan. The bankers are at their wits end. Every one is hoarding gold — the nation, the bankers, the Jews. We of the producing and debtor class are just ground down between the millstones." "Owing as much money as I do, I have to keep quiet simply because any public utterance of my opinions would injure my standing and credit." [16] What a fate for an Adams!

Early in 1895 Adams was privately ranting against gold like a Populist zealot. "The cant of the best money, 'honest money', the money of the 'civilized world.' " A year later he was stretching every nerve to defeat William Jennings Bryan and equating the advocacy of changing a nation's currency with "the most insidious form of treason." One factor in this melodramatic return to his earlier conviction was no doubt a reconnaissance he made through the West in 1896. So rapid had been the reversal of fortune or so intense was Adams' desire to make a case, that Kansas City, recently dark with doom, was now "jubilant with 90 cent wheat at each street corner." Further west the mountain states and the Pacific coast had completed the readjustment. The tide "has changed." And then on July 9 the Democratic party nominated Bryan for the presidency and demanded in its platform a currency of silver and gold at a parity of sixteen to one. Adams waited some months before he penned his portrait of the Democratic standard bearer. It began with perception and ended with petulance. "Among political characters, Bryan strikes me as almost typical of our present,

American stage of development. Naturally kindly and sympathetic, very ambitious and only half educated, of quick intelligence and ready speech, he reflects his surroundings, he embodies his environment. His model is Abraham Lincoln, and he really strives to shape his thoughts and gives utterance to them after the fashion of his model: yet, instead of rising to the desired altitude, he sinks under his environment into continual demagoguery. I can't help wondering whether he realizes it. He is a pinchbeck Christ. American civilization and American freshwater colleges are responsible for a lot of them. Half-bakedness is the crying evil of the day." Whatever may have been the "evil," the "crying" need was for stability. The country had adjusted to gold: "It is Burke who somewhere refers to 'tampering' as the vice of unstable and ignoble minds." [17]

"The success of the Democratic Party in this election would, in my judgment, surely entail upon the country financial and political consequences the disastrous consequences of which I cannot try to measure or hope to outlive," wrote Adams to Carl Schurz. The note of despair, here so sharp and clear, shows that the depression years were not ones of calm calculation and detailed diagnosis, but phases of an emotional drama. For Adams this had been a time of "financial nightmares," of "thinking, scheming, devising, and tossing" at night, of taking "brohmides" [sic] for the first time, of hurling himself on horseback for one of his "medical rides," of "Nerves! Nerves!" [18] In these periodic "turns of terror" he feared he had lost all judgment and was living in a world of fantasies.

Though the outcome of the election dispelled one peril, Adams was not done with crises. In 1897 danger converged upon two of his important enterprises. For twenty years he had been an investor and director in the Kansas City Smelting and Refining Company. By the century's end this company had extended to other centers: Leadville, El Paso, and Mexico. These plants worked Mexican ore and marketed the lead in foreign and domestic markets. Before 1890 and the "protection orgy" then introduced by the McKinley Bill, this ore had come into the country free. The McKinley Bill slapped on a duty which Adams calculated was one of 100 percent. The Dingley Act of 1897 increased the duty. According to the company's president, A. R. Mayer, the previous duty had cut profits by $1,000,000. In 1897 also the Kansas Legislature decided to set the prices charged for handling animals at large stockyards within the state. These were declared "public" stockyards and rates were fixed at so much a head. The only stockyards really regulated by the law were those of the Kansas City Stockyards Company, "almost the largest and altogether the most profitable investment I have." In operation the legislative rates reduced the company's annual income by half.[19]

Luckily for Adams' well-being the Kansas City Smelting and Refining Company forthwith joined the American Smelting and Refining Company, a consolidation which ultimately included the Guggenheims and H. H. Rogers of Standard Oil fame. The deal reminded Adams in its deviousness of his "Chapter of Erie" and he assailed the Guggenheims as "Jews from Jerusalem" and Rogers as a self-made "cutthroat and pirate in Wall Street" who started life driving a delivery wagon for a grocery store in New Bedford. The American Smelting and Refining was a trust. "I feel no compunction. Congress . . . tried to rob us — despotically, brutally, avowedly of all the fruits of a legitimate enterprise, honestly conducted and intelligently devised . . . I hope it is a monopoly; and out of that monopoly I trust to make much money." The Kansas City Stockyards Company brought suit in the courts on the ground that the Kansas Act of 1897 was confiscatory, discriminatory, and unconstitutional. The litigation was prolonged. Adams was present to hear the final arguments before the Supreme Court. The majority of the learned Justices did not impress him favorably — Harlan was a "beefy product of the Ohio grass country"

— but Justice Brewer was an exception; he "argued our case for us" and also wrote the decision invalidating the Kansas law as a denial of the equal protection of the laws.[20]

Though Adams cackled at downing the Kansas Legislature and euchring Congress, these two triumphs did not mark the moment when he emerged from the jungle of his financial woes. It is impossible to date his deliverance with precision, for financial entries in the diaries drop away after 1900, perhaps because in the family tradition he had transferred responsibility in these matters to his son-in-law, Grafton Abbott. Meanwhile the general prosperity of the first decade of the twentieth century brought many of his argosies to safety. The ownership of land now contained recuperative factors, for a fortunate sale or lease hit the jackpot. On his return from Europe in 1905 he found "his goose hung higher and higher." His western land was moving. And the projected sale of the Grand Avenue property in Kansas City, the site for a new Union Station, and some coal lands would bring him enough to get "out from under the financial harrow." [21]

His melancholy experience with the repercussions of political circumstances and considerations upon business enterprise of course led Adams to formulate general conclusions. The election of McKinley in 1896 resulted from "the craving, now epidemic, for government interference in all industrial pursuits. The old political economy is wholly out of date; everyone is now to be protected, everything is to be regulated, and McKinley is the prophet of this dispensation." When the assassin's bullet elevated Roosevelt to the presidency, Adams detected no shift in direction. The "strenuosity of the day and its empty loquacity" did nothing to commend the regime to him. When Roosevelt brought his program to full flower, Adams was certain: "Every single one of the propositions advanced in Roosevelt's Confession of Faith has to me a hollow ring, and the best that can be said of any of them is that it would be likely to prove innocuous. The great mass of them would be in my judgment altogether injurious . . . The whole tendency of the day is opposed to both my experience and judgment. It is based on charlatanism, pure and simple; and is altogether empirical in its method . . . If you have an ailment today, you do not take a vote of the club, or of your immediate neighborhood — counting noses, as to the best method of treatment. On the contrary you call in a physician in whose judgment you have confidence. When, however, it comes to the body politic, whose ills are far more hidden, complicated, and interwoven than those of the physical body, the cry today is to solve everything on the democratic plan, taking a periodical count of noses and following the prescription which the majority favor." [22] Thus Charles discovered, as had earlier Adamses, that much of the argument for democracy was cant.

As Adams and a few of the like-minded had understood it, their program of reform — tariffs, civil service, currency — had reached a certain finality at the turn of the century. Suddenly another issue touched anew their fundamental ideals and stirred them to action. It came from an unexpected direction — Grover Cleveland, for whom Adams had spoken and worked in 1892 as a man of character and courage. Three years later when a dispute between Venezuela and Great Britain over Venezuela's western boundary was moving toward crisis, Cleveland in a message to Congress proposed, with considerable verbal truculence, that he take steps to settle the issue by arbitration. Adams read the "jingo" message in New York. "I fairly rubbed my eyes over it. Could it be or was I dreaming?" Cleveland's "drunken rhodomontade" imparted an unpleasant tremor to the delicate equilibrium of Adams' business affairs. More dishearteningly it was a symptom of the nation's temper. "The average American, it would appear, thinks it the correct course to rush into a man's office with a big stick, shake it at him, and threaten him with personal castigation if he does not either immediately do, or desist from doing, something which may be brought about more certainly in a less rude and offensive way." [23]

The McKinley administration soon confronted Adams with a graver example of national militancy and mission: the recognition of Cuban independence, the Spanish-American War, the annexation of Hawaii, and the proposed acquisition of the Philippines. Like the Venezuela affair, some of these incidents upset Adams' plans for recouping his fortunes. More important, a great-grandson of John Adams, who had signed the Declaration of Independence, could hardly endorse an American empire, built without the consent of the governed. Nor did he. "We are blood guilty; and we are doing to others, in violation of our traditional policy and all the teachings of history what we have protested against when attempted on us or doing elsewhere . . . I feel I ought to bear witness." [24]

To defeat the territorial articles of the peace treaty was the first objective. To create and marshal public opinion, Adams helped organize the Boston Committee of the Anti-Imperialist League, carried on a wide correspondence, wrote and signed addresses and petitions, and planned overall strategy. But he was not sanguine. The movement in Boston was directed by Edward Atkinson, "who is, in my judgment, not quite the right man. Like Gamaliel Bradford he has injured his useful effectiveness by too great activity, always in evidence." As for Gamaliel Bradford he is "considerable of a bore. He has a decided tendency crankward." When he regarded his closest associates thus dubiously, it is not surprising that he felt the Democratic party of the South and West was "honeycombed with imperialism." Bryan's artful maneuvers in behalf of the treaty made certain its ratification. "The country will go into the 'open door', colonies, dependency craze. They think it will all be plain sailing . . . Then will come rebellions, scandals, vast appropriations for larger, overpaid armies, the Chinese syphilis and typhoid." [25]

In the light of this forecast and the outbreak of the Philippine struggle for independence, there was a continued need for oversight by the anti-imperialists. Adams, Carnegie, Schurz, and others realized this and promoted every effort to reveal the costs of subjugating the islands in terms of atrocities and humane considerations and the threat to American economic interests. In the end the post-treaty period was the most important phase of their activity. Adams gave a shout of victory in 1902: "We have won. Roosevelt has established civil government and the army has been brought up short . . . I am not disposed to continue" the record. In reality the anti-imperialist crusade had left him mortified and disillusioned. "We are the most impracticable set of cranks probably to be found on the face of the earth. By 'we' I refer to our imperialist crowd. We cannot agree on anything: and the standards we set up are so exalted and all embracing, and any infringements upon them are so objectionable, that to reach an agreement is impossible, and our influence is, therefore, wasted." [26]

As he approached his seventies, the dream of an intellectual elite, of the "sophists," advising and directing democracy, which he had formulated in his young manhood and sought to fulfill over the years, sometimes singlehanded, began to crumble. He fell into the habit of writing epitaphs. Only a few years before this appraisal of the anti-imperialists, he had made a more dismal surrender: "I can influence no one. Everyone I could possibly influence . . . thinks as I do, while those who think otherwise regard me as belonging essentially to the 'classes', and as, therefore, not even entitled to a hearing, much less to any degree of confidence, on the part of what they are pleased to call the 'masses.' " [27]

Nonetheless where state rather than national matters were involved, Adams had once set so strong and so successful a precedent with the Railroad Commission that the Commonwealth still called upon him to apply intelligence in defining a problem and disinterestedness in recommending solutions. Whether or not he was liked or even known by the voters, state officials had to acknowledge his talents and sought his assistance. In the 1890's, for instance, the application of the electric motor to the omnibus or horsecar had led to the expansion of urban and inter-urban trolley and cable cars, and opened new vistas in the operation and control of these enterprises. There was a considerable movement for the "municipalization" of these systems. The presence in Massachusetts of Edward Bellamy, the author of *Looking Backward*, a Utopian novel picturing the blessings of collective enterprise, and of Frank Parsons, an advocate of municipal ownership who achieved the distinction of simultaneously holding positions on the faculty of the Boston University Law School and that of the Kansas State Agricultural College, gave point and leadership to the agitation. Since Adams had once, on the Railroad Commission, had the responsibility of regulating horse railroads and was now, through Westinghouse, acquainted in a general way with the fundamental technical progress in the electrical industry, the governor appointed him in 1897 as chairman of a three-man committee to investigate and report "on the relations between cities and towns and street railway companies." So Adams wrote one more report. It stressed the familiar necessity of thorough preliminary investigation. Adams took advantage of a trip abroad to inform himself of European precedent and practice.[28]

The report derided the idea of competition as a possible regulator and expressed a preference for consolidation. Insofar as government regulated these public utilities, the power should remain in the hands of communities; they had the advantages of a knowledge of local conditions and of "concernment." If the community were to start over again in these matters, Adams thought it might well follow the German precedent under which the municipality owned the tracks, as well as the rest of the street, and leased the lines to private enterprise for operation. With many a touch of the old fire and shrewdness, he dismissed "municipalization" in general and particular; its advantages were based upon "loose assertions" rather than proof. "The members of the Committee have only to say that, if a street railway utopia anywhere exists, they have in the course of their investigations failed to find it. That the street railways of Massachusetts have, as a whole, cost much more than they could now be replaced for, is as indisputable as it has been unavoidable; that in some cases they have been overcapitalized, through questionable processes of financiering, is more than probable; but those, after all, are to a greater or less extent incidents inseparable from an unusually rapid development along new lines and in untried fields." [29]

Adams' other bureaucratic assignment in the 1890's was somewhat less a recapitulation of earlier attitudes and recommendations. According to his assertion he rather "blundered into it." Actually his interest in parks, his long and friendly association with F. L. Olmsted and other landscape architects, his despair at the despoilment of the natural beauty around Quincy, made him a logical choice to head a wider effort "to conserve and to make accessible to the people, the brooks, ponds, beaches, and bits of wilderness still left untouched" by those he was wont to call the "development fiends." Since the landscapes or open spaces suitable for preservation did not fall necessarily within the exact boundaries of metropolitan Boston or of any one of the suburban towns or cities around it, an agency greater than the localities had to be created to take land and finance its purchase, if the process of saving "real country" and "beautiful scenery" were to continue. Community leaders joined with professors from Harvard University to get under way the agitation for such an innovation.[30]

In 1892 the General Court authorized a commission of three individuals to investigate the "advisability of laying out ample open spaces" and to prepare maps and plans. Adams became chairman, and for its chief expert, the commissioners chose Charles Eliot, son of the president of Harvard. Young Eliot, trained in landscape architecture, had helped start this movement, and in 1893 the Olmsted firm made him a member. Adams, his fellow commissioners, and their advisers traveled over the Blue Hills, the Middlesex Fells, Revere Beach, and elsewhere in the neighborhood of Boston by train, by boat, by barge, and by horseback, in fair weather and in foul. Early in 1893 they were ready to report, and Adams, as was his wont, had the obligation to write the document. Also as was his wont, he worried about it. His fellow commissioners, however, accepted it "with effusion and relief." Then, as in Railroad Commission days, Adams had to help push the design "through the gauntlet of legislative stupidity, suspicion, and greed." [31]

The result was a resounding triumph. The report attained the status of a best seller, as the General Court ordered 9000 copies printed and distributed. Even more spectacular was the resulting legislation. A statute of 1893 became a Magna Charta for parks. It established a Metropolitan Park Commission of five members to lay out "open spaces for exercise and recreation" and appropriated $1,000,000 in state bonds for their purchase. In proportions recurrently determined, the towns and cities were to meet half the costs of interest and a sinking fund for the principal and of care and maintenance; Boston's share was to be 50 percent of the whole. Adams headed the new commission. Almost at once the depression of 1893 gave it an embarrassment of riches, for the General Court sought to relieve distress by stimulating public works. In 1894 one act appropriated $500,000 for boulevards to connect communities with the new reservations — an activity which the commissioners were not particularly enthusiastic about assuming; and another statute appropriated $500,000 for open spaces along the Charles River above Cottage Farm Bridge, a step in the ultimate development of the Charles River Basin.[32]

By the end of 1895 Charles Eliot was able to write that "the various public open spaces now or soon to be controlled by the Metropolitan Park Commission include more numerous large public pleasure grounds than are governed by any other public authority in northern America, excepting the governments of the United States and Canada." By this time Adams had resigned from the commission: "I have done what I set out to do." A difference of opinion had also arisen with Eliot over the rate of acquisition and development. Besides, as usual, day-to-day administration vexed Adams. Large landowners refused to put their holdings into the reservations; expenses for purchases in public funds were ten cents a foot, instead of the two cents which they might have been in private money.[33]

Since he could never quite shake off the specter of the Union Pacific, Adams feared the Metropolitan Park Commission was diverting him from his real interests. One of these interests had been education. His work on the school committee in Quincy had resulted in the "new departure" there; in 1882 his election to the Board of Overseers of Harvard College opened perchance a similar vista. In some ways the opportunity for change seemed limited. In the government of Harvard, the Board of Overseers is a larger body than the Corporation — the President and the Fellows — but an inferior one as far as making decisions is concerned. It discusses and ratifies the acts of the Corporation; only rarely does it initiate changes. Adams also was bewildered as to how a constituency, presumably as intelligent as Harvard alumni, could elect a body of such mediocrity. He visited his particular scorn upon the "foreign representation" from New York, who did not discuss matters in the wonted conversational style, but substituted "some of the worst declamations ever listened to by mortal man . . . It must be, I suppose, the New York style — and its a devilish bad style." [34]

But there were compensations for the human inertia and unreason, "the conservative, reactionary spirit" which Adams was accustomed to encounter everywhere. Frequently re-elected, he served on the board until 1907. Since the board did most of its work by committees, he attained strategic position as chairman of the committee which selected individuals, from the overseers and from distinguished outsiders, for the visiting committees to each department; and as chairman of the committee on reports and resolutions he brought these separate surveys together. During Adams' long service Charles W. Eliot, president of the university and ex-officio a member of the Board of Overseers, was transforming the whole institution. In the college a greater freedom in the choice of subjects, the elective system, was washing away the old required curriculum. Up to a certain point Eliot and Adams thought and felt alike. They both believed in liberty and individuality. Early in the 1890's Adams was concluding: "Eliot is a very remarkable man. He has force, will, purpose, and I have always found him straightforward." "It is rather surprising how much I like and respect Eliot." [35] Since Eliot himself was often under fire, however, conceivably the president of the university was a liability rather than an asset to Adams.

To an individual accustomed, as Adams was, to thinking in large terms and far ahead, his initial introduction to the Board of Overseers must have been discouraging. At the first meeting the chief item was "a lively debate over rows on Commencement." A week later "the honorable and reverend, the overseers" were "settling the question of Commencement drunkenness." A year later the question of whether the college at commencement should give the customary honorary degree to Ben F. Butler, governor of the Commonwealth, tore reason to tatters. Surprisingly Adams voted for the award, but he was in a minority. At this very moment, June 1883, Adams succeeded in breaking away from such trivialities. On the invitation of the Harvard chapter, he delivered the annual Phi Beta Kappa address to that society.[36] His theme was the continued existence of the requirement in Greek for admission to Harvard College. The title, "A College Fetich," though provocative, gave little idea of the savagery of the performance. This full-scale attack upon "the species of sanctity" hedging about the classics was designed to inflict the maximum of pain upon the classicists. The argument was eloquent and did not refrain from assigning blame to individuals, including the speaker. For Adams asserted Greek had done him no good. Like other educational reformers, he was here elevating a personal grudge into an abstract issue. Without doubt his Phi Beta Kappa address was the most important single document in the "Greek War" flaring in academe in the last decades of the nineteenth century.

Aligning himself with the "modernists," Adams asserted it was the business of the college to fit men for "the work of today." That life was not understood in terms of the dead languages or their structures. Most of the professions required as "essential tools of their trade" a knowledge of French and German. The inordinate emphasis upon the classics prevented time being given to the study of modern languages at an age when adolescent boys could naturally master them. "Latin I will not stop to contend over. That is a small matter. — Not only is it a comparatively simple language . . . it has its modern uses." But the compulsory study of Greek is "a superstition," "a positive wrong." The arguments for it as an intellectual discipline are largely cant. According to the speaker, the experience of his brothers, of his father, his grandfather, and his great-grandfather proved the uselessness of this study. In fact John Adams wrote Jefferson that he learned only two things from Plato, one of which was "that sneezing is a cure for the hiccough." Adams concluded: "I am practical and of this world enough to believe, that in a utilitarian and scientific age the living will not forever be sacrificed to the dead. The worship even of the classical fetich draweth to a close." [37]

On the day he spoke Adams noted he had "exploded my

bomb not without success." This estimate did not spring from the mere glow of the moment. Adams claimed privately that his attack "practically represents the view of the President and the majority of the ruling boards of the College." This assertion was affirmed early in 1884 when Eliot delivered a paper at Johns Hopkins entitled, "What is a Liberal Education?" In it he proposed so to arrange the college curriculum and admission requirements that more subjects might be judged "liberal and put on terms of equality with the old." He strengthened his argument by persuasive examples from the history of knowledge and employed a tone more conciliatory and persuasive than had Adams. Eliot's paper was published in June 1884.[38]

Meanwhile, bomb or no, Adams' speech fell into the limbo populated by academic addresses made on the eve of the long summer vacation. Still he had spoken out with such force and in such harmony with the ferment of the times that the argument was sure to be picked up later. It was "Greek, Greek, Greek" when his various clubs met in the fall, or held a reception for Matthew Arnold, who was in the United States on a lecture tour, in the course of which he defended the classics. Soon Adams' "mind was in a perfect muddled whirl of irritated excitement over Greek, U.P. and everything else." But the contagion spread. Appraisals, hostile or friendly, appeared in print, the most magisterial and numerous of which came from the pen of Noah Porter, president of Yale. Porter treated Adams and Eliot as unruly undergraduates for their attack upon the "divine language." He dismissed Eliot as "adventurous." Elsewhere he added, "Even Mr. Charles Francis Adams, Jr., must be astonished that his guerilla raid upon the sacred shrine of the long-worshiped Fetich has resulted in so speedy a surrender to the rampant iconoclast. We would suggest that a commemoration service be held at Sanders Theatre for the manes of the Fetich, by some antique dramatic representation in Attic Greek — only once and for the last time . . . At all events, let not the oldest and most literary University of America be wholly unmindful of the honor which it paid to Greek in the past before it formally marches over into the camp of the Philistines . . . We trust that the partial abandonment of it [Greek] in the oldest American University does not signify a weakening of faith in the supernatural facts of the New Testament History, or in the Eternal Truths which that History illustrates and enforces." [39] Harvard is not apt to resort to Yale to learn its own duty, particularly when it can listen to statements just as silly from Cambridge sources.

One of Adams' fellow overseers identified the continuation of the study of Greek with the continuation of the United States as a Christian country. This argument was not likely to take Adams aback. The author went on to express amazement at the claim that classics had done the Adams family harm. "When a member in the fourth generation of the most successful family in America ascribes to Greek all the misfortunes and failures of his ancestors and kindred, we might almost suspect him of anti-republican aspirations; for the only misfortune that can be conceived of in the history of that family is their failure to become a race of hereditary monarchs." In addition to such sportive irrelevancies, the overseers had before them a petition signed by the presidents of eight New England colleges from Yale to Boston University praying Harvard would make no change in the Greek requirement for "it would injuriously affect every classical college in America and the work which they are now able to do for the cause of a truly liberal education." The petitioners excused their intrusion by adding that they "were jointly responsible with yourselves for the educational standards and work and reputation of our country." [40]

The discussion in the board disclosed an inclination to permit a scientific substitute for Greek or Latin, "one of the two languages always being required." When the faculty took up the question the exponents of the natural sciences followed the same line. J. P. Cooke, professor of chemistry, pleaded that "science-culture" be granted an equal chance with linguistic culture; and with many a shrewd insight appraised the social forces and status-seeking which stood behind the classical program. He ended his plea to his colleagues with the assertion, "I would welcome every form of culture which had vindicated its efficiency and value, and in so doing I feel that I should best promote the interests of the special department which I have in charge." [41] Though the last motive was usually present in faculty power struggles, this avowal was exceptional for its candor.

When the academic shoving stopped it was clear that something had been done. The college adopted in 1886 a "new plan" of admissions. Adams' intervention had at least helped loosen a log jam. In the narrower area of the classics it was hard to identify the victor. A student could now enter without taking examinations in both elementary Greek and Latin. If he omitted the former, he had to "pay double" by taking more examinations in more advanced subjects, one of which must be advanced mathematics or physical science. The science alternative was "so difficult as to suggest that it was intended to be prohibitory," and Eliot commented that it required twice as long to master as did Greek. The college took an oath of allegiance to the traditional subjects: "Greek, Latin, and Mathematics will continue to have, as they now have, much greater weight than any of the rest of the elementary subjects." There was also an agreement that the requirements of admission adopted in 1886 be left for six years "without material change." By the time the truce ran out Eliot was dissatisfied with the results of the new plan which he blandly labeled "transitional." The percentage of students entering without Greek had increased, but the figure was far short of revolutionary. There had also been some improvement in instruction in the sciences in the preparatory schools and a larger number of public schools had sent their graduates to Harvard. Though Eliot looked forward to further alterations in this area, Adams hung back. The "Greek War" had given him a success: "For once I touched there a chord to which many minds responded." [42]

A different crusade, the teaching of English composition, now excited Adams and gave him the opportunity to attack from a different angle another of the pretensions of the classics, that the mastery of them was essential to a fine English style. Adams was a member of the overseers' visiting committee on composition and rhetoric; a distinguished associate on the committee was E. L. Godkin, editor of the *Nation*. A dinner party at which Adams entertained Godkin and instructors Wendell, Briggs, Baker, and Kittredge seems to have kindled Adams' interest in the matter. After the occasion he was writing: "The English work at Harvard is better than when I was there and the zeal of the instructors remarkable. But there is an apparent absence of result." The explanation, Adams at first thought, was that "the English literary mind is lying fallow." Since his temperament could not long accept limitations, especially those about which he could do something, he went back to the methods of the Quincy "new departure" and of the Railroad Commission.

Naturally the first step was a thorough preliminary investigation. He and the other members of the committee on composition and rhetoric read entrance examinations, freshman themes, and student replies to questionnaires. Adams took some 1300 themes, at present bound in nine volumes in the Harvard archives, with him to Florence where he read them over the months in a villa he had rented. He was probably the only man who ever conceived of renting a foreign villa in which to read Harvard themes. In spite of the change in setting, the task remained "a terror." [43] The committee made three reports, in 1892, 1895, and 1897. At Adams' expense facsimiles of the student performances formed an appendix to some of these reports. Though student names were omitted, a similar oblivion did not hide the schools from which they came.

Thus informed, the committee advanced its argument and its proposal. The college should neither teach the mechanics of writing English — if it did, "Chairs of Orthography, Chirography, and Punctuation" would "supplement the existing chairs of Rhetoric and Belles-Lettres" — nor in its elementary courses seek to produce literary figures, for "the University could not make new lights." The object of English instruction should be to teach "the habit of talking with the pen instead of with the tongue." The reason this objective had not been attained was the fault of the methods of instruction in the preparatory schools. Even the best of these proceeded upon the false premises that periodic oral recitations and formal compositions and the rendering of Greek and Latin into English gave a student facility in writing. They did not. The last device resulted in "translation English," "a grotesque jargon"; the first two proceeded upon the analogy that you could teach speech by one declamation a week and spend "the rest of the time in Trappist silence." Consequently the committee on composition and rhetoric invited the preparatory schools so to reform themselves that Harvard would not feel compelled to give English A — that "intermediate stage between school and College." [44]

As these three reports of the committee were issued, tension mounted. Adams apparently started the campaign with a self-denying ordinance. As he wrote Eliot, he did not want "merely to stir up a commotion without reaching any beneficial results, and it is these only I care for." The reports of 1892 and 1895, however, stung John Tetlow of the Girls' High and Latin Schools in Boston to deliver before the Massachusetts Classical and High School Teachers' Association an attack upon the method of publishing the reports with facsimiles of translations from Latin and Greek and with identification of the schools. This method falsely applied to education the idea of "remorseless competition by which the material interests of great corporations are promoted." Moreover, he implied, Adams had lost his temper, and he warned: "Unless the Committee means completely to forfeit the respect of the schoolmasters whose work it hopes to influence, it will do well to give no further exhibitions of its ungracious, illogical, and indiscreet zeal." Within three months the overseers received a protest from six schoolmasters. The signers asserted that the explanation for poor English preparation was "the growing illiteracy of American boys" and that the schools were unjustly blamed "for the absence of literary interests and of literary standards in the community." Opposition of this sort raised Adams' temperature and the argument infuriated him: "An opponent having thus delivered himself into your hands, it is more than human nature can stand to ask the average man . . . and I do not profess to be more or less . . . to withhold his hand." [45]

Adams forthwith wrote a reply to the protest sneering at the explanation of the schoolmasters "as a somewhat wide generalization," assailing secret talks rather than open publication as a means of reform, and declaring that the schools must be judged by their results. In the autumn Adams and his committee requested the overseers to pass a resolution that no one should be admitted to Harvard "who cannot, as evidenced by his examination papers as a whole, write the English language with such degree of neatness & skill in penmanship, correctness in spelling & grammar, & with such facility of expression" as would enable him to pursue advanced courses. At the suggestion of Eliot the overseers adopted a substitute motion, stressing the same attainments but dropping the link with the examination papers. At the same time the overseers laid on the table a resolution by one of their members prohibiting the publication of admission examinations in facsimile or in other ways or the attribution of such samples to particular schools. There was the sound of trumpets in the air as Adams readied the committee report of 1897.[46]

Anticlimax ensued. The report which dealt with the 1308

Harvard freshman themes concluded with the intention to deposit this evidence. "It will hereafter speak for itself," particularly "to the Committee which in 1920 or thereabouts may then examine Composition and Rhetoric to know whether our satisfaction with the trend is correct." The relegation of English A to secondary schools the committee believed was both certain and "not remote." "But it is not likely to be hastened by further action on its part. When, however, it is attained, — be that time five years hence, as the Committee hopes, or fifty as may prove to be the case," the school and university can both do their appropriate work better.[47] No word or move could mask so unmistakable a retreat. English A still stands.

As chairman of the committee on reports and resolutions Adams was quite aware that reports of the visiting committees consisted of "one long and somewhat varied, and yet withal extremely monotonous, cry for aid and additional means to do the work in hand." One of the factors, although a subordinate one, in his campaign to get rid of English A was "that it would save the University a whole staff of instructors and some $30,000 a year." The need for economy played like lightning about his growing concern with libraries. Justin Winsor, the librarian of the university, was always asking for more room and money. Adams was against granting either request, until the librarians of Boston adopted a joint policy for "differentiating their acquisitions." "When London, Paris, and St. Petersburg get along with one library apiece, why should . . . little Boston support Harvard, the Public Library, and the Athenaeum. — Our libraries are none of them a century old — yet already they are clogged with strata of worthless literary mud. They are becoming Augean stables." [48] In the 1890's the word "mausoleums" became Adams' favorite designation for libraries. But he scolded without any immediate or visible results.

Early in the twentieth century, however, Harvard's deficits made a consideration of remedies inevitable. Instead of false economies Adams preferred that the tuition fee of $150 be raised to $225 and that the number of prizes or scholarships be enlarged to meet the hardship of students of merit from poorer families. The rich, felt Adams, could afford to pay in a higher tuition the real costs of educating their sons. However familiar and enduring the dilemma and the arguments, the issue then gained importance for its repercussions upon the relations between Eliot and Adams. The president feared an increase in tuition would in fact act to exclude the children of the less well-to-do and harm the better relationships the university was securing with the public schools. Inevitably the concepts of "democracy" versus a "rich man's college" entered the controversy. "I have been trying to see things Eliot's way. Eliot believes in Liberty, Individuality, and Democracy — all spelled with capital letters. He wants to bring Harvard into line with its time and its environment. Liberty means the elective system, Individuality choice according to induction, Democracy — a minimum of barriers to university education. The elective system has led to the 'line of least resistance' and 'soft-snap'. As for his Democracy, it is a catch-word, largely cant. Democracy has no place in education. Fitness is there the only test and rule. In this respect I go far beyond Eliot. My own line is distinctly socialistic . . . And so Eliot and I part company. Eliot has done a great work and will leave a permanent record. But he has materialized rather than elevated it [the University] and organized more than stimulated." In the Greek War it had been "one equal temper of heroic hearts"; in the battle over English Adams got the impression Eliot feared his companion was riding too hard; [49] and finally appreciation had cooled into appraisal.

Since the thrill and warmth had gone, in the summing-up Adams underestimated his own work for the university. He had found it "a hard and distinctly ungrateful subject on which to spend force . . . I might, I now think, have been more profitably employed." More accurate than this disparagement would have been another of his many phrases, "I did good work." He was dedicated, energetic, and foresighted, and his innovating tendencies did something to counter the traditional conservatism of the overseers. Though he often apologized for bringing a material or practical approach to bear upon problems — "I am not a scholar; I am not an educator; I am not a philosopher" — his concreteness of mind was one factor in his unique value. He was also enough of a scholar and littérateur to appreciate that a place of learning was "a wholly other world" [50] and to respect those who lived and worked in it. Informed and sensitive in the areas of business and of education, Adams' career as an officer of Harvard had few equals in distinction and usefulness.

❖ VII ❖

INTO HARBOR AT LAST

1890-1915

AS he "rowed against wind and tide" on the Union Pacific, lived through the financial reverses of the 1890's, or on Sunday trips to Quincy burned his youthful diaries, Adams came to a belated recognition of his real vocation. "I am an artist, that is, it is out of the exercise of the artistic qualities that are in me, that I have always got the greatest enjoyment of life. My work may be very indifferent; but still it gives me pleasure." Then again after John's death: "I am in my sixtieth year. I must be up and doing, — and doing persistently, systematically, constantly. I have but ten years left." "My course now is well enough marked out, — biography, history, and Europe." [1]

Thanks to Adams' habit of self-dramatization, we know the time and occasion when history first stirred him. "I perfectly well remember in the winter of 1848 my father returning from a journey to Washington, and bringing in his hand a paperbound copy of Harper Bros.' cheap reprint of the first volume of Macauley's *England*, then just out. I was thirteen; and of Macauley I had never even heard the name. Boy-like, I picked the book up, and began to turn over its pages. I can see the room and the day now — the dining-room in the Mt. Vernon Street house, the fire in the grate, the hair-covered rocking-chair in which I sat, the table, set for dinner. I took the book up, and almost instantly got absorbed in it. Though I did not the least in the world realize it, I then and there quickened, my aptitude asserted itself. The only trouble afterwards was that, being a mere aptitude and not an overpowering call, this tendency, or inclination, never dominated me to the exclusion of all else." [2]

Later, circumstances drew Adams back to the path of history. Since he came from a distinguished Massachusetts family and was, after all, a Civil War veteran, he had the obvious qualifications for a commemorative or Fourth of July address. The Fourth of July oration, blending history with inspiration, is now as dead as Fast Day; but in the 1860's and 1870's it was still a part of the holiday protocol. Though he had, according to his estimation, general success in this field, Adams regarded as critically significant in his career the oration he delivered at Weymouth. "The Weymouth address of 1874 . . . first set me in motion that way [historical investigation], and I have always felt ever since I owned Weymouth." Adams took nearly a month to write his paper, going over to Weymouth by train, carriage, or afoot. He examined the town records and talked with the natives, particularly the older ones. "All this research interests me greatly, — I hate to have to think of anything else." The address and other ceremonies, including eating, took place on Great Hill in Weymouth. Adams took the precaution of visiting this knoll a few days before and found preparations "truly colossal." On the day itself he drove over with his father and, after the customary prelude of hymns, prayers, poems, and preliminary addresses, he was allowed to speak. Though the local reporter felt Adams held the "undivided attention" of his audience of 2500 adults and 700 school children, Adams was not so sure. It was a "curiously mismanaged affair, a vast tent, a stolid audience, a fairground. Had to change my whole plan and speak extemporaneously." Two days later, still tired and worried, he was sure that his Weymouth address — "the

longest thing I have ever done" — "had fallen flat." "Everything
has gone wrong." [3]

If there were a mode of historical expression lower in the
esteem of modern scholars than the Fourth of July oration, it
would be the collaborative local histories of the late nineteenth
century. These were the fat volumes put together for purely
commercial reasons; the tops of the pages were usually gold-
dipped and the numerous steel engravings of local worthies
wore an expression as if the subject were refusing a "touch"
for five dollars. Adams first wrote a long paper on Massachusetts transportation, by his own admission in a rather slipshod
manner, for the *Memorial History of Boston,* which Justin
Winsor edited. Hardly was this enterprise completed when he
undertook to write a sketch of Quincy for a history of Norfolk
County. As he proceeded, he lost his initial lack of interest and,
gathering momentum, he wrote between November 1883 and
the middle of February 1884 a first draft of 500 pages — "the
most sustained heavy work I ever yet did." In print this sketch
occupies a little over 100 pages. As these essays were done at a
time when his professional and business life was unpleasant
and frustrating, it is little wonder that he looked upon historical work as a lifeline to sanity and continuity. "This is the
great pleasure of my life now — these few morning hours when
I go out of the present world, which I can't manage, into the
past where I am master." He was in the same mood three years
later, when he was on the edge of his presidency in the Union
Pacific and correcting proof on the Quincy article — "For me,
history alone pays." [4]

Clearly his interest in history, which he had once regarded
as merely "a facility in a certain direction," was deepening and
tempting him to a more exclusive commitment. A series of
coincidences hurried him along. When Richard Henry Dana,
once his mentor in the law, died in 1882, Adams presented before the Massachusetts Historical Society an impromptu obitu-

ary which was so effective that it won applause, a response without precedent in that setting. In the end the family solicited Adams to prepare a biography. He nibbled away at this assignment as he traversed his wasteland of the Union Pacific. By 1890 the project was almost completed. It had been quite an ordeal. Business worries brought constant interruptions, and the Dana descendants supervised and altered the manuscript. "These infernal Danas [are] at me again — they are the most infernal crowd of female cranks I ever struck." Providentially the two-volume work appeared at the very moment of his being thrown out of the Union Pacific. "It was literally on two successive days that I ceased to be a railroad man and appeared as an author. A case of out of the darkness and into the light — it could not have been better arranged!" [5]

Without pausing to discover that the biography was "the literary success, at least locally of the season," Adams turned at once to a rewriting and expansion of his earlier piecemeal articles on Quincy. Entitled *Three Episodes in Massachusetts History*, the new treatment in two volumes was easily Adams' single most important historical work. In 1892, when it appeared, Adams was fifty-seven.

Like most productive historians with impressive bibliographies, Adams used the same material over and over. *The Three Episodes* was a case in point. This is really a history of Quincy, put frequently in so large a setting that the history of the town is diffused into that of the Commonwealth. The book is in three parts. The first on the settlement of Massachusetts Bay derives from Adams' Weymouth address. Though interesting in places — particularly on Thomas Morton of Wollaston — the profusion of Indian names and the antiquarian concern in locating the exact point where events took place and in tracing the marches or voyages of Captain Miles Standish hardly distinguish the treatment from more conventional narratives of colonial days. The second part — the Antinomian Controversy

— seems a little lugged in, for the connection with Quincy of two of the rebels, John Wheelwright and Anne Hutchinson, was tangential or episodic. Nevertheless their difficulties with the established church of the Bay Colony gave Adams a magnificent opportunity to air his secularism. Adams had little sympathy with the fine points of theological doctrine but to make explicable the dramatic confrontation between those rebellious individuals and a persecuting clergy he labored hard to comprehend what was meant by a covenant of grace and a covenant of works; according to his diary he "solved the question." Adams' successive treatments of Mrs. Hutchinson as "essentially transcendental" — she might perhaps "not inaptly be termed the great prototype of that misty school" — as "a born social leader," and finally as the forerunner of the late nineteenth century women's rights activist, were diverting as well as enlightening. The third episode, "A Study of Church and Town Government," is more specifically located in Quincy. This part derives largely from Adams' sketch in the Norfolk County history and is somewhat franker in regarding the author's century and his own activities and accomplishments as part of history.[6]

The review of *Three Episodes* by Herbert Osgood, a scholarly authority on American colonial history, hailed the two volumes as "probably the most original and suggestive town history ever written in this country." The critical notices were numerous and always enthusiastic. Incident to this major work and certain editorial duties, Adams had written a sort of postscript, *Massachusetts: Its Historians and Its History*.[7] It would be impossible to characterize this thin volume as a grace note, for the author was far from gracious about most early Massachusetts settlers or those, particularly John G. Palfrey, who had written about them.

Then Adams turned to a family obligation. "I must write my father's life and work the material he left into its proper place in the record. Five years I am prepared to devote to them.

Then we will see what use we can make of life's afternoon." Adams grossly underestimated the length and magnitude of the task. The documentation was staggering. While perusing the 1308 Harvard themes in his Florentine villa in 1891–92, he also finished reading his father's 56-year diary, "a work . . . rather longer than Gibbon's 'Decline and Fall.' " It had taken Charles two years. Other documents and other readings were in the Quincy "mausoleum," the edifice built on the grounds of the "old house" by Charles' father pursuant to a bequest of John Quincy Adams. "Why any man in possession of his ordinary faculties, would, in this climate, have constructed such a cheerless, ill-arranged, and ill-adapted a library building will always remain a mystery to such as did not know my father." [8]

Charles' research burdens and his discontent with his father's character and temperament apparently came through to those in a position to judge. For Henry wrote of the compact single volume Charles succeeded in writing for the American Statesmen series: "These biographies are murder . . . They belittle the victim and the assassin equally." The larger life and the edition of his father's papers forever eluded Charles. A deep diffidence hampered him. Did he have the ability to show his father as he really was? "Now for me comes the test. I will forget he is my father here. I cannot, and should not do so in public." Furthermore the work enlarged as he shaped it. The details of the events and times through which "the governor" moved must be correctly clarified and the characters of the participants understood. By 1912, when Charles had got as far as the Battle of Bull Run, he realized if he were to comprehend his father's mission to England, he must go to Great Britain to consult the public records as well as papers in private hands. Meanwhile there flowed from tongue and pen a series of studies, military and diplomatic. I "see my way clearly through the narrative. The only question is whether I will hold out to get through it." [9]

He did not finish the course. He lacked the will to prevent himself from dissipating his force. He had begun his career of historian as a talker; he finished it in the same way. Naturally he had moved beyond the local scene. In 1900, as president of the Massachusetts Historical Society, the mother society in the country, he brought felicitous greetings to the celebration at Madison dedicating the new building for the Wisconsin Historical Society, and in the evening delivered an address, "The Sifted Grain and the Grain Sifters." Far too long, it encompassed an application of Darwinism to the western movement, an estimate of every major historian who had ever written, and the most careful and systematic statement Adams ever made of his creed as a practitioner of history. Characteristically not wishing his effort to go unnoticed, Adams published 3000 copies of the address at his expense and had the society distribute it.[10] Equally characteristically, he moaned over the amount of work required for this address and over the unlikelihood of any good coming from it.

These dejected reactions fled in 1907 when Washington and Lee invited him to give the address at the university on the centennial observance of Lee's birth. Adams felt a strong pull of duty, because of the historic connections between Massachusetts and Virginia. He had also an unflawed admiration for Lee. Except for Lee, all the Confederate leaders were "failures." "Lee was a great man, — great in defeat, a noble, moral character. The nearer I get to him, the more I admire him. I consider him well-nigh of the highest type of human development." The occasion at Lexington turned out to be "the success of my life!" Adams delivered "Lee's Centennial" in the college chapel with Lee's tomb and recumbent statue behind him. Two days later he left by train. All the students were at the station to give him a send-off and he got away "amid an ovation." [11]

Eventually Adams talked overseas. In 1912–1913 the Rhodes

Scholarship Foundation invited the old man to deliver a few lectures at Oxford. He gave four: all but the last, given in competition with a race of the college eights, went well. Of course he encountered the peculiar circumstances of an English audience trying to understand why they should listen to American history. In the end he observed: "Oxford is, in many respects, a very droll place, and I think those that dwell there are, as a rule, somewhat in doubt as to whether George Washington figured in the late Civil troubles, while Robert E. Lee was in some way connected with the revolutionary war. As to other American notables, I think a reference to the Century Dictionary of names as an elementary source of information, would just about meet requirements." When, on his return to the United States, Adams was invited to lecture at the Johns Hopkins University, he took the Oxford lectures as a starting point. Under his reshaping the four become ten. "I have found cause to modify, if not change, almost every conclusion I had heretofore reached . . . In doing this I am free to confess I get a species of real enjoyment . . . I take almost an absolute pleasure in revising my conclusions and then letting the world . . . into the secret that in my opinion all history, including my own, needs to be rewritten once in ten years." [12]

The addresses were but the highlights of a regime of speaking on civic issues and historical subjects. His "memoirs," addresses, and "contributions" for the Massachusetts Historical Society alone would literally fill volumes. Few have given a more vivid picture of the discomforts and boredom of a career of public speaking: "the long tremors of anticipation," the coming home early to dress, the reception where the speaker grasps "warm, moist, clammy hands, longing, when the shake is done, to rub your sore defiled paw in the hidden folds of your coat-tail," the "banquet" where "there is nothing to drink but water and bad coffee, while the food seems to turn to pulp in your mouth and smites your appetite with the blow of a sandbag." In reflective moments Adams was certain that "If there is one form of literary work which appears to me less profitable than another it is orations and occasional addresses . . . If there is a drearier and, on the whole, less valuable residuum of a life's work than Edward Everett's four volumes of orations and addresses, I am not acquainted with it. Its rhetoric flavors of the past, and, for historical research, it is valueless." Sound though the conviction was, Adams could no more resist an invitation to speak than he could one to buy stock on borrowed money. He had almost as much ability in one field as the other. "I have no histrionic power, I am unable to arouse! I cannot give happy turns, or make a striking point. My efforts are never accentuated by responsive applause. But I do interest." In the end, however, his gift for saying the unpredictable and his intensity gave him the success he craved. On the last day of 1912 he addressed a session of the American Historical Association in Boston and then went on to New York and to bed at his club. "The year ended very pleasantly, the sound of applause still ringing in my ears." [13]

Adams' chief exemplar as a historian was Gibbon's *Decline and Fall of the Roman Empire*, which he read through at least twice. Of the other writers in the English school he had reservations. Carlyle was "a poet rather than an historian," "fatally biased"; Froude, whom Adams read aloud to his wife over a four-month period, had "literary form" but "his judgment was fatally defective"; Macaulay, Adams' early inspiration, was "unquestionably the most popular historian that ever wrote," but he magnified dramatic episodes disproportionately and "the pigments he used are indisputably Whig." Of contemporaries Adams most admired John Richard Green. He had read Green's *Short History of the English People* in 1875 and found it "a very remarkable work"; a quarter of a century later he still esteemed Green for his combination of judgment, dedication to research, and his "well-developed literary sense." [14]

Adams also passed in review the American stalwarts, and though he respected their character he generally found their performance wanting. Irving, Prescott, Hildreth, Bancroft, Motley, and Palfrey either lacked judgment, did not follow correct methods of investigation, or more commonly were deficient in "form and finish." The only exception was Parkman, "perhaps the most individual of all our American historians, the one tasting most racily of the soil," but even with him "the appreciation of form was radically defective." Those interested in intrafamily rivalries may be curious about Charles' reactions to the work of his brothers. Henry's massive work on the Jefferson and Madison administrations Charles found "surprisingly good; he has used his time better than I have mine." As for Brooks's *Emancipation of Massachusetts*, which forecast Charles' own work, it was "poor stuff" by a "writer not to the manor born." [15]

Of the academics who were making history a profession, often after training abroad, Adams knew and respected many — and not only those from Harvard. But the directions they were taking disturbed him. They were apt to write books from libraries rather than from a study of "men in action." The results were frequently fine spun, farfetched, and remote from life. In an evaluation of Confederate leaders, Adams had once dismissed Alexander Stephens, the Confederate vice-president, with the epitaph, "the ideal southern abstractionist. He was a college professor." More alarming among college professors was the habit of ignoring literary presentation: "Everything runs into the monograph, and form is distinctly 'bad form.' " Adams was reminded of Burke's comparison "between the bullocks quietly grazing under the oaks of England and the noisy call of the grasshoppers. I do not mean to say that the professors in our universities resemble more nearly the grasshopper than the bullock, but there is certainly something which suggests the possibility." [16] Ironically, the very year this stigma was applied

to them these noisy, and presumably futile, creatures tendered
their homage to Adams by electing him president of the American Historical Association.

In some ways it did not make much difference whether or not
Adams was thoroughly versed in writings by other historians.
As Edward Channing once informed a meeting of the Massachusetts Historical Society, Charles Francis Adams, Jr., belonged to the "New Historical School," if by that was meant
"that we of the 'New' base our theories on the records while
the older writers copied from one another." Adams certainly
built his work upon the records, though whether such a course
was the novelty that Channing asserted is open to question.
However bookish he was, Adams was sharp enough to realize
that the historian's life was a part of his education. Edward
Gibbon from "an experience among the yeomen's militia of
England derived a certain comprehension of the legionnaires
of Rome," and American historians generally failed to understand the way British trade restrictions worked because of "the
historian rarely having been himself engaged in trade." Action
as financier, government official, and businessman had certainly
given Adams an exceptional variety of experience, and from
these activities had come "much hard common-sense" which
along with erudition and a "developed literary sense" Adams
thought the prerequisites of "the ideal historian." [17]

Inevitably Adams applied the reform temperament to history. One can imagine him impatiently pushing aside Frothingham's *Rise of the Republic* as he exclaimed: "This is a book
of a class out of which I get small profit. There is a good statement of events and much research, but neither interest of nar-
ration nor philosophy of thought. What is the good of annals
except for philosophers to work on." Though in his reform of
American history Adams wasted no time speculating about
the applicability to human affairs of the second law of thermo-
dynamics, he believed that historical events conformed to law:

"All is sequence, all order, all law." When Adams proceeded to concrete causes leading to ordained results, he was apt to select the geographical environment and the details of occupation and employment. Perhaps here he reflected the influence of Buckle. But he did not advance so far along the path of economic determinism as to ignore the moving power of ideas or of individual "character." Massachusetts history, for instance, was a centuries-long struggle toward Religious Toleration and Equality before the Law, both of which he capitalized. Whence came these ideas? After an examination of the origins of the New England town Adams concluded that the ultimate origin of the town's institutions has "to be looked for not in any village or tribal usages, no matter how primitive, but embedded deep in the animal instincts of developed man." Or as he wrote in another connection: "History thus becomes largely a study of character. Insight into temperament is hardly less important than the probing of 'original materials.' " [18]

Adams sought to enlarge, as Macaulay and Green had done, the range of areas included in history. He gave attention to population growth, religion, education, and the way men earned their livelihood and divided their society into classes. The town drunk was in his pages as well as the gentry. The novelty of such inclusiveness reached its apogee in his paper of 1891 before the Massachusetts Historical Society on "Some Phases of Sexual Morality and Church Discipline in Colonial New England." Before the time of Freud and Kinsey such a topic required so much daring that Adams felt he ought "to write this last out with my own hand." The society took the paper with an aplomb which was perhaps a little disappointing to its author. Adams also extended the time range of historical narrative. So far from being exclusively preoccupied with the colonial period, he brought his history of Quincy down to the date when a Knights of Labor political caucus took the town meeting of Quincy out of the hands of the wise, the true, and the good, and incidentally nearly defeated Adams as a trustee of the Crane Library. The *Episodes,* in the words of Herbert Osgood, was "a most interesting sociological study." The book was indeed the history of a people.[19]

Adams pointed out again and again that the real enemy of "scientific history" was sentiment. "The historian invariably scrutinizes the record through eyes jaundiced by faith or patriotism or filial affection or partisan zeal; and he is even lauded for so doing!" "In the literature of our mother tongue there is one great example of the opposite method of historical treatment . . . The History of the Decline and Fall of the Roman Empire still remains the most delightful, instructive, and refreshing of all works of the kind, simply because the man who wrote it — a scholar, an investigator, and a thinker — chanced also to be nothing else — not even what is known in common parlance as a Christian." [20] The campaign against filiopietism in American history was Adams' greatest contribution as a historian. Few were better fitted, by family and by position, to be influential in a crusade against ancestor worship and the notion that the good old days were best. That this cause turned a patrician into a debunker is all the more piquant.

It is tempting to trace the cause of Adams' hostility to filiopietism in history back to his feelings against his father. Actually the sequence should be reversed. The son was bothered by the fact that his own historical principles compelled him to portray his father as he actually was. More certain is the connection of Adams' beliefs about history with his immersion in general reform. He once urged Schurz to write up the anti-imperialist case because: "We are not prepared to enter upon the development of the future until the past is summarized in a philosophical spirit." The functional relation between Adams' historical and reform ideas may have been one explanation for the uneasiness the former occasioned; subversion works by indirection. When Adams read a paper on religious toleration to the Thomas Shepard Society in Cambridge, its members "listened with silent astonishment to my screed on ancestor-worship in history." [21]

The members of the Massachusetts Historical Society were of sterner or more articulate stuff. At the December meeting of 1893 R. C. Winthrop, Jr., in the course of a communication apparently unsolicited, "let off his blunderbuss at my Massachusetts." Though Winthrop willingly admitted that both he and his venerated father had enjoyed the book, he went on to say, "My long intimacy with Mr. Adams has led me to attach a peculiar value to his opinions but I cannot quite consent to regard them in the light of historical data." Toward the close Winthrop added, "I have already drawn attention to several of the flowers of rhetoric distributed by him among his co-workers past and present, but they convey but an imperfect idea of the vigor of a recital which fairly entitles its author to be henceforth regarded in this community as the very Boanerges of iconoclasm. His lectures teem with such additional amenities as 'maze of sophistry', 'self-satisfied complacency', 'cant', 'self-deception', 'systematic narrowness of vision', 'jaundiced eyes', 'perversion of facts', 'distortion of record', 'pages pervaded by degrading beliefs', 'they knew better', 'they had no excuse for not knowing better', 'knowing better, they sinned', and so on." Adams, quite obviously taken by surprise, stalled for time in which to reply. Perhaps what caught him off-balance was the "distinctly impertinent" character of these remarks, or perhaps it was the recapitulation of epithets which he so constantly directed against those who differed with him or had other shortcomings that he thought nothing of their use.[22]

Many motives brought Adams to dedicate himself to history. One was present in all his activities — a desire for success. He craved the approval of experts and was sensitive to the unprofessional opinions of his circle in the Saturday Club and the

Massachusetts Historical Society. But he also was frank to "confess myself a strong advocate of what is sometimes rather contemptuously referred to as the popularization of history. I have but a limited sympathy with those who, from the etherealized atmosphere of the cloister, whether monkish or collegiate, seek truth's essence and pure learning only, regardless of utility, of sympathy or of applause." Consequently he hung like a hawk over sales figures. The *Dana* gave him the first test. About 1300 copies were sold the first year. "Highly encouraging that to an author! Le Roi s'amuse!" He then shifted his hopes to the *Episodes*. "If I could have heard that 20,000 copies of the 'Three Episodes' had been sold, my dearest ambition would have been satisfied; but I didn't hear it, and I never shall hear it." Though he blamed many trivial or extraneous factors for this outcome, he later sensed that modern taste had turned to the sensationalism of current events away from an interest in the past.[23] He did not acknowledge, however, that a family dilemma was at work. With the Adamses, the problem of how to be superior and popular has always been difficult.

In history, as elsewhere, Adams was a doer and organizer rather than a mere talker and dilettante. His instrument was the Massachusetts Historical Society. Its resident membership was co-optative. On June 10, 1875, "My father and I went to Charlestown together to my introductory meeting of the Massachusetts Historical Society, — we met at Mr. Frothinghams and the battle of Bunker Hill was discussed and we visited the ground." Membership in the society was very nearly a prescriptive right for Adamses, for although Charles' older brother had "escaped belonging," to one member "a conundrum which I cannot answer," Charles represented the fourth generation on its roster. He became a member of its council in 1884, soon after he became president of the Union Pacific. In 1890, a few months before he left the railroad, he became a vice-president of the society and was "thus put in line for the succession."

Five years later the expectation was fulfilled. His selection as president filled him with little elation. "More work! — More details!" These might be made palatable if they fell into a grand design.[24]

Whatever the members may have felt about the shift of command, Adams thought his succession a revolution. One of his predecessors, Robert C. Winthrop, had occupied the office from 1855 to 1885. "I liked Mr. W. and from certain points of view admired him; but —." The presidency of the Reverend George E. Ellis, Winthrop's successor, was clearly that of a caretaker government. In a tribute which Adams privately thought "a very neat piece of work," he implied that his predecessor was somewhat of a bumbler — "he discoursed discursively," "he was rather of the antiquarian type" — but he could not dismiss as entirely negligible a clergyman and a former professor in the Harvard Divinity School who, on bequeathing his estate to the university as residuary legatee specified that none of it was to be used for the theological department. The deaths of Winthrop and Ellis marked in Adams' eyes an epoch in the society's history, "for, of necessity, it then passed from the hands of the men of the first half of the century into the hands of the men of its second half. And, in the case of this nineteenth century of ours, that signifies much." [25] Like Ellis, Adams lived to a ripe old age and died in harness as president of the society.

Since presidents of the Massachusetts Historical Society do not deliver programmatic inaugural addresses, Adams stated his intentions piecemeal. Before the first year was out, he presented a long paper on whether the society should remove the limitations on the numbers of its resident members; in this address Adams veiled his own attitude with a primarily historical discussion. If the society wanted to know what its new leader felt on this matter, it could recall Adams' tribute to Robert Winthrop a year back, in the course of which he said, "I am of those who think that neither democracy, as it is called, nor democratic methods, have to do with literature, science, or art. These, in their highest form are the ultimate results of a great concentration of life, wealth and thought, — of evolution, and the survival of the intellectual fittest." [26]

Even if the sacred circle could not be stretched, different tests could be applied as new members were selected to fill vacancies left by death. Since the membership was not large enough to constitute a random sample, there were lags and spurts in mortalities. One of the spurts coincided with Charles' accession to the presidency: "I seem of late to have had imposed upon me more than enough of mortuary reflection amid the urns and sepulchres." Adams proposed that the society depart from the practice of electing only those with an interest, however varied, in history. It should seek out eminence wherever displayed. Apparently he accomplished something, for heretics, radicals, and even those abstractionists, the professors, now joined existing members who continued to think of the society "as a fortress" to hold against lesser breeds without the law. Retrospectively Adams felt that he had been remiss in not altering the quality of the membership more. The society had a tendency to elect "figureheads and mummies." Sometimes it chose a Maecenas. "In the great majority of cases they fail to 'Maecenas' worth a cent." [27]

Historical societies, particularly in New England, tend to accumulate "characters" as administrators. The individual who fulfilled this role par excellence for the Massachusetts Historical Society was Dr. Samuel A. Green. The society had made him librarian in 1868, and in 1895, when Adams became president, Dr. Green became also a vice-president. "The everlasting and inescapable Big Medicine Man," as Adams once derisively designated him, was a singular aggregate of experiences and talents. He was an M.D., and he had had one term as a reform mayor of Boston. Like many old-style librarians, he regarded the society's library as a personal "abiding place." As for policy, he believed in "masterly inactivity." Acquisitions were often unacknowledged, papers were "guarded" rather than catalogued. As the years went by, Green's unsystematic habits and his old age built up a faction in the society bent upon his dismissal. But their plans, even when sweetened with the bribe of a possible honorary degree from Harvard, always went awry. Actually Adams rather liked the flavor of the old man and thought his years entitled him to tender treatment. Green not only had endurance, he had money which the society needed. Adams at one time thought he should "temporarily" resign the presidency and transfer it to Dr. Green in order to rivet tight the hoped-for bequest. Finally in 1913 Green resigned as vice-president, but not as librarian; Adams' resolutions on this change were thought by some to be so kind as to be insincere. When Green died in 1918, he left his accumulations to Lawrence Academy in Groton, Massachusetts, a town for which his passion was so great that, it was said, he never read a novel unless the scene was laid there. But his friendship with John L. Sibley, the librarian of Harvard University, had led Sibley, in his anger at Harvard, to leave his money to the Massachusetts Historical Society, a bequest which today is the largest item in the society's endowment.[28]

During this farce Adams had had a chance to appoint an editor for the society's publications. He chose Worthington C. Ford, sometime of the Boston Public Library and the Congressional Library. Ford was more than a "counterforce" for the "Doctor." His editorship of Bradford's *History of Plymouth Plantation* was one of the scholarly landmarks of the Adams administration. Adams had other tangible successes. In some way, too detailed for chronicling here, enough money was got together from bequests, sales, and contributions to enable the society in 1899 to move out of its "old quarters," nestled among the churches, graveyards, and more congenial bars in the center of Boston, to a building of its own on the edge of the Fenway in Boston's West End. Adams, perhaps trying to match with words the importance of the occasion, gave one of the few really pompous addresses of his career. The "Genius of History" and Charles Darwin wander about in it, and the president of the Massachusetts Historical Society, appraising the Commonwealth's contributions "towards the evolution of man" in the equality of man before the law, in the town meeting, and in the common school, boasted "that the passage of the Red Sea was, from this point of view, not a more momentous event than the voyage of the Mayflower, and that the founding of Boston was fraught with consequences hardly less important than those which resulted from the founding of Rome." Although he added, "I am a prejudiced witness," he did not retract.[29]

"I set a good deal of store by the social side of the Society," wrote Adams in 1914. Customarily he had the members to luncheon after the annual meeting. When he sold the Gloucester Street house in 1896, he had to discontinue the entertaining, which Winthrop had also once proffered. The impossibility of observing this tradition stood him in good stead in 1912, when the American Historical Association held its annual meeting in Boston. A "reception" by the Massachusetts Historical Society was clearly called for. But the president of the American Historical Association was Theodore Roosevelt. "I look forward to it with no considerable satisfaction, as I look upon the President of the Association as a sciolist in history and a fraud in politics." Adams solved his dilemma by running off to his Washington home, forgetting the reception, and entrusting preparations to others. The only specification Adams insisted upon was a champagne or claret cup: "Of course we do not wish . . . to have wine in the morning, unlimited." [30]

By this time Adams was nearing his eighties and fearing if he did not resign the presidency of the society, he might become as great a nuisance in his way as the "Big Medicine Man." For several years, with a composure unexpected in one so impatient, he had noted the checkpoints on the path to oblivion. They flashed by more frequently now. In 1912 he was "utterly unequal to the drudgery of historical investigation. I must have things brought to me and set before me. I can no longer hunt them up. Much less can I rummage and root amid that vast accumulation or refuse known as 'the original material of history.'" He was beset by "eye shortage" and "a certain noticeable physical impairment." He had nevertheless the physical and mental resilience to go to England and deliver his Oxford lectures. "As a result of the excessive strain to which I was subjected and the very infernal weather . . . I contracted an influenza in the nature of a grippe which has sent me home with manifestly impaired strength. I am too old for that sort of fun!" [31]

On his return he recovered from the impairment enough to resume his "talky-talky dinners." In the spring of 1915 he made a swing through the North during which he attended a Lincoln town meeting and addressed the voters on taxation and economy, and for the last time got up from the long oval table in the Dowse Library of the Massachusetts Historical Society and presented some remarks on the death of an associate. All the while he kept flowing his heavy stream of correspondence and his reading. Among the volumes he finished was *Embattled Germany*, a war book justifying the German cause, by Oswald Garrison Villard, the son of his old associate and railroad competitor. "It makes me very tired," snapped Adams, "these chosen people of the Teutonic God; — in fact they are the common enemies of mankind." Two days later, on March 14, 1915, he wrote in his diary: "Spring didn't come but winter wore itself out, clear and fresh. Lost the day for I was not well . . . Read the Sunday papers, and at 1.30 to Lodges for lunch. Got back at 3 o'cl. and then out on Red Oak from 4.15 to 6 o'cl. but was very tired and out of breath. Dined with Henry — he and I alone and very dull. Glad to get to bed at 10.30." [32] It was the last entry. Pneumonia set in.

On March 20, 1915, the impatient, inquiring mind and busy pen fell still. Adams was buried in Quincy in the cemetery which lies on the slope of Mount Wollaston. In November the Massachusetts Historical Society arranged a formal memorial service in the First Church of Boston, and Senator Henry Cabot Lodge, Adams' successor in the presidency of the society, delivered a long memorial address. [33]

Whether Adams would have approved of these obsequies any more than he had previously those of others is problematical. He had his own test for achievement. Really great men "at the end of their labors, leave their profession or calling perceptibly changed and elevated through what they have done in it." Perhaps his disclaimers of reaching this level of achievement were understandable in view of the multitude of his professions. Still this very virtuosity requires a discriminating appraisal. Though he had not invented the commission, no man had done more as prophet, expositor, and practitioner to extend or popularize this instrument of government. It was not confined to railroads. As Governor Russell said in 1891, "With much truth Massachusetts has been described as a commission-governed state." Two decades later a letter to the *Survey* commenting on the labor turmoil of the day, concluded, "Only by commissions shall we learn comprehensively the whole truth." Ironically, though Adams was unlikely to have approved of another utterance in the magazine, there was not a better compact statement of his faith and his reasons for it, than this simple sentence. As a business executive he treaded water. Of himself in this capacity he truly wrote that he "just didn't do it. The last little something was wanting." [34] As a historian he helped keep alive the literary tradition until it fused with the scientific history he also believed in.

The enumeration of categories lets the whole man escape. Adams was memorable for the range of his interests, the intensity of his industry, the incisiveness of his style, his zest and reach for a future, neither catastrophic nor utopian, but one which could be attained by man's reason and efforts. Since they made him "other-minded," these traits were not necessarily endearing, as Adams was the first to recognize. Nor did they completely accord with a time which tended to overvalue materialism and equalitarianism and assume progress was inevitable. But Adams insisted that what he believed was important. That America made as much use of his dissent as it did was a tribute to itself as well as to the merit and force of a distinguished patrician.

Notes

Index

NOTES

I. Catching the Step, 1835–1869

1. C. F. Adams, Diary, Adams Papers (Microfilm Edition, no. 62), May 27, 1835.

2. C. F. Adams, Diary, Adams Papers (Microfilm Edition, no. 78), June 5, 1865.

3. S. E. Morison, "Peter Chardon Brooks," *Dictionary of American Biography*, III, 83; C. F. Adams, Diary, Adams Papers (Microfilm Edition, no. 71), January 4, 1849; C. F. Adams, Jr., to Henry Adams, March 9, 1860, Adams Papers (Microfilm Edition, no. 548).

4. C. F. Adams, Jr., *Charles Francis Adams by His Son* (Boston, 1900), pp. 93–95.

5. C. F. Adams, Jr., Memorabilia, 1888–1893, May 31, 1891, Adams Papers (Massachusetts Historical Society), p. 293; *ibid.*, 1894–1897, August 25, 1894, pp. 539–542.

6. C. F. Adams, Jr., to Henry Adams, Quincy, May 14, 1859, Adams Papers (Microfilm Edition, no. 546); Henry Adams to C. F. Adams, Jr., Rome, May 19, 1860, Adams Papers (Microfilm Edition, no. 549); Adams, Memorabilia, 1888–1893, May 3, 1891, p. 283; C. F. Adams, Jr., Diary, April 27, 1873, Adams Papers (Massachusetts Historical Society); Henry Adams to Elizabeth Cameron, Washington, March 26, 1915, *Letters of Henry Adams, 1892–1918*, ed. W. C. Ford (Boston, 1938), II, 636n.

7. C. F. Adams to Henry Adams, Boston, January 15, 1859, Adams Papers (Microfilm Edition, no. 546). C. F. Adams, Jr., Diary, August 24, 1877; May 23, 1883; June 27, 1886; July 25, 1886; September 18, 1889; September 5, October 10, 1893; February 16, 1894.

8. Henry Adams to C. F. Adams, Boston, December 17–18, 1858, *Letters of Henry Adams, 1858–1891*, ed. W. C. Ford; C. F. Adams, Jr., to Henry Adams, Boston, January 15, 1859, Adams Papers (Microfilm Edition, no. 546).

9. Adams, Diary, May 5, 1896; Adams, Memorabilia, 1894–1897, March 14, 1897, pp. 944–953; "Remarks of John Torrey Morse, Jr.," *Proceedings of the Massachusetts Historical Society*, 60 (1926–1927): 174.

10. Adams, Diary, October 26, 1889; Adams, Memorabilia, 1888–1895, October 22, 1893, p. 498.

11. C. F. Adams, Jr., *Autobiography* (Boston, 1916), pp. 15–16, 19–21; Adams, Memorabilia, 1888–1895, January 24, 1893, p. 413; Henry Adams,

The Education of Henry Adams, An Autobiography (Boston, 1918), p. 54; Phillips Brooks, "The Boston Latin School," *Essays and Addresses, Religious, Literary, and Social* (New York, 1894), p. 418; George Santayana, *Persons and Places* (New York, 1944), pp. 151–158; Charles W. Eliot, "A Conservative School," *Two Hundred and Seventy-fifth Anniversary of the Boston Latin School* (n.p., 1910), pp. 26–27.

12. Adams, Diary, October 20, 1889; Adams, *Autobiography*, pp. 22–23; Adams, Memorabilia, 1889–1893, January 24, 1893, p. 419; *Two Hundred and Seventy-fifth Anniversary*, p. 43.

13. Adams, Memorabilia, 1889–1893, June 1, 1893, p. 480; Adams, Diary, June 15, 1893, June 26, 1895; Adams, Memorabilia, 1889–1893, June 17, 1893, p. 488; C. F. Adams, Jr., "The Journeyman's Retrospect," *Three Phi Beta Kappa Addresses* (Boston, 1907), p. 152.

14. *Twenty-ninth Annual Report of the President of Harvard College to the Overseers, 1853–1854*, p. 27; *Thirty-first Annual Report of the President of Harvard College to the Overseers, 1855–1856*, p. 25; *Thirty-second Annual Report of the President of Harvard College to the Overseers, 1856–1857*, p. 13; Henry James, *Charles W. Eliot, President of Harvard University, 1869–1909* (Boston, 1930), I, 236–237.

15. C. B. Frothingham, "Memoir of Rev. James Walker, D.D., LL.D.," *Proceedings of the Massachusetts Historical Society*, second series, 6 (1890–1891): 454–468; C. F. Adams, Jr., *Richard Henry Dana, A Biography* (Boston, 1890), II, 151–152; *Thirty-first Annual Report of the President of Harvard College to the Overseers, 1855–1856*, pp. 4–5; Adams, Memorabilia, 1887–1893, March 10, 1891, p. 247.

16. *Twenty-eighth Annual Report of the President of Harvard College to the Overseers, 1852–1853*, p. 24; *Thirty-second Annual Report of the President of Harvard College to the Overseers, 1856–1857*, p. 22; C. F. Adams, Jr., "A College Fetich," *Three Phi Beta Kappa Addresses* (Boston, 1907), pp. 3–11.

17. S. E. Morison, *Three Centuries of Harvard, 1636–1936* (Cambridge, Mass., 1936), pp. 260, 263; Adams, *Autobiography*, p. 26; G. S. Hillard, "Memoir of Cornelius Conway Felton, LL.D.," *Proceedings of the Massachusetts Historical Society*, first series, 1867–1869, pp. 360–361.

18. Adams, *Autobiography*, pp. 33–34.

19. Adams, Memorabilia, 1894–1897, November 25, 1895, pp. 676–679; Adams, *Autobiography*, pp. 24–30; *Harvard Graduates' Magazine*, 23 (1914–1915): 677.

20. Adams, "The Journeyman's Retrospect," p. 153; Adams, *Autobiography*, p. 26; *Harvard Graduates' Magazine*, 23 (1914–1915): 677; Adams, Memorabilia, 1894–1897, November 25, 1895, p. 710.

21. Adams, Diary, December 12, 1864, and February 10, 14, 17, 24, 1889; Adams, *Autobiography*, pp. 27–28.

22. C. F. Adams, Jr., to Henry Adams, Quincy, October 9, 1858, Adams

Papers (Microfilm Edition, no. 545); *Report of the Harvard Class of 1853, 1849–1913* (Cambridge, Mass., 1913), pp. 15–16.

23. "Remarks of John Torrey Morse, Jr.," pp. 172–173; T. W. Higginson, *Cheerful Yesterdays* (Cambridge, Mass., 1898), pp. 62–63.

24. Adams, *Dana*, II, 138; Adams, *Autobiography*, pp. 38–39, 41–42; C. F. Adams, Jr., to Henry Adams, Boston, December 1859, Adams Papers (Microfilm Edition, no. 547).

25. C. F. Adams, Jr., to Henry Adams, Boston, December 19, 1858, Adams Papers (Microfilm Edition, no. 543); same to same, Boston, March 13, 1859, Adams Papers (Microfilm Edition, no. 547).

26. C. F. Adams, Jr., to Henry Adams, Boston, July 29, 1859, Adams Papers (Microfilm Edition, no. 547).

27. C. F. Adams, Jr., to Henry Adams, Boston, November 25, 1858, Adams Papers (Microfilm Edition, no. 545); same to same, Boston, November 3, 1859, Adams Papers (Microfilm Edition, no. 547); same to same, Boston, November 1, 1859, Adams Papers (Microfilm Edition, no. 547); same to same, Boston, November 3, 1859, Adams Papers (Microfilm Edition, no. 547).

28. C. F. Adams, Jr., to Henry Adams, Boston, December 19, 1858; same to same, Boston, January 15, 1859, Adams Papers (Microfilm Edition, no. 546); same to same, Boston, July 2–9, 1859, Adams Papers (Microfilm Edition, no. 547); same to same, Boston, January 15, 1857, Adams Papers (Microfilm Edition, no. 544); Adams, Memorabilia, 1894–1897, February 6, 1896, p. 706; Samuel A. Drake, *Old Landmarks and Historic Personages of Boston* (Boston, 1873), p. 394.

29. C. F. Adams, Jr., to Henry Adams, Boston, April 25, 1859, Adams Papers (Microfilm Edition, no. 546); same to same, Boston, December 1859, Adams Papers (Microfilm Edition, no. 547); C. F. Adams to C. F. Adams, Jr., Washington, April 21, 1860, and same to same, Washington, May 9, 1860, Adams Papers (Microfilm Edition, nos. 548, 549).

30. Martin B. Duberman, *Charles Francis Adams, 1802–1886* (Boston, 1961), pp. 139–215.

31. C. F. Adams, Jr., to Henry Adams, Boston, March 9, 1860, Adams Papers (Microfilm Edition, no. 548); same to same, Boston, January 15, 1859, Adams Papers (Microfilm Edition, no. 546).

32. Adams, *Autobiography*, pp. 57–65; C. F. Adams, Jr., "Campaigning with Seward in 1860," ed. T. C. Blegen, *Minnesota History*, 8 (1927): 165–171.

33. Adams, *Autobiography*, pp. 85, 89, 107–113; Adams, Diary, March 4, 1861.

34. Adams, *Autobiography*, p. 41; C. F. Adams, Jr., "The Reign of King Cotton," *Atlantic Monthly*, 7 (April 1861): 450–465; F. L. Olmsted to C. F. Adams, Jr., Central Park, New York, March 25, 1861, Adams Papers (Microfilm Edition, no. 553).

35. Unsigned letter to C. F. Adams, Jr., Cambridge, March 27, 1861, Adams Papers (Microfilm Edition, no. 553); T. S. Clark to C. F. Adams, Jr., Boston, March 5, 1861, Adams Papers (Microfilm Edition, no. 553); Adams, *Autobiography*, p. 41.

36. Adams, *Autobiography*, pp. 114–115; C. F. Adams, Diary, November 16, 1861, Adams Papers (Microfilm Edition, no. 76).

37. Adams, *Autobiography*, p. 125.

38. Adams, Memorabilia, 1894–1897, February 6, 1896, p. 707; C. F. Adams, Jr., to J. Q. Adams, November 28, 1862, *A Cycle of Adams Letters, 1861–1865*, ed. W. C. Ford (Boston, 1920), I, 197–198.

39. Adams, *Autobiography*, p. 124; C. F. Adams, Diary, January 2, 1861, Adams Papers (Microfilm Edition, no. 76).

40. John T. Morse, "Memoir of Henry Lee," *Proceedings of the Massachusetts Historical Society*, second series, 19 (1905): 235–253.

41. B. W. Crowninshield, *A History of the First Regiment of Massachusetts Cavalry Volunteers* (Boston, 1891), pp. 317–324; C. F. Adams, Jr., to F. W. Palfrey, Beaufort, S.C., February 7, 1862, Adams Papers (Microfilm Edition, no. 557); Adams, *Autobiography*, pp. 130–132, 137.

42. C. F. Adams, Diary, January 22, 1861, Adams Papers (Microfilm Edition, no. 76); C. F. Adams, Jr., to F. W. Palfrey, Beaufort, S.C., February 7, 1862, Adams Papers (Microfilm Edition, no. 557).

43. Adams, *Autobiography*, p. 153; C. F. Adams, Jr., to C. F. Adams, Beaufort, February 28, 1862, *A Cycle of Adams Letters*, I, 115–117; Jere Abbott to C. F. Adams, Jr., Boston, May 22, 1863, Adams Papers (Microfilm Edition, no. 564).

44. Adams, *Autobiography*, pp. 148, 153–154; Crowninshield, *First Regiment of Massachusetts Cavalry*, pp. 143–160; Adams, Diary, July 2, 3, 4, 1863; Adams, "The Journeyman's Retrospect," pp. 156–157.

45. C. F. Adams, Jr., to C. F. Adams, Potomac Run, January 28, 1863, *A Cycle of Adams Letters*, I, 246–247; C. F. Adams, Jr., to Abigail B. Adams, Potomac Creek, May 12, 1863, and C. F. Adams, Jr., to Henry Adams, Harpers Ferry, July 18, 1863, *A Cycle of Adams Letters*, II, 3–5, 50.

46. C. F. Adams, Jr., to Henry Adams, Armiesville, Va., August 2, 1863, *A Cycle of Adams Letters*, II, 68; C. F. Adams, Jr., to C. F. Adams, Potomac Creek Bridge, Va., May 24, 1863, *A Cycle of Adams Letters*, II, 13; *The Report of the Secretary of the Class of 1856, Harvard, January 1865* (Boston, 1865), pp. 5–6; Adams, Diary, January 23, 29, 1864.

47. Adams, Diary, February 16, 18, 25, March 7, 8, 9, 10, 1864.

48. C. F. Adams, Jr., to C. F. Adams, Potomac Run, Va., December 2, 1862, *A Cycle of Adams Letters*, I, 218; Caspar Crowninshield to C. F. Adams, Jr., Gloucester Point, Va., April 14, 1865, Adams Papers (Microfilm Edition, no. 563); Adams, *Autobiography*, pp. 154–155.

49. Adams, Diary, May 6, 25, 1864; C. F. Adams, Jr., to Abigail B.

Adams, Petersburg, August 27, 1864, *A Cycle of Adams Letters*, II, 185.
50. Henry G. Pearson, *The Life of John A. Andrew, Governor of Massachusetts, 1861–1865* (Boston, 1904), II, 90–94; Adams, Diary, September 1, 2, 1864; C. F. Adams, Jr., to C. F. Adams, Point Lookout, Md., November 2, 1864, *A Cycle of Adams Letters*, II, 213; same to same, Hillsboro, Va., July 22, 1863, and same to same, near Warrenton, Va., October 31, 1863, *A Cycle of Adams Letters*, II, 52–53, 99; C. F. Adams, Jr., to Henry Adams, Point Lookout, Md., September 18, 1864, and C. F. Adams, Jr., to C. F. Adams, Point Lookout, Md., November 2, 1864, *A Cycle of Adams Letters*, II, 194–195, 214–219.

51. Adams, Diary, October 7, 12, 16, November 6, 16, 19, 24, December 25, 1864; Adams, *Autobiography*, pp. 165–167; C. F. Adams, Jr., to C. F. Adams, near Petersburg, April 10, 1865, *A Cycle of Adams Letters*, II, 261–262; Adams, *Autobiography*, pp. 166–167; Crowninshield, *First Regiment of Massachusetts Cavalry*, p. 322.

52. C. F. Adams, Jr., to C. F. Adams, John's Island, South Carolina, June 18, 1862, *A Cycle of Adams Letters*, II, 156; Adams, *Autobiography*, p. 167; Adams, Memorabilia, 1894–1897, April 10, 1895, p. 621.

53. *Report of the Secretary of the Class of 1856, January, 1865*, p. 6; C. F. Adams, Jr., to C. F. Adams, January 16, 1864, *A Cycle of Adams Letters*, II, 118–119.

54. Adams, Diary, January 29, 30, 31, December 13, 14, 15, 1864.

55. Adams, Memorabilia, 1894–1897, February 13, 1895, pp. 577–585.

56. *Washington Wife: Journal of Ellen Maury Slayden from 1897–1919*, ed. Walter P. Webb (New York, 1963), p. 275.

57. C. F. Adams, to C. F. Adams, Jr., London, March 17, 1865, Adams Papers (Microfilm Edition, no. 573); Adams, Memorabilia, 1901–1905, April 5, 1905, p. 2682; *ibid.*, 1888–1893, June 30, 1889.

II. Railroad Reformer, 1869–1890

1. C. F. Adams, Jr., to Henry Adams, Boston, February 14, 1859, Adams Papers (Microfilm Edition, no. 546); C. F. Adams, Jr., to Henry Adams, Potomac River, Md., January 23, 1863, *A Cycle of Adams Letters, 1861–1865*, ed. W. C. Ford (Boston, 1920), I, 238–239; Henry Adams to C. F. Adams, Jr., London, November 21, 1862, *A Cycle of Adams Letters*, I, 196.

2. C. F. Adams, Jr., "An Undeveloped Function," *American Historical Review*, 7 (January 1902): 214–215, 232.

3. C. F. Adams, Jr., to C. F. Adams, Quincy, November 26, 1861, *A Cycle of Adams Letters*, I, 73; C. F. Adams, Jr., to Henry Adams, March 22, 1863, *A Cycle of Adams Letters*, I, 266–267; Adams, Diary, August 21, 1887 (Massachusetts Historical Society); C. F. Adams, Jr., *A College Fetich* (Boston, 1884), p. 13.

4. U.S. Bureau of the Census, *Historical Statistics of the United States*,

Colonial Times to 1957 (Washington, 1960), p. 427; Massachusetts, *First Annual Report of the Board of Railroad Commissioners, January, 1870,* pp. 43–44.

5. Edward C. Kirkland, *Men, Cities and Transportation* (Cambridge, Mass., 1948), I, 362–432; II, 32–71.

6. Kirkland, *Men, Cities and Transportation,* I, 226–284; F. L. Merk, "Eastern Antecedents of the Grangers," *Agricultural History,* 23 (January 1949): 1–8.

7. Adams, Diary, April 14, 1869, August 21, 1887; A. D. Chandler, *Henry Varnum Poor, Business Editor, Analyst, and Reformer* (Cambridge, Mass., 1956), pp. 20–185.

8. C. F. Adams, Jr., "The Railroad System," *North American Review,* 104 (April 1867): 479–480.

9. *Ibid.,* pp. 507–508.

10. *Ibid.,* p. 497n.

11. C. F. Adams, Jr., "Boston," *North American Review,* 106 (January 1868): 25; 106 (April 1868): 591.

12. C. F. Adams, Jr., "Legislative Control over Railway Charters," *American Law Review,* 1 (April 1867): 451–476; C. F. Adams, Jr., "Railroad Legislation," *American Law Review,* 2 (October 1867): 25–46; C. F. Adams, Jr., "Railroad Inflation," *North American Review,* 108 (January 1869): 130–164.

13. C. F. Adams, Jr., "A Chapter of Erie," *North American Review,* 109 (July 1869): 30–106.

14. Adams, Diary, April 11, 14, 1869.

15. *Ibid.,* January 8, March 19, 20, 24, April 5, May 12, 15, July 20, 21, 23, October 9, 1869; January 24, 1870; January 8, 1872.

16. *Ibid.,* May 28, June 9, 11, 18, 20, 28, July 5, 1869; C. F. Adams, Jr., *Autobiography* (Boston, 1916), p. 173.

17. C. F. Adams, Jr., *Railroads: Their Origin and Problems* (New York, 1878), p. 138; *Acts and Resolves Passed by the General Court of Massachusetts in the Year 1869,* pp. 699–703.

18. Adams, *Railroads,* p. 138.

19. *Ibid.,* p. 138; Adams, Diary, July 13, 1869, August 2, 1869, and May 2, 1871; C. F. Adams, Jr., Memorabilia, 1888–1893, December 29, 1891, p. 343, Adams Papers (Massachusetts Historical Society); Kirkland, *Men, Cities and Transportation,* II, 244.

20. Adams, Diary, July 1, September 13, December 13, 1869; November 10, 11, 1871; February 23, 1881. Adams, Memorabilia, 1888–1893, December 29, 1891, p. 345. Kirkland, *Men, Cities and Transportation,* II, 244.

21. C. F. Adams, Jr., "Boston," *North American Review,* 106 (January 1868): 24; Kirkland, *Men, Cities and Transportation,* II, 32–54.

22. Kirkland, *Men, Cities and Transportation,* I, 387–432.

23. Adams, Diary, August 20, 1869, May 31, 1870.

24. Adams, Diary, March 27, 1875, September 3, 1878; Kirkland, Men, Cities and Transportation, I, 417.

25. Kirkland, Men, Cities and Transportation, II, 44–46; Adams, Diary, April 12, May 7, 1870.

26. Adams, Railroads, p. 140; Adams, Diary, January 20, 1870, March 7, 1871, and May 8, 1872.

27. Acts and Resolves of Massachusetts, 1869, index, pp. xxx–xxxiv; Acts and Resolves of Massachusetts, 1874, pp. 347–406; Massachusetts, Fifth Annual Report of the Board of Railroad Commissioners, January, 1874, pp. 45–46.

28. Acts and Resolves of Massachusetts, 1872, pp. 40–45.

29. Massachusetts, Third Annual Report of the Board of Railroad Commissioners, January, 1872, pp. lxxxvii–lxxxix; Massachusetts, Seventh Annual Report of the Board of Railroad Commissioners, January, 1876, pp. 25–27; Acts and Resolves of Massachusetts, 1870, pp. 226–227.

30. Fifth Annual Report of the Railroad Commissioners, 1874, p. 21.

31. Ibid., pp. 15–16.

32. Seventh Annual Report of the Railroad Commissioners, 1876, pp. 27, 34; Acts and Resolves of Massachusetts, 1876, pp. 156–157; Eighth Annual Report of the Railroad Commissioners, 1877, pp. 12–17, 83–102.

33. Kirkland, Men, Cities and Transportation, II, 235.

34. C. F. Adams, Jr., Notes on Railroad Accidents (New York, 1879), pp. 141–142; Second Annual Report of the Railroad Commissioners, 1871, p. xxx; Third Annual Report of the Railroad Commissioners, 1872, pp. xcv–cv, cxxix–cxlv.

35. Adams, Notes on Railroad Accidents, pp. v–vi, 248–249; Kirkland, Men, Cities and Transportation, II, 360f.

36. Third Annual Report of the Railroad Commissioners, 1872, pp. xcv–xcix, cxxxvi–cxxxvii.

37. Kirkland, Men, Cities and Transportation, II, 412–415; Adams, Diary, February 15, 16, 17, 18, 19, 20, 23, 1877; Adams, Autobiography, pp. 174–175.

38. Ninth Annual Report of the Railroad Commissioners, 1878, pp. 46–65; W. F. Bucknam, A History of Boston Division Number Sixty-one Brotherhood of Locomotive Engineers (Boston, 1906), p. 108.

39. First Annual Report of the Railroad Commissioners, 1870, pp. 58–63; Fourth Annual Report of the Railroad Commissioners, 1873, pp. 79–81; Fifth Annual Report of the Railroad Commissioners, 1874, pp. 48–50, 58–60; Fifteenth Annual Report of the Railroad Commissioners, 1884, p. 151; C. F. Adams, Jr., "The Granger Movement," North American Review, 120 (April 1875): 394–424.

40. First Annual Report of the Railroad Commissioners, 1870, pp. 46–47, 121–122; Second Annual Report of the Railroad Commissioners, 1871, pp. vii–x, xlvi–lxx; Fifth Annual Report of the Railroad Commissioners,

1874, pp. 22–27; *Seventh Annual Report of the Railroad Commissioners, 1876*, pp. 52–60; *Ninth Annual Report of the Railroad Commissioners, 1878*, p. 124.

41. *Tenth Annual Report of the Railroad Commissioners, 1879*, pp. 54–55.

42. Adams, Diary, April 24, 1870; March 26, August 8, 1878; January 18, March 29, 1879. Adams, *Autobiography*, pp. 173–174. Adams, Memorabilia, 1888–1893, June 30, 1889, p. 80. W. D. Mallam, "The Fight for the Old Granite Block," *New England Quarterly*, 36 (March 1963): 42–62. E. C. Kirkland, *Industry Comes of Age, Business, Labor and Public Policy, 1860–1897* (New York, 1961), pp. 116–120.

43. Adams, *Autobiography*, pp. 175–176.

44. Adams, Memorabilia, 1888–1893, June 30, 1889, p. 81.

45. C. F. Adams, Jr., to Carl Schurz, Boston, May 5, 1879, Carl Schurz Papers, Library of Congress.

46. Testimony of Albert Fink, *Report of the Committee of the Senate, on Labor and Capital, 1885*, II, 463f; Kirkland, *Industry Comes of Age*, pp. 86–88.

47. Adams, *Railroads*, pp. 191–196.

48. Adams, Memorabilia, 1888–1893, June 30, 1889, p. 82, and November 23, 1890, p. 142; Adams, Diary, April 28, May 2, 1879; *Proceedings and Circulars of the Joint Executive Committee*, [of the Trunk-Line Railroads], January 19, February 1, March 2, 1882.

49. Adams, Diary, May 23, September 17, 1879.

50. Adams, Memorabilia, 1888–1893, June 30, 1889, p. 83; Adams, Diary, August 20, December 6, 9, 28, 31, 1881; January 7, 1882; June 27, 1884.

51. Testimony of C. F. Adams, Jr., Report of the [Cullom] Senate Select Committee on Interstate Commerce, 49 Cong., 1 Sess., *Senate Report*, no. 46, vol. II (serial no. 2537), pp. 1207–1208.

52. Adams, Memorabilia, 1888–1893, February 24, 1889, p. 48, and June 30, 1889, pp. 83–84; Adams, Diary, December 22, 1887.

53. "Mr. Adams and Mr. Thurber," *Nation*, April 2, 1881, pp. 294–295.

54. Adams, Memorabilia, 1888–1893, January 13, 1889, pp. 18–20.

55. Adams, *Autobiography*, p. 176.

III. Making a Fortune, 1869–1890

1. C. F. Adams, Jr., "The Protection of the Ballot in National Elections," *Journal of Social Science*, 1 (June 1869): 108.

2. C. F. Adams, Jr., Memorabilia, 1888–1893, June 30, 1889, p. 81, Adams Papers (Massachusetts Historical Society); C. F. Adams, Jr., Diary, February 24, 1871, April 12, 1873, Adams Papers (Massachusetts Historical Society).

3. Adams, Diary, March 31, 1876; Adams, Memorabilia, 1888–1893, November 13, 1891, p. 321.

4. William B. Gates, Jr., *Michigan Copper and Boston Dollars* (Cambridge, Mass., 1951), pp. 43–45, 217–224; Adams, Diary, April 7, 1872, April 3, 1875, December 14, 1877, and May 30, 1878; *Geological Survey of Michigan, Upper Peninsula, 1869–1873* (New York, 1873), I, 47, 117; Henry R. Mussey, *Combination in the Mining Industry: A Study of Concentration in Lake Superior Iron Ore Production* (New York, 1905), pp. 50–102, 167.

5. Adams, Diary, February 2, August 15, October 4, 1880; September 15, December 9, 15, 22, 1881; June 26, 1882.

6. *Ibid.*, June 15, 1871; January 9, May 3, July 22, August 30, 1872; October 30, 1873; March 31, November 24, 1874; January 4, 9, 14, 1878; December 5, 1880. *Geological Survey of Michigan, 1869–1873*, I, 21–23, 61–64.

7. Adams, Diary, August 14, 15, 16, 1872; Julius Grodinsky, *The Iowa Pool. A Study in Railroad Competition, 1870–84* (Chicago, 1950), pp. 9–11; *Poor's Manual of Railroads, 1874–1875*, p. 615; *Poor's Manual of Railroads, 1876–1877*, p. 408.

8. Adams, Diary, December 31, 1888; "Southern Regeneration and the English Land Question," *Nation*, November 13, 1879, p. 323.

9. W. W. Belcher, *The Economic Rivalry between St. Louis and Chicago, 1850–1880* (New York, 1947), p. 79; C. W. Glaab, *Kansas City and the Railroads, Community Policy in the Growth of a Regional Metropolis* (Madison, Wis., 1962), pp. 103–123; U.S. Bureau of the Census, *Compendium of the Tenth Census (1880)*, pp. 4, 5, 6; Joseph C. McCoy, *Historic Sketches of the Cattle Trade of the West and Southwest*, ed. Ralph P. Bieber (Glendale, Calif., 1940), pp. 111–134, 347–348.

10. F. W. Blackmer, *Kansas, A Cyclopedia of State History* (Chicago, 1912), II, 50–52. McCoy, *Cattle Trade*, pp. 329–333. Cuthbert Powell, *Twenty Years of Kansas City's Live Stock Trade and Traders* (Kansas City, Mo., 1893), pp. 15, 18–20. Adams, Diary, August 28, 1872; October 31, November 28, 1873; September 4, 1878.

11. Charles F. Morse, *A Sketch of My Life Written for My Children* (Cambridge, Mass., 1927), pp. 7–42, 65.

12. McCoy, *Cattle Trade*, pp. 348–349; C. F. Adams, Jr., *Autobiography* (Boston, 1916), pp. 187–188; Adams, Diary, June 10, 1877.

13. Morse, *A Sketch of My Life*, pp. 49–55. Adams, Diary, October 22, 1878; March 7, 15, 17, 18, 24, October 12, 13, 14, 15, December 29, 1879; April 1, 9, 1880; June 19, 22, 1882; June 9, 29, 1885; October 3, 1887. Adams, *Autobiography*, p. 188.

14. Adams, Diary, January 25, 1888 (entry follows December 31, 1888), August 27, 1888, and September 7, 1889.

15. Morse, *A Sketch of My Life*, p. 61. Adams, Diary, April 28, December 24, 1865; July 26, 1867; August 10, September 2, 6, 7, 1889.

16. Adams, Diary, August 31, 1888; July 12, 17, August 23, 27, September 21, 1889; March 18, 1896. Adams, Memorabilia, 1888–1893, October 8, 1889, pp. 90–92 and July 4, 1890, p. 125.

17. Adams, Diary, May 15, 20, 21, 1870; May 25, June 4, 1871; August 25, 1872; May 12, September 18, 23, 1874; September 7, 30, 1875; October 18, 1879; October 12, 1882; July 25, 1885; May 15, 1887; March 27, April 3, 1888; September 15, 1889.

18. Edward C. Kirkland, "Boston during the Civil War," *Proceedings of the Massachusetts Historical Society*, 71 (1953–1957): 201–202; Adams, Diary, March 16, May 12, 13, 15, 1886.

19. Adams, Diary, December 1, 1871; October 23, 1873; February 24, 1881; September 17, 1888; January 13, December 31, 1889; September 10, 1893; August 28, 1896.

20. Adams, Diary, March 25, April 9, 1874; April 1, 2, 1881; January 31, May 1, 1884; November 25, 1886; March 17, 1897.

21. Adams, Memorabilia, 1888–1893, June 18, 1889, pp. 72–73.

22. Adams, Diary, March 6, 1872, and March 25, 1896; T. Jefferson Coolidge, *Autobiography, 1851–1920* (Boston, 1923), pp. 86–87.

23. Adams, Diary, October 15, 1879; March 30, October 9, 1880; November 28, 29, 1881; September 7, 1888; January 25, 1888 (entered after December 31, 1888). Assessor's Valuation List, Quincy Archives, May 1, 1890. Adams, *Autobiography*, p. 188.

24. Adams, Diary, December 10, 1877.

25. *Ibid.*, February 18, 1869; December 31, 1881; December 31, 1886; August 21, December 31, 1887; January 13, December 31, 1889.

26. Adams, Diary, February 24, 1871, December 31, 1886, and August 21, 1887; Adams, Memorabilia, 1888–1893, November 26, 1891, pp. 329–331.

IV. The Union Pacific Failure, 1883–1890

1. 4 *United States Statutes at Large*, 70; 12 *United States Statutes at Large*, 489–498; 13 *United States Statutes at Large*, 356–365; Report of the Select Committee [Wilson] on the Credit Mobilier, 42d Cong., 3d Sess., *House Report*, no. 78 (serial no. 1577), p. xx.

2. *Poor's Manual of the Railroads for 1884*, pp. 773–774; 13 *Statutes at Large*, 358, 360, 361.

3. *Report of the Directors of the Union Pacific Railway Company to the Stockholders for the Year Ending December 31, 1885*, p. 147; "Oakes Ames," *Dictionary of American Biography*, I, 251–253; "Oliver Ames," *Dictionary of American Biography*, I, 253–254; "Frederick Lothrop Ames," *Dictionary of American Biography*, I, 246–247; testimony of C. T. Sherman, C. S. Bushnell, Oliver Ames and J. B. Alley, Report on the Credit Mobilier, 42d Cong., 3d Sess., *House Report*, no. 78 (serial no. 1577), pp. 40–41, 55, 252, 557–558, 664.

4. *Report of the Union Pacific, 1885*, p. 147; testimony of Jay Gould, *Report of the United States Pacific Railway Commission*, 50th Cong., 1st Sess., *Senate Executive Document*, no. 51, vols. I and II (serial no. 2505), pp. 447, 449–466; *Commercial and Financial Chronicle*, 40: 570; C. F. Adams, Jr., to J. H. Wilson, Boston, February 20, 1881, J. H. Wilson Papers, Library of Congress; same to same, Boston, undated.

5. J. F. Rhodes, *History of the United States from the Compromise of 1850* (New York, 1906), VII, 4–9; Solon J. Buck, *The Granger Movement* (Cambridge, Mass., 1913), pp. 194–199.

6. Report of the Select Committee [Poland] To Investigate the Alleged Credit Mobilier Bribery, 42d Cong., 3d Sess., *House Report*, no. 77 (serial no. 1577), pp. v–xix; testimony of Oakes Ames, *ibid.*, pp. 15–23; Report on the Credit Mobilier, *House Report*, no. 78 (serial no. 1577), pp. i, iii, xx; Robert W. Fogel, *The Union Pacific Railroad, A Case in Premature Enterprise* (Baltimore, 1960), pp. 69, 70, 72, 84–90.

7. *Report of the Union Pacific, 1885*, p. 147; 17 *United States Statutes at Large*, 508–509; Remarks of Senator Morgan, *Congressional Record*, 45th Cong., 2d Sess., vol. VII, pt. 2, p. 1860.

8. United States v. Union Pacific Railroad Company, 91 *United States*, 78; United States v. Union Pacific Railroad Company, 98 *United States*, 601.

9. 98 *United States*, 601.

10. 20 *United States Statutes at Large*, 56–61, 169–171; C. F. Adams, Jr., to Carl Schurz, Boston, April 5, 1880, Schurz Papers, Library of Congress.

11. C. F. Adams, Jr., "Railroad Inflation," *North American Review*, 108 (January 1869): 144–147. C. F. Adams, Jr., to Carl Schurz, Boston, March 23, 1878; same to same, Boston, October 31, 1878; same to same, Boston, May 5, 1879, Schurz Papers, Library of Congress. C. F. Adams, Jr., to J. H. Wilson, Omaha, October 29, 1883, J. H. Wilson Papers, Library of Congress. Boston *Daily Advertiser*, December 19, 1882, p. 3. Adams, Diary, March 16, 23, 1878; November 16, 1882; January 26, February 5, 23, 27, March 7, 1883.

12. *Commercial and Financial Chronicle*, April 18, 1884, p. 480, May 17, 1884, p. 582, and June 7, 1884, p. 669; Union Pacific Railway Company v. United States, 104 *United States*, 662; letter from the Secretary of the Interior, 48th Cong., 1st Sess., *Senate Executive Documents*, no. 121 (serial no. 2167), p. 4; *Congressional Record*, 48th Cong., 1st Sess., vol. XV, pt. 5, pp. 5319, 5325, 5517.

13. Adams, Diary, April 20, 22, May 2, 5, 26, 27, 28, 29, 30, 31, and June 22, 23, 24, 1884; Annual Report of the Commissioner of Railroads, 48th Cong., 2d Sess., *House Executive Document*, no. 1, pt. 5 (serial no. 2286), pp. 289–291; *Report of the Union Pacific, 1884*, p. 6.

14. *Commercial and Financial Chronicle*, September 19, 1885, p. 506.

15. Testimony of F. G. Dexter, Elisha Atkins, F. L. Ames, and E. H.

Baker, *Report of the Pacific Railway Commission*, I and II, 687, 688, 730, 745, 774; Adams, Diary, April 28, July 6, 1888, and March 19, 27, 1889; *Commercial and Financial Chronicle*, June 28, 1884, p. 764; *Report of the Union Pacific, 1884*, pp. 148–149; *Report of the Union Pacific, 1885*, pp. 147–148.

16. *Commercial and Financial Chronicle*, March 28, 1885, p. 385; Adams, Diary, March 20, 25, 1885; testimony of Jay Gould, *Report of the Pacific Railway Commission*, I and II, 588.

17. *Report of the Union Pacific, 1884*, p. 175. Adams, Diary, September 15, 22, 24, 25, 29, October 22, 1885; April 6, 1886; April 30, 1888. C. F. Adams, Jr., Memorabilia, 1888–1893, April 19, September 10, 1891, pp. 263, 300, Adams Papers, Massachusetts Historical Society.

18. *Report of the Union Pacific, 1884*, p. 175; *Report of the Union Pacific, 1885*, p. 48; Adams, Memorabilia, 1888–1893, September 10, 1891, p. 310.

19. "John Sharp," *Dictionary of American Biography*, XVII, 23–24; C. F. Adams, Jr., to G. M. Dodge, Boston, May 1, 1889, Dodge Papers, Iowa State Department of History and Archives.

20. *Commercial and Financial Chronicle*, August 30, 1884, p. 235; Adams, Memorabilia, 1888–1893, June 18, 1889, pp. 64–65, January 14, 1891, pp. 192–193, and January 25, 1891, p. 199; Adams, Diary, December 27, 1889; F. L. Ames to G. M. Dodge, Boston, July 8, 1887, Dodge Papers.

21. Richard C. Overton, *Burlington West* (Cambridge, Mass., 1941), p. 403; Adams, Memorabilia, 1888–1893, June 18, 1889, p. 65; Adams, Diary, February 29, March 9, October 5, 1888; *Report of the Union Pacific, 1887*, p. 10.

22. Adams, Memorabilia, 1888–1893, July 4, 1890, pp. 117, 127–129; November 23, 1890, p. 169.

23. *Ibid.*, June 18, 1889, p. 68.

24. *Ibid.*, pp. 64, 70; Adams, Diary, October 19, 20, 1889; C. F. Adams to Charles W. Eliot, Boston, April 2, 1889, Eliot Papers, Harvard Archives; Adams, Memorabilia, 1888–1893, July 4, 1890, pp. 125–126.

25. Adams, Diary, February 28, 1887; Ellen M. Slayden, *Washington Wife*, ed. Walter P. Webb (New York, 1963), p. 166; Adams, Memorabilia, 1888–1893, June 18, 1889, p. 65; "A Theoretical Experiment," *Railway Age*, 15 (1890): 836.

26. *Report of the Union Pacific, 1884*, p. 176; *Commercial and Financial Chronicle*, June 26, 1884, p. 764.

27. C. F. Adams, Jr., "The Prevention of Railroad Strikes," *Scribner's Magazine*, 5 (1889): 424–430; Donald L. McMurry, *The Great Burlington Strike of 1888. A Case History in Labor Relations* (Cambridge, Mass., 1936), pp. 12–16.

28. F. W. Taussig, "The South-western Strike of 1886," *Quarterly Jour-*

nal of Economics, 1 (January 1887): 124–219; *Commercial and Financial Chronicle*, May 8, 1886, p. 566.

29. McMurry, *The Great Burlington Strike*, pp. 9–69, 110–111, 116–121; C. F. Adams, Jr., to T. L. Kimball, Boston, March 5, 1888, Dodge Papers.

30. Adams, Memorabilia, 1888–1893, August 18, 1891, p. 322; Adams, Diary, March 19, April 1, 4, 1888.

31. Adams, Diary, November 12, 1886.

32. Nelson Trottman, *History of the Union Pacific. A Financial and Economic Survey* (New York, 1925), pp. 223–224; Adams, Diary, November 8, 1884, February 15, 1889; remarks of Senator Van Wyck, *Congressional Record*, 48th Cong., 1st Sess., vol. XV, pt. 5, p. 5434.

33. Adams, Memorabilia, 1888–1893, February 3, 1889, p. 84, and June 30, 1889, p. 85; Report of the Commissioner of Railroads, 52d Cong., 1st Sess., *House Executive Documents*, no. 1, pt. 5, pp. 144–145.

34. Testimony of Elisha Atkins, *Report of the Pacific Railway Commission*, I and II, 748–749.

35. Remarks of Representative Outhwaite, *Congressional Record*, 49th Cong., 1st Sess., vol. XVII, pt. 5, pp. 5316–5322; vol. XVII, pt. 8, appendix, pp. 215–222.

36. C. F. Adams, Jr., to G. M. Dodge, Boston, March 18, 1886; same to same, Boston, January 25, 1887, February 5, 1887, Dodge Papers. *Congressional Record*, 49th Cong., 2d Sess., vol. XVIII, pt. 1, p. 775; pt. 2, p. 1358; pt. 3, pp. 2069–2070, 2268, 2277–2288, 2568. Adams, Diary, February 4, 13, 26, 1887.

37. *Congressional Record*, 49th Cong., 2d Sess., vol. XXIII, pt. 3, p. 2262; Adams, Diary, February 28, 1887; C. F. Adams, Jr., to G. M. Dodge, Boston, March 11, 1887, Dodge Papers.

38. C. F. Adams, Jr., to Carl Schurz, Boston, March 9, 1887, Schurz Papers; "Robert Emory Pattison," *Dictionary of American Biography*, XIV, 313–314; "William Miskey Singerly," *Dictionary of American Biography*, XIV, 313–314; Majority Report, *Report of the Pacific Railway Commission*, I, 106; Adams, Diary, July 10, 1887.

39. Majority Report, *Report of the Pacific Railway Commission*, I, 117; Adams, Diary, May 24, 1887, and July 5, 6, 9, 16, 17, 19, 21, 1887.

40. Adams, Diary, April 25, September 11, 17, 18, October 13, November 5, 10, 1887; February 29, 1888; February 27, 1889.

41. Majority Report, *Report of the Pacific Railway Commission*, I, 117; testimony, *Report of the Pacific Railway Commission*, I, 440.

42. Majority Report, *Report of the Pacific Railway Commission*, I, 34; Minority Report, *Report of the Pacific Railway Commission*, I, 149–153.

43. Majority Report, *Report of the Pacific Railway Commission*, I, 50; Minority Report, *Report of the Pacific Railway Commission*, I, 180.

44. Adams, Diary, December 3, 8, 14, 21, 1887; January 3, 4, 10, 13, February 17, 1888. *Report of the Pacific Railway Commission*, I, v.

45. J. M. Wilson to C. F. Adams, Jr., Washington, July 19, 1888, Dodge Papers; C. F. Adams, Jr., to G. M. Dodge, Boston, April 18, 1888, Dodge Papers; Adams, Diary, March 24, June 30, July 1, 2, 1888; *Congressional Record*, 50th Cong., 1st Sess., vol. XIX, pt. 3, pp. 2572–2576, and pt. 4, p. 3249.

46. Adams, Memorabilia, 1888–1893, February 3, 1889, p. 40; Adams, Diary, July 26, October 17, 23, 1888.

47. Adams, Memorabilia, 1888–1893, February 3, 1889, pp. 35–36, and April 14, 1891, pp. 256–257; "Preston B. Plumb," *Dictionary of American Biography*, XV, 10–11.

48. "George Franklin Edmunds," *Dictionary of American Biography*, VI, 24–27; Adams, Memorabilia, 1888–1893, February 3, 1889, pp. 39–40, and April 14, 1891, p. 258.

49. Adams, Diary, February 2, 5, 1889; Adams, Memorabilia, 1888–1893, February 3, 1889, pp. 29–40; *Congressional Record*, 48th Cong., 1st Sess., vol. XV, pt. 5, p. 5435.

50. Adams, Memorabilia, 1888–1893, December 23, 1888, p. 10, October 6, 1889, pp. 95–96, and April 14, 1891, p. 253; Adams, Diary, June 23, 25, 1888, November 6, 1889; C. F. Adams, Jr., to G. M. Dodge, Boston, January 15, 1887, Dodge Papers; *Commercial and Financial Chronicle*, April 2, 1887, p. 435; C. E. Perkins to J. M. Forbes, December 1, 1889, Perkins Papers, Richard C. Overton.

51. *Report of the Union Pacific, 1884*, p. 150; Boston *Daily Advertiser*, December 19, 1882, p. 3; 13 *United States Statutes at Large*, 365; 14 *United States Statutes at Large*, 293; 16 *United States Statutes at Large*, 574.

52. Adams, Memorabilia, 1888–1893, December 23, 1888, p. 10, January 13, 1889, p. 11, and April 21, 1889, p. 52; Adams, Diary, September 8, 1887, January 27, 1888.

53. Testimony of John C. Stubbs, *Report of the Pacific Railway Commission*, V and VI, 3307–3310; testimony of Richard Gray, *Report of the Pacific Railway Commission*, V and VI, 573.

54. Adams, Memorabilia, 1888–1893, January 13, 1889, pp. 9, 12–13.

55. Testimony of C. F. Adams, Jr., Report of the Senate Select [Cullom] Committee on Interstate Commerce, II, 1221.

56. *Ibid.*, II, 1210–1214; testimony of C. F. Adams, Jr., *Report of the Pacific Railway Commission*, III and IV, 2000.

57. *Report of the Pacific Railway Commission*, III and IV, 1999; testimony of C. F. Adams, Jr., Report of the Senate Select [Cullom] Committee, II, 1216; C. F. Adams, Jr., to Henry Villard, August 3, 1888, quoted in J. B. Hedges, *Henry Villard and the Railways of the Pacific Northwest* (New Haven, 1930), p. 178; *Commercial and Financial Chronicle*, September 30, 1884, p. 310, December 20, 1884, pp. 695–696, April 18, 1885, p. 465, and May 2, 1886, p. 576.

58. Testimony of C. F. Adams, Jr., *Report of the Pacific Railway Com-*

mission, I and II, 45, 55; testimony of C. F. Adams, Jr., Report of the Senate Select [Cullom] Committee, II, 1218.

59. *Report of the Pacific Railway Commission,* I and II, 47; *Report of the Union Pacific Railway, 1884,* p. 31; *Report of the Union Pacific Railway, 1889,* p. 136.

60. Testimony of C. F. Adams, Jr., *Report of the Pacific Railway Commission,* I and II, 102–104; *Report of the Union Pacific Railway, 1884,* p. 148.

61. Hedges, *Henry Villard,* pp. 56–63; testimony of C. F. Adams, Jr., *Report of the Pacific Railway Commission,* I and II, 90–95.

62. C. F. Adams, Jr., to G. M. Dodge, Boston, September 2, 1886, Dodge Papers.

63. *Report of the Union Pacific, 1884,* p. 166; *Report of the Union Pacific, 1889,* p. 104; "Review of the Decision of the Supreme Court of the United States in the Sinking Fund Cases," *Poor's Manual of the Railroads of the United States for 1880,* pp. xxvi–xxvii.

64. Adams, Memorabilia, 1888–1893, December 25, 1888, pp. 4–9; January 12, 1889, pp. 11–17.

65. *Ibid.,* January 13, 1889, pp. 18–23; Julius Grodinsky, *Transcontinental Railway Strategy, 1889–1893* (Philadelphia, 1963), p. 342.

66. Adams, Memorabilia, 1888–1893, January 13, 1889, pp. 23–25, and February 24, 1889, p. 43; Grodinsky, *Transcontinental Railway Strategy,* pp. 346–350.

67. Adams, Diary, February 22, 1889; Testimony of C. F. Adams, Jr., Report of the Senate Select [Cullom] Committee, II, 1214–1215; Adams, Memorabilia, 1888–1893, December 23, 1888, p. 9.

68. *Commercial and Financial Chronicle,* January 18, 1890, p. 107, and June 7, 1890, p. 801; Adams, Diary, May 14, 15, 1889.

69. Adams, Diary, April 12, 22, June 18, September 13, October 13, 1890; Hedges, *Henry Villard,* pp. 202–203.

70. C. F. Adams, Jr., to G. M. Dodge, Boston, October 23, 1889, Dodge Papers; *Commercial and Financial Chronicle,* October 26, 1889, pp. 526, 539; Grodinsky, *Transcontinental Railway Strategy,* p. 384; Julius Grodinsky, *Jay Gould, His Business Career, 1867–1892* (Philadelphia, 1957), p. 575.

71. *Poor's Manual of the Railroads of the United States for 1891,* p. 567; testimony of Oliver Ames, *Report of the Pacific Railway Commission,* I and II, 805; *Commercial and Financial Chronicle,* November 29, 1890, p. 731; Adams, Diary, April 7, 1890; *Commercial and Financial Chronicle,* November 15, 1890, p. 681.

72. Adams, Diary, August 24, 1886; *Report of the Union Pacific Railway, 1886,* p. 19; Adams, Memorabilia, 1888–1893, November 23, 1890, p. 168; testimony of C. F. Adams, Jr., *Report of the Pacific Railway Commission,* I and II, 389.

73. *Commercial and Financial Chronicle*, April 2, 1897, p. 413; Adams, Memorabilia, 1888–1893, November 23, 1890, p. 153.

74. Adams, Diary, May 1, October 25, 1889.

75. Adams, Memorabilia, 1888–1893, November 23, 1890, p. 157, and November 25, 1890, pp. 164–177; Adams, Diary, November 13, 14, 15, 17, 18, 21, 1890.

76. Adams, Diary, November 26, 1890; Adams, Memorabilia, 1888–1893, January 14, 1891, pp. 191–193.

77. Adams, Diary, January 5, 1887; Adams, Memorabilia, 1888–1893, January 14, 1891, p. 197.

78. Adams, Memorabilia, 1888–1893, June 30, 1889, p. 86; November 25, 1890, p. 171; December 14, 1890, pp. 182–183; January 14, 1891, p. 196. Adams, Diary, August 21, 1887.

79. Adams, Memorabilia, 1888–1893, January 14, 1891, p. 193.

80. C. F. Adams, Jr., *An Autobiography* (Boston, 1916), p. 190; Adams, Memorabilia, 1888–1893, November 23, 1890, pp. 164–167; *Poor's Manual of the Railroads of the United States for 1891*, p. 991.

81. John T. Morse, Jr., "Remarks on His Fiftieth Anniversary of Membership," *Proceedings of the Massachusetts Historical Society*, 60 (1926–1927): 175; Adams, Memorabilia, 1888–1893, March 23, 1890, p. 171, November 23, 1890, pp. 147, 159, and January 25, 1891, p. 198; C. F. Adams, Jr., to G. M. Dodge, Boston, November 22, 1890, Dodge Papers, Free Public Library, Council Bluffs, Iowa; Adams, Diary, October 24, 1894.

82. Adams, Memorabilia, 1888–1893, November 23, 1890, p. 172.

83. Adams, Memorabilia, 1888–1893, January 14, 1891, p. 195; Adams, Diary, March 25, 1891.

V. The House on President's Hill, 1870–1893

1. "John Adams," *Dictionary of American Biography*, I, 72–73; C. F. Adams, Jr., *Autobiography* (Boston, 1916), pp. 8–9.

2. C. F. Adams, Jr., Diary, July 23, August 13, 27, 28, September 30, November 12, 20, 1870, Adams Papers (Massachusetts Historical Society).

3. *Ibid.*, November 27, 1870; May 3, 11, 23, June 11, 1875; April 14, 30, May 9, 1877. S. F. Bemis, *John Quincy Adams and the Union* (New York, 1936), p. 346.

4. Adams, Diary, March 24, April 16, December 28, 1871; December 2, 3, 1873; July 17, 1875.

5. *Ibid.*, May 10, 11, 1869; April 10, 1870; May 24, 1872; March 12, April 1, October 19, 1875.

6. *Ibid.*, November 22, 1871; December 13, 1874; April 10, December 12, 1875; November 7, 1889. Adams, *Autobiography*, pp. 12, 13, 18, 27. Adams, Memorabilia, 1888–1893, January 1, 1890, p. 100, Adams Papers (Massachusetts Historical Society).

7. Adams, *Autobiography*, pp. 13, 18; Adams, Diary, August 9, 1880, and August 21, 1887.

8. Adams, Memorabilia, 1894–1897, September 18, 1895, pp. 667–670; Adams, Diary, September 26, 1883.

9. Adams, Memorabilia, 1888–1893, September 21, 1891, p. 314, January 17, 1893, p. 403, and February 1, 1893, p. 726; *ibid.*, 1894–1897, February 13, 1895, p. 598; Adams, Diary, September 26, 1869.

10. Henry Adams, *A Catalogue of the Books of John Quincy Adams Deposited in the Boston Athenaeum* (Boston, 1938), pp. 13, 15n; Adams, Memorabilia, 1888–1893, June 17, 1893, p. 488; Adams, Diary, September 25, 1888.

11. Adams, Memorabilia, 1888–1893, April 20, 1892, p. 34; *ibid.*, 1894–1897, June 9, 1895, pp. 652–658; Adams, Diary, August 12, 1864, October 23, 1870, June 1, 1871, November 7, 1881, and March 12, 1889; C. F. Adams, Jr., to Carl Schurz, Washington, April 15, 1901, Schurz Papers, Library of Congress; Adams, *Autobiography*, p. 27; C. F. Adams, Jr., to Brander Matthews, Lincoln, August 11, 1911, Matthews Papers, Columbia University Library.

12. C. F. Adams, Jr., to Henry Adams, Boston, January 15, 1859, Adams Papers (Microfilm Edition, no. 546). Adams, Diary, February 8, 1864; February 7, 15, July 22, 1870; January 26, 1871; January 26, 1873; March 15, 1885. C. F. Adams, Jr., *Richard Henry Dana, A Biography* (Boston, 1890), II, 135.

13. Adams, Diary, May 25, 1869, March 21, 1875, and August 21, 1887; C. F. Adams, Jr., *The Sifted Grain and the Grain Sifters. An Address at Madison*, October 19, 1900.

14. C. F. Adams, Jr., *Three Phi Beta Kappa Addresses* (Boston, 1907), p. 45; Adams, Diary, January 27, 1883; C. F. Adams, Jr., to Frederic Bancroft, Lincoln, November 27, 1908, and Lincoln, April 27, 1909, Frederic Bancroft Papers, Columbia University Library.

15. Adams, Memorabilia, 1888–1893, March 18, 1893, pp. 447–448; *ibid.*, 1901–1905, March 31, 1901, p. 1863; *Washington Wife: Journal of Ellen Maury Slayden from 1897–1919*, ed. Walter P. Webb (New York, 1963), pp. 166–167.

16. Adams, "Quincy," *History of Norfolk County, Massachusetts*, ed. D. H. Hurd (Philadelphia, 1884), pp. 354–355; Bemis, *John Quincy Adams and the Union*, p. 194; Adams, *Autobiography*, pp. 13–15.

17. Adams, "Quincy," pp. 275, 364; Adams, *Autobiography*, p. 179.

18. Adams, Diary, December 7, 1886, February 5, 1888, and February 17, 1889; Adams, *The Sifted Grain and the Grain Sifters*, p. 6; "Remarks by Mr. Charles Francis Adams," *Proceedings of the Massachusetts Historical Society*, second series, 9 (1894, 1895): 248.

19. Adams, Diary, January 30, 1881; November 10, 1889.

20. Adams, *Autobiography*, pp. 15–16.

21. Adams, "Quincy," pp. 257–269; *Abstract of the Census of Massachusetts, 1865,* p. 74.

22. Adams, "Quincy," pp. 354, 371; Adams, Memorabilia, 1894–1897, August 25, 1894.

23. Quincy *Patriot,* March 27, 1880. Adams, Diary, March 3, 1873; March 16, 1874; March 1, 22, 1880; March 10, 28, 1881; March 5, 1884. Adams, "Quincy," p. 371.

24. Adams, Diary, March 3, 1878, February 26, 1879, March 7, 1881, and March 11, 1888; Adams, "Quincy," p. 371.

25. Adams, Diary, June 1, July 9, 10, 1872; C. F. Adams, Jr., *The New Departure in the Common Schools of Quincy* (Boston, 1879), pp. 32–35.

26. Adams, "Quincy," p. 362; F. A. Fitzpatrick, "Francis Wayland Parker," *Educational Review,* 24 (1902): 24.

27. Adams, *The New Departure,* pp. 37–44; B. G. Northrop, "The Quincy Methods," *Education,* 1 (November 1880): 124–125; "Mr. C. F. Adams, Jr., and the Quincy Schools," *New-England Journal of Education,* October 9, 1879, p. 197.

28. Adams, Diary, March 1, 1875; November 6, 1876; March 10, 12, 18, 1877. Quincy *Patriot,* March 27, 1880.

29. Adams, *The New Departure,* pp. 31–36; C. F. Adams, Jr., "The Development of the Superintendency," *The Addresses and Journal of Proceedings of the National Educational Association, 1880, at Chautauqua, New York* (Salem, Ohio, 1880), pp. 61–76; Adams, Diary, March 14, 1880, and January 5, 1881; J. D. Philbrick, "Which Is the True Ideal of the Public School?" *Education,* 1 (January 1881): 303; C. F. Adams, Jr., "Scientific Common School Education," *Harper's New Monthly Magazine,* 61 (October 1880): 934–942; *New-England Journal of Education,* December 11, 1879, p. 339.

30. George A. Walton, "Examinations of Norfolk County Schools," *Forty-third Annual Report of the* [Massachusetts] *Board of Education, January, 1880* (Boston, 1880), pp. 123–248; *The Nation,* March 25, 1880, p. 235; Adams, *New Departure,* p. 45.

31. Adams, "Scientific Common School Education," pp. 935, 937, 939–940.

32. Adams, *New Departure,* pp. 41–51; F. W. Parker, "Remarks," *Addresses and Journal of the National Educational Association, 1880, at Chautauqua, New York,* pp. 49–50; Northrop, "The Quincy Methods," pp. 128, 133–137; *New-England Journal of Education,* November 6, 1879, p. 260; "Mr. C. F. Adams and the Quincy Schools," p. 197; Fitzpatrick, "Francis Wayland Parker," pp. 23–30; C. H. Judd, "Francis Wayland Parker," *Dictionary of American Biography,* XIV, 221.

33. Philbrick, "Which Is the True Ideal of the Public School?" pp. 300–305.

34. Adams, Diary, March 22, October 8, 1881; *Forty-fourth Annual Report of the* [Massachusetts] *Board of Education, January, 1881*, p. 80.

35. Adams, "Quincy," pp. 362–363; Henry Adams, *Catalogue of the Books of John Quincy Adams*, p. 5; Adams, Diary, March 11, 1888; Philbrick, "Which Is the True Ideal of the Public School?" p. 302; *Report of the Trustees of the Public Library for the Year Ending February 1, 1872.*

36. C. F. Adams, Jr., *The Public Library and the Public Schools. A Paper Prepared for the Teachers of the Public Schools of Quincy, 19th of May, 1876* (Boston, 1879); C. F. Adams, Jr., *Fiction in Public Libraries and Educational Catalogues, July 1, 1879* (Boston, 1879); Adams, Diary, March 29, 30, June 7, July 10, 13, August 27, 1875; *Nation*, October 21, 1875, pp. 251–252, and November 4, 1875, p. 291.

37. *Address of Charles Francis Adams, Jr., and Proceedings at the Dedication of the Crane Memorial Hall, at Quincy, Mass., May 30, 1882* (Cambridge, Mass., 1883); Adams, Diary, February 22, March 30, April 2, 1881, and May 30, 1882; *Report of the Trustees of the Quincy Public Library, 1894.*

38. Adams, Diary, March 10, April 6, June 12, 1881; March 27, July 1, 1882; January 21, September 13, 25, 1885; March 11, 1888. C. W. Eliot, *Charles Eliot, Landscape Architect* (Boston, 1902), p. 432.

39. Adams, "Quincy," p. 375; Adams, Diary, March 11, 1888.

40. Adams, Diary, December 2, 1884; February 23, April 13, 16, October 3, 5, 1885; January 5, February 19, November 9, 19, December 9, 1886; December 31, 1887; September 18, 1888.

41. *Ibid.*, April 30, 1883; September 27, October 1, 1889.

42. *Ibid.*, March 25, 1878; March 11, 1888.

43. *The Census of Massachusetts, 1885*, vol. I, pt. 1, p. 74; Adams, Diary, November 16, 28, 1890, and November 13, 1891.

44. Adams, "Quincy," pp. 356–359.

45. Adams, "Quincy," pp. 365–369; Bemis, *John Quincy Adams and the Union*, pp. 445–446; *Address of Charles Francis Adams, Jr., at the Crane Memorial Hall*; C. F. Adams, Jr., *Charles Francis Adams by His Son* (Boston, 1900), pp. 1, 104.

46. Adams, Memorabilia, 1888–1893, October 22, 29, 1893, pp. 498, 544, and May 29, 1892, p. 371; C. F. Adams, Jr., *The Centennial Milestone. An Address in Commemoration of the One Hundredth Anniversary of the Incorporation of Quincy. Delivered July 4, 1892* (Cambridge, Mass., 1892), pp. 17–18; Adams, Diary, January 5, 1885, June 11, 1888, and January 7, 1889.

47. Adams, Diary, August 2, 1871, and November 2, 1875; W. S. Robinson, *"Warrington." Pen Portraits* (Boston, 1877), pp. 419–420; *Harvard Graduates' Magazine*, 3 (March 1895): 388; *Appletons' Annual Cyclopedia, 1868*, pp. 459–460; *ibid., 1869*, pp. 415–417; *ibid., 1870*, pp. 473–477; *ibid., 1871*, pp. 492–494; *ibid., 1879*, p. 605.

48. Adams, Diary, April 18, 1870, and August 21, 1887; C. F. Adams, Jr., "The Government and the Railroad Corporations," *North American Review*, 112 (January 1871): 40–47.

49. Adams, Diary, February 14, 15, 1869.

50. C. F. Adams, Jr., "The Protection of the Ballot in National Elections," *Journal of Social Science*, 1 (June 1869): 91–111.

51. L. L. Bernard and Jessie Bernard, *Origins of American Sociology* (New York, 1943), pp. 540–544; *Journal of Social Science*, 1 (June 1869): 195–200.

52. Adams, Diary, April 20, November 22, 1870; C. F. Adams, Jr., to Carl Schurz, Boston, March 17, 1873, Schurz Papers, Library of Congress.

53. C. F. Adams, Jr., "What Mr. Cleveland Stands For," *Forum*, 13 (June 1892): 661–662; Adams, Memorabilia, 1888–1893, December 21, 1891, p. 339; Adams, Diary, April 23, 26, May 3, 1872; M. B. Duberman, *Charles Francis Adams, 1807–1886* (Boston, 1960), pp. 354–366.

54. Adams, Diary, May 4, August 3, September 30, October 9, November 6, 1872.

55. Adams, Diary, May 14, 15, 16, 1876; New York *Tribune*, May 15, 16, 1876.

56. Adams, Diary, June 17, July 10, October 13, 1876; C. F. Adams, Jr., to Carl Schurz, Boston, July 11, 1876, Schurz Papers; C. F. Adams, Jr., "The 'Independents' in the Campaign," *North American Review*, 123 (October 1876): 426–467.

57. Adams, Diary, November 8, 12, 27, 28, December 6, 1876; C. F. Adams, Jr., to Carl Schurz, Boston, December 18, 1876, Schurz Papers; C. F. Adams, Jr., to Carl Schurz, Boston, June 30, 1877, Schurz Papers.

58. C. F. Adams, Jr., to Carl Schurz, Boston, July 7, 1877, Schurz Papers; Adams, Diary, November 3, 1880, and June 7, 1884; C. F. Adams, Jr., "The Opposition and the Unknown Quantity in Politics," *Nation*, February 17, 1881, p. 111; Adams, Memorabilia, 1888–1893, July 26, 1891, pp. 313–316; Adams, "What Mr. Cleveland Stands For," p. 670.

59. Edward Channing, *A History of the United States* (New York, 1925), VI, 237; "Benjamin Franklin Butler," *Dictionary of American Biography*, III, 357–359.

60. Adams, *Dana*, II, 341–342; *Appletons' Annual Cyclopedia, 1871*, pp. 492–494; *ibid., 1878*, pp. 530–536; *ibid., 1879*, p. 604.

61. Adams, *Autobiography*, p. 160. Adams, *Dana*, II, 344. Adams, Diary, September 21, 27, 28, 1871; November 8, 1882; November 7, 1883.

62. Adams, Memorabilia, 1888–1893, August 22, 1891, p. 267.

63. Adams, "The Protection of the Ballot," pp. 105–106; Adams, Diary, November 5, 1889; Adams, Memorabilia, 1888–1893, February 15, 1891, p. 206, and March 18, 1893, pp. 446–450.

64. Adams, *Dana*, II, 252; C. F. Adams, Jr., "More Sentimentalism," *Nation*, November 3, 1870, p. 297.

65. Adams, Memorabilia, 1888–1893, December 21, 1891, p. 340; C. F. Adams, Jr., "President Garfield and the Independents," *Nation*, February 24, 1881, p. 129; C. F. Adams, Jr., to Carl Schurz, Boston, June 1, 1903, Schurz Papers.

66. Adams, "What Mr. Cleveland Stands For," p. 663; Adams, Memorabilia, 1888–1893, December 21, 1891, pp. 339–340.

VI. An Aversion to Reformers of the Wrong Sort, 1890–1915

1. C. F. Adams, Jr., Diary, December 25, 1892, Adams Papers (Massachusetts Historical Society).

2. *Ibid.*, November 13, 16, 28, 1890; April 24, May 1, July 11, 1892; April 28, May 20, 24, 1893. C. F. Adams, Jr., *Autobiography* (Boston, 1916), p. 204.

3. C. F. Adams, Jr., Memorabilia, 1888–1893, October 29, 1893, Adams Papers (Massachusetts Historical Society), p. 517; Adams, Diary, May 20, July 23, November 7, 1893, and June 7, 1895.

4. Adams, Memorabilia, 1888–1893, May 29, 1892, pp. 367–388; October 29, 1893, p. 517. *Ibid.*, 1894–1897, October 7, 1894, p. 575; December 31, 1896, p. 883; May 18, 1897, p. 964. Adams, Diary, April 14, May 10, 1896. C. F. Adams, Jr., to Carl Schurz, Lincoln, October 10, 1901, Schurz Papers, Library of Congress.

5. Adams, Diary, July 25, 27, 28, October 10, 19, 23, 31, November 4, 5, 6, 12, 14, 17, 1892; January 13, 24, February 12, April 22, 1893; March 23, June 9, 10, 13, 19, August 14, 1894; April 22, May 24, 1895. Adams, Memorabilia, 1888–1893, December 31, 1893, pp. 524–525. *Ibid.*, 1894–1897, August 25, 1894, pp. 552–560.

6. Adams, Diary, December 31, 1890; December 31, 1891; December 30, 1895.

7. Adams, Memorabilia, 1888–1893, December 2, 1891, pp. 337–338; *ibid.*, 1894–1897, February 17, 1895, p. 596; Adams, Diary, April 29, 1891, December 25, 1892, and November 6, 1893.

8. Adams, *Autobiography*, pp. 189–190. Adams, Diary, April 25, 26, June 8, May 12, 1891; December 25, 1892; December 23, 1893; February 23, October 11, 1894. *Poor's Manual of the Railroad's of the United States for 1895*, pp. 869, 873. Adams, Memorabilia, 1888–1893, April 19, 1891, pp. 262–263; September 10, 1891, p. 307; November 26, 1891, p. 327.

9. Adams, Diary, March 10, 1896.

10. Adams, Memorabilia, 1888–1893, November 13, 1891, p. 321. Adams, Diary, February 6, 13, May 6, October 16, November 5, 21, December 18, 22, 1891; April 28, 1892; March 2, 1894; December 19, 1895.

11. Harold C. Passer, *The Electrical Manufacturers, 1875–1900* (Cambridge, Mass., 1953), pp. 327–329, 331–334; Adams, Memorabilia, 1894–1897, March 24, 1895, pp. 607–608; Adams, Diary, June 26, 1896.

12. Adams, Memorabilia, 1888–1893, December 7, 1890, p. 177; Adams, Diary, December 31, 1890, and December 31, 1893.

13. Adams, Memorabilia, 1888–1893, September 17, 1893, pp. 494–495; *ibid.*, 1894–1897, February 17, 1895, p. 587; Adams, Diary, June 30, July 4, August 5, August 15, October 23, November 17, 23, December 5, 1893, and December 31, 1896.

14. Adams, Diary, December 31, 1893.

15. Adams, Memorabilia, 1888–1893, November 25, 1890, pp. 153–157; October 22, 1893, pp. 501–509; December 31, 1893, p. 527.

16. C. F. Adams, Jr., to Carl Schurz, Boston, September 10, 1896, Schurz Papers. Adams, Memorabilia, 1893–1897, September 23, 1894, pp. 562–566; February 17, 1895, pp. 589–594; March 24, 1895, pp. 602–610.

17. Adams, Memorabilia, 1894–1897, March 24, 1895, p. 611, October 17, 1896, p. 828, and November 22, 1896, pp. 859–860; Adams, Diary, March 16, 19, 1896; C. F. Adams, Jr., to Carl Schurz, September 10, 1896, Schurz Papers.

18. Adams to Schurz, September 10, 1896; Adams, Diary, March 12, 1891, and July 4, 13, 27, 1895.

19. Adams, Memorabilia, 1895–1897, July 12, 1897, pp. 972–973, and July 20, 1897, pp. 976–977; *Commercial and Financial Chronicle,* May 20, 1899, p. 675; *State of Kansas, Session Laws, 1897,* pp. 448–450.

20. Adams, Memorabilia, 1901–1905, February 1, 1901, pp. 1838–1843, and April 29, 1901, pp. 1870–1877; Cotting v. Kansas City Stock-yards Company, 79 *Federal Reporter,* 679; 82 *Federal Reporter,* 850; Cotting v. Goddard, 46 *Cases in the Supreme Court, Lawyer's Edition,* 83.

21. Adams, Memorabilia, 1894–1897, May 5, 1895, p. 628. *Ibid.,* 1901–1905, February 1, 1901, p. 1838; April 29, 1901, p. 1884; April 23, 1905, p. 2683. Adams, Diary, January 1, 5, 1895.

22. Adams, Memorabilia, 1894–1897, October 17, 1896, p. 845; C. F. Adams, Jr., to Carl Schurz, Boston, August 8, 1903, Schurz Papers; C. F. Adams, Jr., to Frederic Bancroft, Boston, August 10, 1912, Bancroft Papers, Columbia University.

23. C. F. Adams, Jr., "What Mr. Cleveland Stands For," *Forum,* 13 (July 1892): 662–670; C. F. Adams, Jr., "Mr. Cleveland's Tasks and Opportunities," *Forum,* 15 (May 1893): 298–303; Adams, Diary, December 17, 1895; Adams, Memorabilia, 1894–1897, June 24, 1896, p. 825; C. F. Adams, Jr., to Charles W. Eliot, Boston, January 1, 1896, Eliot Papers, Harvard Archives.

24. Adams, Memorabilia, 1901–1905, February 1, 1901, pp. 1843–1844.

25. C. F. Adams, Jr., to Carl Schurz, Boston, October 22, 1898, Schurz Papers; same to same, November 14, 1898, Schurz Papers; same to same, Boston, November 24, 1898, Boston, December 24, 1898, and Boston, October 11, 1900, Schurz Papers.

26. C. F. Adams, Jr., to Carl Schurz, Boston, April 21, 1902; C. F.

Adams, Jr., to C. E. Norton, Boston, April 15, 1902; C. F. Adams, Jr., to Carl Schurz, Boston, May 12, 1902; same to same, Boston, June 21, 1902; C. F. Adams, Jr., to Herbert Wilson, Boston, August 4, 1902; C. F. Adams, Jr., to Carl Schurz, Boston, August 8, 1903, Schurz Papers.

27. C. F. Adams, Jr., to Carl Schurz, Boston, September 10, 1896, Schurz Papers.

28. Arthur Mann, *Yankee Reformers in the Urban Age* (Cambridge, Mass., 1954), pp. 139–144; 1897 *Acts and Resolves of Massachusetts*, 535–537; Report of the Special Committee Appointed to Investigate the Relations between Cities and Towns and Street Railway Companies, [Massachusetts] *House Document*, 1898, no. 475, pp. 9–10; Adams, *Autobiography*, pp. 186–187.

29. Report of the Special Committee, [Massachusetts] *House Document*, 1898, no. 475, *passim*.

30. Adams, Diary, September 27, 1889; Adams, Memorabilia, 1888–1893, May 31, 1893, p. 479.

31. 1892 *Acts and Resolves of Massachusetts*, 335; Charles W. Eliot, *Charles Eliot, Landscape Architect* (Boston, 1902), p. 355; Adams, Diary, January 14, 1893, and April 5, 1895.

32. 1893 *Acts and Resolves of Massachusetts*, 135, 1447, 1463; 1894 *Acts and Resolves of Massachusetts*, 283, 655; Adams, *Autobiography*, pp. 185–186.

33. Eliot, *Charles Eliot*, pp. 541–542. Adams, Diary, February 27, 1893; October 3, December 29, 1894; May 23, June 15, 1895. C. F. Adams, Jr., to Charles W. Eliot, Boston, August 18, 1902, Eliot Papers.

34. S. E. Morison, *The Development of Harvard University since the Inauguration of President Eliot, 1869–1929* (Cambridge, Mass., 1930), pp. xxvii–xxx; C. F. Adams, Jr., to Charles W. Eliot, Boston, July 23, 1901, Eliot Papers; Adams, Memorabilia, 1888–1893, March 10, 1891, p. 245.

35. Adams, Memorabilia, 1888–1893, March 10, 1891, pp. 246–247; April 22, 1891, p. 269.

36. Adams, Diary, November 16, 23, 1882; April 24, May 20, May 31, June 19, 1883.

37. C. F. Adams, Jr., "A College Fetich," *Three Phi Beta Kappa Addresses* (Boston, 1907), pp. 5–48.

38. Adams, Diary, June 28, 1883; C. F. Adams, Jr., to Carl Schurz, Boston, June 21, 1883, Schurz Papers; C. W. Eliot, "What Is a Liberal Education?" *Century Magazine*, new series, 6 (June 1884): 203–212.

39. Adams, Diary, November 24, December 2, 1883; J. M. Morse, "Greek in American Colleges," *Critic*, August 25, 1883, pp. 340–341; "Mr. Adams on the Classics," *American*, July 14, 1883, pp. 214–215; Noah Porter, "Greek and a Liberal Education," *Princeton Review*, 6 (September 1884): 195–218; Noah Porter (?), "Greek and the Bachelor's Degree," *New Englander and Yale Review*, new series, 8 (May 1885): 424–435.

40. A. P. Peabody, "The Study of Greek," *Atlantic Monthly*, 53 (January 1884): 78; Records of the Overseers of Harvard College, XII, 141–143, Harvard Archives.

41. Records of the Overseers, XII, 201; J. P. Cooke, "Further Remarks on the Greek Question," *Popular Science Monthly*, 25 (October 1884): 772–777; J. P. Cooke, "The Greek Question," *Popular Science Monthly*, 24 (November 1883): 1–6.

42. *Annual Reports of the President and Treasurer of Harvard College, 1885–86* (Cambridge, Mass., 1887), pp. 7–8; *Annual Reports of the President and Treasurer of Harvard College, 1888–89* (Cambridge, Mass., 1890), p. 6; *Annual Reports of the President and Treasurer of Harvard College, 1889–90* (Cambridge, Mass., 1891), pp. 9–10; *Annual Reports of the President and Treasurer of Harvard College, 1890–91* (Cambridge, Mass., 1892), p. 73; *Annual Reports of the President and Treasurer of Harvard College, 1892–93* (Cambridge, Mass., 1894), pp. 23–24; C. H. Grandgent, "The Modern Languages as an Alternative in College Admission Requirements," *Educational Review*, 11 (May 1896): 439; *The Harvard University Catalogue, 1886–1887* (Cambridge, Mass., 1886), p. 75; C. F. Adams, Jr., to C. W. Eliot, Boston, May 15, 1896, Harvard Archives; Adams, Diary, February 10, 1885.

43. C. F. Adams, Jr., to C. W. Eliot, Boston, May 10, 1896; Adams, Memorabilia, 1888–1893, April 22, 1891, pp. 265–266; Adams, Diary, April 21, 28, 1891, and January 23, 1892.

44. *Reports of the Visiting Committees of the Board of Overseers from 1890 to 1902*, pp. 117–121, 150–157, 275–287, 401–402, 407–424; C. F. Adams, Jr., "Preparatory School Education, The Classics and Written English," *Harvard Graduates' Magazine*, 1 (January 1893): 177–189; *Reports of Visiting Committees, 1890–1902*, p. 412.

45. C. F. Adams, Jr., to C. W. Eliot, Boston, June 11, 1892; same to same, October 19, 1896, Eliot Papers; John Tetlow, "Sight Translation from the Classics as a Test of Proficiency in English Composition," *Educational Review*, 12 (June 1896): 75–84; Protest of Six Schoolmasters, June 26, 1896, against the Report of the Committee on Composition and Rhetoric, Harvard Archives.

46. Reply of the Committee on Composition and Rhetoric to the Six Schoolmasters, Harvard Archives; Records of the Overseers of Harvard College, XIII, 298, 300–301, Harvard Archives; C. F. Adams, Jr., to C. W. Eliot, Boston, March 18, 1896, Eliot Papers.

47. *Reports of Visiting Committees, 1890–1902*, pp. 423–424.

48. C. F. Adams, Jr., *Three Phi Beta Kappa Addresses* (Boston, 1907), p. 191; C. F. Adams, Jr., to C. W. Eliot, Boston, September 30, 1896, Eliot Papers; Adams, Memorabilia, 1888–1893, April 16, 1893, pp. 462–466.

49. C. F. Adams, Jr., "The Proposed Increase of the Tuition Fee," *Harvard Graduates' Magazine*, 13 (September 1904): 6–22; Adams, Memora-

bilia, 1901–1905, January 11, 1905, pp. 2572–2575; C. F. Adams, Jr., to C. W. Eliot, Boston, March 26, 1892; same to same, Boston, June 11, 1892, Eliot Papers.

50. Adams, *Autobiography*, pp. 200–201; Adams, "A College Fetich," pp. 17, 42–43; Adams, Diary, November 8, 1886.

VII. Into Harbor at Last, 1890–1915

1. C. F. Adams, Jr., Diary, August 21, 1887, Adams Papers, Massachusetts Historical Society; C. F. Adams, Jr., Memorabilia, 1894–1897, August 25, 1894, p. 558, and February 17, 1895, p. 598, Adams Papers, Massachusetts Historical Society.

2. C. F. Adams, Jr., *Autobiography* (Boston, 1916), p. 25.

3. Adams, Memorabilia, 1888–1893, July 17, 1891, pp. 312–313; Adams, Diary, June 9, July 1, 4, 6, 1874; *Proceedings on the Two Hundred and Fiftieth Anniversary of the Permanent Settlement of Weymouth, with an Historical Address by Charles Francis Adams, Jr., July 4th, 1874* (Boston, 1874), p. 81.

4. C. F. Adams, Jr., "The Canal and Railroad Enterprise of Boston," *The Memorial History of Boston*, ed. Justin Winsor (Boston, 1881), IV, 111–150. Adams, Diary, June 17, 1881; November 9, 1883; January 12, February 21, March 23, May 10, 1884. C. F. Adams, Jr., "Quincy," *History of Norfolk County, Massachusetts, with Biographical Sketches*, ed. D. H. Hurd (Philadelphia, 1889), pp. 257–375.

5. Adams, Memorabilia, 1888–1893, September 1, 1890, pp. 135–141; Adams, Diary, November 8, 1890; Adams, *Autobiography*, p. 198.

6. Adams, Diary, January 1, 16, 1891, July 14, 1891; C. F. Adams, Jr., *Three Episodes of Massachusetts History* (Boston and New York, 1892), I, 395, 398–399, and II, 569.

7. *Political Science Quarterly*, 8 (June 1895): 346–349; *Critic*, November 5, 1892, p. 246; *Dial*, January 1, 1893, pp. 15–17; *Nation*, November 24, 1892, pp. 394–395; Williston Walker, "A Study of a New England Town," *Yale Review*, 1 (February 1, 1893), 368–380; C. F. Adams, Jr., *Massachusetts: Its Historians and Its History* (Boston and New York, 1893).

8. Adams, Memorabilia, 1894–1897, August 25, 1894, p. 559, and March 14, 1897, p. 944; Adams, Diary, February 22, 1896.

9. *The Letters of Henry Adams, 1892–1918*, ed. W. C. Ford (Boston and New York, 1938), p. 271; C. F. Adams, Jr., to Frederic Bancroft, Boston, August 6, 1912, and August 10, 1912, Bancroft Papers, Columbia University Library.

10. R. G. Thwaites, *The State Historical Society of Wisconsin. Exercises at the Dedication of the New Building. October 19, 1900* (Madison, 1901); C. F. Adams, Jr., *The Sifted Grain and the Grain Sifters. An Ad-*

dress at the Dedication of the Building at Madison, October 19, 1900
(Cambridge, Mass., 1900).

11. Adams, *Autobiography*, p. 207; C. F. Adams, Jr., to John C. Reed, Boston, December 29, 1905, Bancroft Papers, Columbia University Library; Adams, Diary, January 19, 26, 1907.

12. C. F. Adams, Jr., to Frederic Bancroft, Boston, June 21, 1913, Bancroft Papers; C. F. Adams, Jr., *Trans-Atlantic Historical Solidarity* (Oxford, 1913), pp. 9–18; C. F. Adams, Jr., to J. F. Rhodes, London, October 31, 1915; same to same, Washington, February 25, 1914, Society Papers, Massachusetts Historical Society.

13. Adams, Memorabilia, 1888–1893, June 29, 1892, pp. 374–375, and May 25, 1893, pp. 473–475; *ibid.*, 1901–1905, March 31, 1901, p. 1858; Adams, Diary, December 31, 1912.

14. Adams, *The Sifted Grain and the Grain Sifters*, pp. 32–35; Adams, Diary, April 6, 22, May 2, 1875.

15. Adams, *The Sifted Grain and the Grain Sifters*, pp. 35–39; Adams, Diary, April 20, 1874, January 21, 1887, and March 25, 1890; Adams, *Massachusetts: Its Historians*, p. 57.

16. Adams, Diary, August 17, 1891; C. F. Adams, Jr., to Frederic Bancroft, Lincoln, July 7, 1901, Bancroft Papers; C. F. Adams, Jr., to John C. Reed, Boston, December 29, 1905, Bancroft Papers; C. F. Adams, Jr., to Frederic Bancroft, Boston, July 2, 1900, Bancroft Papers; Adams, *The Sifted Grain and the Grain Sifters*, p. 27; C. F. Adams, Jr., to G. O. Trevelyan, Lincoln, July 21, 1900, Bancroft Papers.

17. Remarks of Dr. Edward Channing, *Proceedings of the Massachusetts Historical Society*, second series, 8 (1891, 1892): 242–243; Adams, *Three Episodes*, II, 697; *Proceedings on the Two Hundred and Fiftieth Anniversary*, p. 47; Adams, *The Sifted Grain and the Grain Sifters*, p. 28; C. F. Adams, Jr., "Review of Mr. Rhodes' Fifth Volume," *Proceedings of the Massachusetts Historical Society*, second series, 19 (1905): 314.

18. Adams, Diary, January 27, 1881; Adams, *Massachusetts: Its Historians*, pp. 1–2, 53, 92, 208; Adams, *The Sifted Grain and the Grain Sifters*, p. 32; Adams, *Three Episodes*, II, 648; Adams to Bancroft, July 14, 1901, Bancroft Papers.

19. Adams, *The Sifted Grain and the Grain Sifters*, p. 47; C. F. Adams, Jr., "Some Phases of Sexual Morality and Church Discipline in Colonial New England," *Proceedings of the Massachusetts Historical Society*, second series, 6 (1890, 1891): 477–516; Adams, Diary, March 11, 1888, and May 22, June 11, 1891; *Political Science Quarterly*, 8 (June 1892): 349.

20. Adams, *Massachusetts: Its Historians*, pp. 40–41.

21. C. F. Adams, Jr., to Carl Schurz, Boston, August 18, 1902, Schurz Papers; Adams, Diary, March 20, 1893.

22. Adams, Diary, December 14, 1893, January 1, 1894; "Remarks by Mr. R. C. Winthrop, Jr.," *Proceedings of the Massachusetts Historical Society*, new series, 8 (1892–1894): pp. 376, 381.

23. Adams, *The Sifted Grain and the Grain Sifters*, pp. 39–40; Adams, Diary, April 7, 1891; Adams, Memorabilia, 1888–1893, March 25, 1893, p. 455; C. F. Adams, Jr., to Frederic Bancroft, Boston, February 19, 1907, Bancroft Papers, Columbia University Library.

24. Adams, Diary, June 10, 1875, April 10, 1890, and December 21, 1894; J. T. Morse, Jr., "Remarks on His Jubilee," *Proceedings of the Massachusetts Historical Society*, 60 (1926–1927): p. 175; Adams, Memorabilia, 1894–1897, February 17, 1895, p. 599.

25. Adams, Diary, December 8, 1894, and January 8, 1895; "Remarks by Mr. Charles F. Adams," *Proceedings of the Massachusetts Historical Society*, second series, 9 (1894, 1895): 244–252.

26. "Remarks by Mr. Charles Francis Adams," *Proceedings of the Massachusetts Historical Society*, second series, 9 (1894, 1895): 258; "Remarks by the President," *Proceedings of the Massachusetts Historical Society*, second series, 10 (1895, 1896): 315–327.

27. "Remarks by Mr. C. F. Adams," *Proceedings of the Massachusetts Historical Society*, second series, 10 (1895, 1896): 9, 325; "Tribute of Mr. Sanborn," *Proceedings of the Massachusetts Historical Society*, 48 (1914, 1915): 408–409; C. F. Adams, Jr., to James F. Rhodes, Washington, February 25, 1914, Society Papers, Massachusetts Historical Society.

28. "Tributes by J. C. Warren, Robert Grant, J. H. Tuttle," *Proceedings of the Massachusetts Historical Society*, 52 (1918–1919): 45–55; Stewart Mitchell, "Worthington Chauncey Ford," *Proceedings of the Massachusetts Historical Society*, 69 (1949–1950): 409–410; C. F. Adams, Jr., to James F. Rhodes, Washington, December 24, 1912, Society Papers, Massachusetts Historical Society; Adams, Memorabilia, 1901–1905, January 1, 1905, pp. 2575–2578.

29. C. F. Adams, Jr., "Address by the President," *Proceedings of the Massachusetts Historical Society*, second series, 13 (1899, 1900): 92–93; *Proceedings of the Massachusetts Historical Society*, 60 (1926–1927), 164–166; *Proceedings of the Massachusetts Historical Society*, 69 (1949–1950): 407–408.

30. C. F. Adams, Jr., to James F. Rhodes, Washington, December 24, 1912; same to same, Washington, February 25, 1914, Society Papers, Massachusetts Historical Society; C. F. Adams, Jr., to Frederic Bancroft, Boston, August 6, 1912, Bancroft Papers, Columbia University Library.

31. C. F. Adams, Jr., to Frederic Bancroft, Lincoln, August 16, 1912; same to same, Lincoln, June 21, 1913, Bancroft Papers.

32. Adams, Diary, March 7, 8, 11, 12, 13, 14, 1915; *Proceedings of the Massachusetts Historical Society*, 48 (1914–1915): 321–325.

33. Adams, *Autobiography*, pp. ix–lx.

34. Adams, Memorabilia, 1888–1893, June 30, 1889, p. 88, and March 22, 1891, p. 224; 1891 *Acts and Resolves of Massachusetts*, 1123; *Survey*, December 30, 1911, p. 1423.

INDEX